W9-BFY-727

Magic Lantern Guides®

Nikon
D60

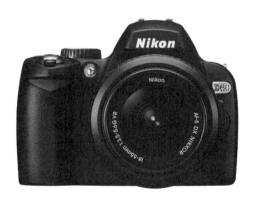

Simon Stafford

LARK BOOKS
A Division of Sterling Publishing Co., Inc.
New York / London

Editor: Frank Gallaugher
Book Design and Layout: Michael Robertson
Cover Design: Thom Gaines – Electron Graphics

Library of Congress Cataloging-in-Publication Data

Stafford, Simon.
  Magic lantern guides : Nikon D60 / Simon Stafford. -- 1st ed.
      p. cm. -- (Magic lantern guides)
  Includes index.
  ISBN 978-1-60059-413-7 (PB-trade pbk. : alk. paper)
  1. Nikon digital cameras--Handbooks, manuals, etc. 2. Digital
cameras--Handbooks, manuals, etc. I. Title. II. Title: Nikon D60.
  TR263.N5S7234 2009
  771.3'3--dc22

                                         2008023392

10 9 8 7 6 5 4 3 2 1

First Edition

Published by Lark Books, A Division of
Sterling Publishing Co., Inc.
387 Park Avenue South, New York, N.Y. 10016

Text © 2008, Simon J. Stafford
Photography © 2008, Simon J. Stafford unless otherwise specified

Distributed in Canada by Sterling Publishing,
c/o Canadian Manda Group, 165 Dufferin Street
Toronto, Ontario, Canada M6K 3H6

Distributed in the United Kingdom by GMC Distribution Services,
Castle Place, 166 High Street, Lewes, East Sussex, England BN7 1XU

Distributed in Australia by Capricorn Link (Australia) Pty Ltd.,
P.O. Box 704, Windsor, NSW 2756 Australia

This book is not sponsored by Nikon Corp. The written instructions, photographs, designs, patterns, and projects in this volume are intended for the personal use of the reader and may be reproduced for that purpose only. Any other use, especially commercial use, is forbidden under law without written permission of the publisher. The works represented are the original creations of the contributing artists. All artists retain copyrights on their individual works, except as noted.

Nikon, Nikkor, Speedlight, and other Nikon product names or terminology are trademarks of Nikon Corp. Other trademarks are recognized as belonging to their respective owners.

Every effort has been made to ensure that all the information in this book is accurate. However, due to differing conditions, tools, and individual skills, the publisher cannot be responsible for any injuries, losses, and other damages that may result from the use of the information in this book. Because specifications may be changed by manufacturers without notice, the contents of this book may not necessarily agree with software and equipment changes made after publication.

If you have questions or comments about this book, please contact:
Lark Books
67 Broadway
Asheville, NC 28801
(828) 253-0467
www.larkbooks.com/digital

Manufactured in USA

All rights reserved

ISBN 13: 978-1-60059-413-7

For information about custom editions, special sales, premium and corporate purchases, please contact Sterling Special Sales Department at 800-805-5489 or specialsales@sterlingpub.com.

Contents

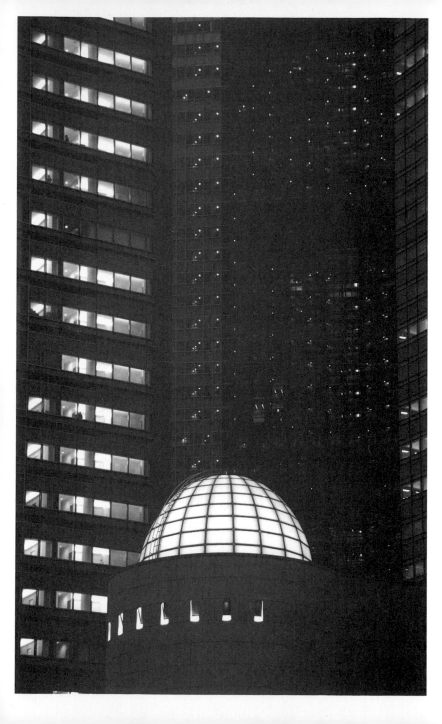

Introduction

The Nikon Corporation has accrued many years of experience building digital cameras beginning with a variety of hybrid cameras produced in collaboration with Kodak and Fujifilm respectively. Nikon's breakthrough to independence came in 1999 with the launch of the Nikon D1. This model represented their first fully independent digital SLR camera design, which not only broke new ground technically but also made high quality digital photography financially viable for many photographers.

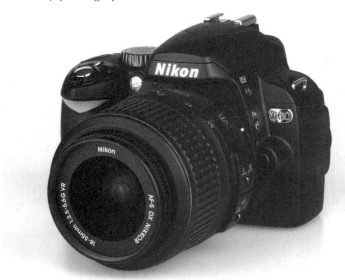

The Nikon D60 with Nikkor AF-S DX 18-55mm f/3.5-5.6G VR lens.

Nikon has a long history of photographic excellence, from its early film cameras to today's highly innovative digital SLRs.

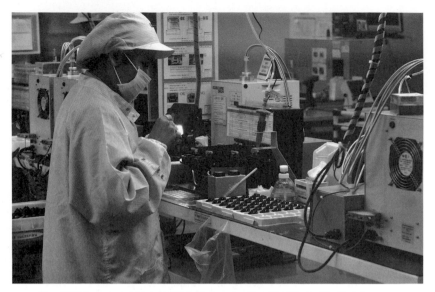

The D60 is assembled at Nikon's production facility in Thailand.

Since then the company has never attempted to introduce new camera models at anywhere near the frequency of some of its well-known competitors; until recently development of Nikon D-SLR cameras has followed a sedate process of steady evolution. A variety of models have been introduced, aimed at different sectors of the market, from the popular D100 launched during 2002 to the phenomenally successful D70 that arrived during 2004, and later to the mid-range D200 and D80, together with the professionally specified D2Xs. However, the rate of change is gathering pace because early in 2008, less than two months are the release of the D300 and D3 models, the Nikon Corporation announced the D60, their 16th digital SLR camera.

Arriving less than a year after the introduction of the D40x, the model it replaces, the D60 offers a specification that surpasses that of it predecessor at no increase in cost, which is an indication of how the economies of scale involved in the manufacture of digital cameras and associated technologies have changed in a short period of time.

The key new features of the D60 include:

- **Expeed image processing** - as well as specifically improving the rendition of color, contrast, and the control of noise, the general concept of Expeed is to enable all Nikon D-SLR cameras that support the feature to achieve the same basic color characteristics in the images they record.

- **Dust Control System** - this utilizes Nikon's image sensor cleaning feature first introduced in the D300, together with Nikon's innovative Air Control System, which directs air inside the mirror box toward ducts set into its base, which helps to draw dust particles away from the low-pass filter located in front of the camera's CCD sensor.

- **Active D-Lighting** - this feature automatically detects situations of high contrast prior to exposure and modifies the exposure level to help retain detail in the brightest highlights, while preserving the shadow and mid-tone values by adjusting in-camera processing.

- **In camera NEF RAW processing** - a new feature in the retouch menu of the D60 is the in-camera processing of NEF RAW files enabling adjustment of image quality, image size, white balance, exposure compensation, and optimize image options. Any copy of the original NEF RAW file, which must have been taken on the D60, can only be saved in the JPEG format.

- **Eye-sensor function** - a new function that detects when a user's eye is close to the viewfinder eyepiece and turns the LCD monitor screen off automatically to prevent it distracting the user and to reduce battery drain; the monitor turns back on again as soon as the user moves their eye away from the viewfinder.

- **LCD monitor display rotation** - the camera detects its orientation (horizontal, or vertical format) and automatically rotates the shooting information display on the LCD monitor accordingly, making it easier to view.

- **Other new features include** - date imprint within the image area, stop-motion animation (rapid playback of a sequence of JPEG format images), and a cross-screen (star-burst) filter effect.

The new Dust Control System, Active D-Lighting, Automatic Eye-sensor, and Expeed image processing all add very useful functionality to the D60; however, in spite of these changes, which required no significant modification to design or key components, the new camera represents a relatively modest update of the highly popular D40X model. As such the D60 is a sophisticated photographic tool with the flexibility to be used in either a completely automated way for point & shoot style photography, or with all its features and functions under the direct control of the user. Therefore, it is capable of meeting a broad range of requirements from those of a complete beginner to the more experienced, dedicated enthusiast seeking to enhance their photographic skills.

Production of the Nikon D60

The D60 is assembled at Nikon's wholly owned production facility, Nikon (Thailand), near Ayuthaya, the old historical capital of Siam, about 50 miles (80Km) north of Bangkok, Thailand's present day capital. I say assembled as a number of core parts of the D60 are manufactured elsewhere, such as the camera's main printed circuit board and its associated electronic components, which is produced at the Nikon factory in Sendai, Japan. The Nikon (Thailand) plant has been involved in precision manufacturing for almost twenty years. Its ability to handle high volume production in the digital era was proven by the tremendously successful D70 and D70s models, with the unprecedented demand for these cameras bringing about a significant expansion in the size of the workforce. Today the factory, which also handles production of the D40, D80, and D300 models, together with a number of lower-priced Nikkor lenses, operates around the clock in three eight-hour shifts and employs about 15,000 people, enabling around 80,000 D60 cameras to be manufactured per month.

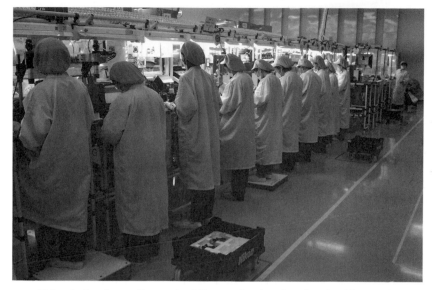

This photo shows the part of the production line for the Nikon D60 camera, which operates around the clock in Thailand.

About This Book

To get the most from your D60 it is important that you understand its features so you can make informed choices about how to use them in conjunction with your style of photography. This book is designed to help you achieve this and should be seen as an adjunct to the camera's own instruction manual. Besides explaining how all the basic functions work this book also provides you with useful tips on operating the D60 and maximizing its performance. The book does not have to be read from cover to cover. You can move from section to section as required, study a complete chapter, or just absorb the key features of functions you want to use.

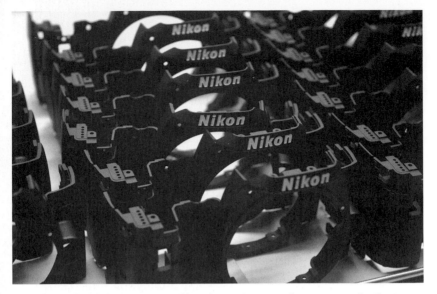

Nikon D60 front plates awaiting the next stage of camera production.

The key to success, regardless of your level of experience, is to practice with your camera. You do not waste money on film and processing costs with a digital camera; once you have invested in a memory card it can be used over and over again. Therefore, you can shoot as many pictures as you like, review your results along with a detailed record of camera settings almost immediately and then delete your near misses but save your successes - this trial and error method is a very effective way to learn!

Conventions Used in This Book
Unless otherwise stated when the terms 'left' and 'right' are used to describe the location of a camera control, it is assumed the camera is being held to the photographer's eye in the shooting position.

When referring to a specific Custom Setting it will often be mentioned in the abbreviated form – CS xx, where xx is the identifying number of the function. In describing the functionality of lenses and external flash units, it is assumed that the appropriate Nikkor lenses, generally D, or G-type Nikkor lenses to ensure full compatibility, and Nikon Speedlight units are being used. Note that lenses and flash units made by independent manufacturers may have different functionality. If you use such products refer to the manufacturer's instruction manual to check compatibility and operation with the D60.

When referring to software, either Nikon, or third-party, it is assumed that the most recent iterations of each application are used. Compatibility between image files recorded by the D60 and Nikon software will require the following, or later versions: Nikon Transfer (version 1.1.0), Nikon View NX (version 1.1.0), Capture NX (version 2.0.0), and Nikon Camera Control Pro (version 2.1.0).

Acknowledgements

Finally I would like to thank the following persons for their assistance and support during the writing of this book. At the Nikon Corporation (Tokyo), I would like to thank Mr. Gen-ichiro Ishii, head of the Nikon D60 development team and Mr. Tetsuro Goto, Chief Operating Officer and Vice President (Nikon Imaging Company); Mr. Goto kindly accompanied me during my recent tour of the Nikon (Thailand) factory. At Nikon UK Limited, Mr. Michio Miwa, Managing Director, Mr. Jeremy Gilbert, Group Marketing Director (Imaging Division), and Mr. James Banfield, Nikon European Technical Support Office.

Simon Stafford
Wiltshire, England

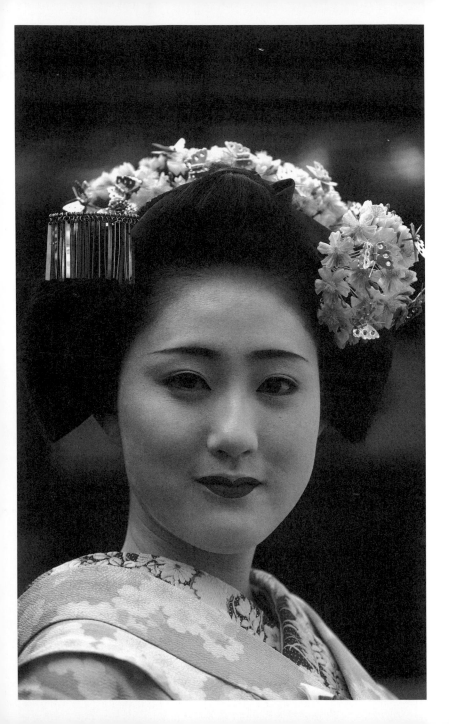

Introducing the Nikon D60

The compact D60 is designed to integrate ease of operation, high performance, and excellent image quality. It possesses a comprehensive set of features and a wide range of menu options that produce outstanding photographic results. Because of its compact size and high resolution the D60 makes an excellent pairing with my D300, especially when I need to carry two cameras for a day long shoot. It is a camera that has the ability to appeal to a wide range of photographers, from the complete beginner who seeks point-and-shoot convenience to the budget conscious professional who requires complete control of their camera. It offers complete automation of exposure and focusing, as well as full manual control of all its features and functions.

The D60 has an all-polycarbonate body that encases a fully mechanical, electronically timed shutter unit, which Nikon tests to perform at least 100,000 cycles. Providing a shutter speed range of 30 seconds to 1/4000 second, with a maximum flash synchronization speed of 1/200 second, it is the same unit used in the Nikon D40x and D80 models. It has a 420-segment RGB sensor for TTL metering and flash exposure control. The D60 uses the same Multi-CAM530 autofocus sensor as the D40 model. The D60 and D40 share the same physical dimensions making them the smallest cameras in the current Nikon D-SLR range due in part to the exclusion of a built-in autofocus motor and LCD control panel on the top of the camera.

Nikon's new Expeed processing regime allows the D60 to offer improved image quality, color, contrast, and noise control.

Nikon has long been trumpeting that image quality in the digital world rests on three pillars: optical quality of the lens, sensor technology, and internal camera processing. In respect of the two latter aspects, the D60 uses the same 10.2MP (effective) sensor as the D80 and D40 models. Nikon has dubbed their entirely new image-processing regime "Expeed" and it is at the heart of the camera's ability to record, process and output high quality images with improved rendition of color, contrast, and the control of noise, consistently.

The approximate dimensions for the D60 (W x D x H) are 5.0 x 2.5 x 3.7 inches (126 x 64 x 94 mm) and it weighs approximately 17 oz (495 g) without battery or memory card. It has a Nikon AF lens mount with the appropriate electrical contacts, however the camera does not have a built-in motor to drive the focusing mechanism of lenses that do not have their own built-in AF motor. Consequently the D60 will only support autofocus with AF-S and AF-I type Nikkor lenses, although many earlier Nikkor lenses can be mounted on the D60.

Used with AF-D or AF-G type Nikkor lenses that do not have a built-in focusing motor, the D60 supports all functions except autofocus. Other AF Nikkor lenses and AI-P type manual-focus lenses can be used but provide a lower level of compatibility in terms of the camera's TTL metering system (i.e. standard Color Matrix metering as opposed to 3D Color Matrix metering). If the D60 is set to the M (Manual) exposure mode, it is even possible to use a number of manual focus AI, AI-S, AI converted, and E-series Nikkor lenses, although the camera's autofocus system, TTL metering system (including TTL flash control), and electronic analog exposure display will not function, and lens aperture must be set via the aperture ring on the lens, see chart on page 275 for more information.

The D60 uses Secure Digital (SD) memory cards and is able to support the new generation of Secure Digital High Capacity (SDHC) cards based on SDA 2.00 specification as

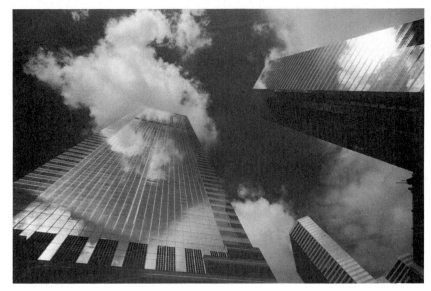

The D60 camera accepts the latest SD memory cards with high capacities.

well, providing support for the latest 4GB SDHC memory cards and, in time, capacities of up to 32GB.

The D60 does not have an LCD screen on its top plate; instead it uses the LCD monitor to show the information about camera settings in what Nikon calls the "Shooting Information Display". All relevant camera settings pertaining to exposure, flash, focus, TTL metering, ISO, white balance, battery status, and image quality are shown on the monitor. Nikon has even included a range of different display style options for the Shooting Information Display.

Nikon D60 – Front View

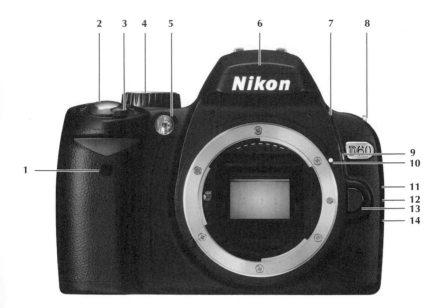

1. Infrared receiver
2. Shutter-release button
3. Power switch
4. Mode dial
5. AF-assist illuminator
   Self-timer lamp
   Red-eye reduction lamp
6. Built-in flash
7. Flash mode button
   Flash compensation button

8. Eyelet for camera strap
9. Self-timer button
   FUNC button
10. Lens mounting index
11. Video connector
12. Reset switch
13. Lens release button
14. USB connector

Nikon D60 – Back View

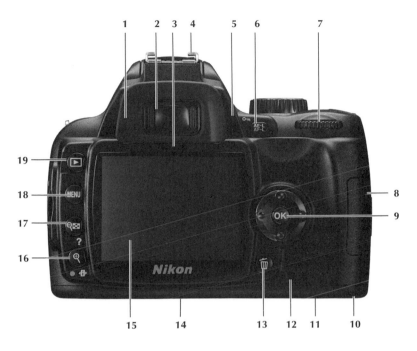

1. Rubber Eyecup DK-20
2. Viewfinder eyepiece
3. Eye sensor
4. Hot Shoe
5. Diopter adjustment control
6. AE-L / AF-l button
   Protect button
7. Command dial
8. Memory card slot cover
9. Multi selector
10. Power connector cover
11. Battery chamber cover
12. Memory card access lamp
13. Delete button
14. Tripod socket
15. LCD monitor
16. Playback zoom in button
    Information display/Quick
    setting display button
    Reset button
17. Thumbnail/Playback zoom
    out button
18. Menu button
19. Playback button

Nikon D60 – Top View

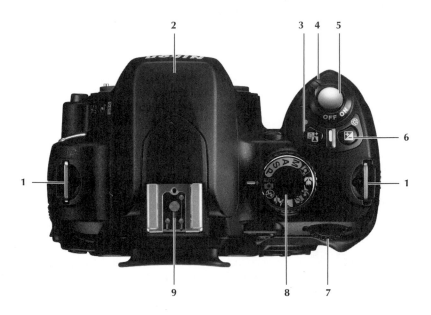

1. Eyelet for camera strap
2. Built-in flash
3. Active D-Lighting
   Reset button
4. Power switch
5. Shutter release button

6. Exposure compensation
   button
   Aperture button
   Flash compensation button
7. Command dial
8. Mode dial
9. Hot shoe

Power

A single Nikon EN-EL9 (7.4V, 1000 mAh) lithium-ion (Li-ion) battery is used to power the D60; it weighs approximately 1.8 oz. (51 g). The D40 and D40x models accept the same battery type. The standard camera body cannot accept any other type of Nikon rechargeable battery, and currently Nikon has no plans to introduce a separate battery pack/grip for the D60, such as the MB-D80 that is available for the standard D80 body.

Battery performance depends on a number of factors, including condition of the battery, the camera functions and features used, and the ambient temperature. It powers up in just 0.18 seconds when the temperature is 68°F (20°C). It is possible to make many hundreds of exposures on a single fully charged EN-EL9. For extended periods of use, the Nikon EH-5, or EH-5a AC adapter can also be used to power the D60, via the EP-5 power adapter cable.

Note: All electronically controlled cameras may occasionally function improperly due an electrostatic charge. To remedy, first switch the camera off, remove and replace the battery (or disconnect then reconnect the AC supply), then switch the camera on again. If this fails to clear the problem, press the reset button located between the video-out and USB terminals, beneath the connector cover on the left side of the camera. If you press this button, the camera's internal clock will need to be reset from the Setup menu.

Sensor

The Charge Coupled Device (CCD) sensor used in the D60 is the same sensor as used in the Nikon D80 model. It has a two-channel output to an analogue-to-digital converter (ADC), which processes the analogue electrical signal from the sensor at a 12-bit depth, there after all further internal camera processing is handled at a 12-bit depth by a single ASIC. Nikon calls their new internal, camera processing regime "Expeed";

as mentioned above this is not the name of the ASIC process-ing engine as "Expeed" involves a range of different compo-nents designed to enable the D60 to produce images with the same basic color characteristics as all other images recorded by Nikon D-SLR cameras that use "Expeed" processing. Pro-duced by Sony (a fact not officially acknowledged by Nikon) the sensor has a total of 10.75 million photosites (pixels) of which 10.2 million are effective in recording light to form an image. Each photo site is just 5.9 microns square (1 micron = 1/1000 millimeter). This gives the camera a maximum resolu-tion of 3872 x 2592 photosites (pixels), sufficient to produce a 16 x 11 inch (40 x 27.5 cm) print at 240ppi (pixel per inch) without interpolation (re-sizing) in software.

The imaging area is 0.66 x 1 in (15.6 x 23.7 mm), which is smaller than a 35mm film frame that measures 1 x 1.5 in (24 x 36 mm) but retains the same 2:3 aspect ratio. Nikon calls this their DX-format (elsewhere it is often referred to as the APS-C format) and use the same 'DX' designation to identify those lenses that have been optimized for use with their digital SLR cameras. Due to the smaller size of the DX-format digital sensor the angle-of-view offered by any focal length is reduced compared with a lens of the same focal length used on a 35mm film camera. If it assists you to esti-mate the angle-of-view for a particular focal length in com-parison with the coverage offered by the same focal on a 35mm film camera, multiply the focal length by 1.5x, see page 272 for a full explanation.

The CCD sensor of the D60 is actually a sandwich of sev-eral layers each with a specific purpose.

Photodiode Layer
The sensor has a layer of photodiodes, which converts the light that falls on them into an electrical signal; this signal is then moved away from the sensor using a method of sequen-tial transfer before it is passed on to the analogue-to-digital converter (ADC) that changes the level of the electrical sig-nal from each photodiode into a digital value using a 12-bit conversion process.

Bayer Pattern Filter Layer

Above the layer of photodiodes is a layer of color filters. The photodiodes on the CCD sensor do not record color; they can only detect a level of brightness, which is dependent on the amount of light that strikes them. To impart color to the image formed by the light that falls on the sensor, a series of minute red, green, and blue filters are arranged over the photodiodes in a Bayer pattern, which takes its name from the Kodak engineer who invented the system. These filters are arranged in an alternating pattern of red/green on the odds numbered rows, and green/blue on the even numbered rows. The Bayer pattern comprises 50% green, 25% red, and 25% blue filters; the intensity of light detected by each photodiode located beneath its single, dedicated color filter according to the Bayer pattern, is converted into an electrical signal before being converted to a digital value by the ADC. If the camera is set to record a NEF RAW file the value for each photodiode is simply saved. When you open this file in an appropriate RAW file converter the software will interpret the value from each photodiode to produce a red-green-blue (RGB) value, which in turn is converted into an image that can be viewed. However, if the camera is set to record JPEG files then the value from each photodiode is processed in the camera by comparing it with the values from a block of surrounding photodiodes, using a process called interpolation. The interpolation process produces a "best guess" for the RGB value for each sampling point (photodiode) on the sensor.

Micro-Lens Layer

Immediately above the Bayer pattern filter there is a layer of micro lenses. Since the photodiodes on the sensor are most efficient when the light falling on them is perpendicular each photodiode has a miniature lens located above it to channel the light into its well to help maximize its light gathering ability.

Optical Low-Pass Filter

Positioned in front of the CCD sensor, comprising the layers of the photodiodes, Bayer pattern filter and micro-lenses but not connected to it is an optical low-pass filter (OLPF), which is sometimes called an anti-aliasing filter.

When the frequency of detail in an image, particularly a small regular repeating pattern, such as the weave pattern in a fabric, alters at or close to the pitch of the photodiodes on the sensor there is often a side effect that produces unwanted data (often referred to as an artifact) due to the way in which the in-camera processing converts the electrical signal from the sensor to a digital value via the analogue to digital (ADC) converter. This additional data is manifest in the final image as a color pattern known as a moiré. Furthermore, the same in-camera processing can also result in a color fringing effect, known as color aliasing, which causes a halo of one or more separate colors to appear along the edge of fine detail in the image.

The OLPF is used to reduce the unwanted effects of color aliasing and moiré. However, the OPLF reduces the resolution of detail, so the camera designers must strike a balance between its beneficial effect and the loss of acuity in fine detail, which increases as the strength of the filter is increased. The OLPF also incorporates a number of important coating layers to help improve image quality:

- To help prevent dust and other foreign material from adhering to the surface of the OLPF it has an anti-static coating made from Indium Tin Oxide.

- To reduce the risk of light being reflected from the front surface of the OLPF onto the rear element of the lens, which could then result in flare effects, or ghost images, the filter has an anti-reflective coating.

- The CCD sensor is sensitive to wavelengths of light outside the spectrum visible by the human eye. This light, which can be either in the infrared (IR) or ultraviolet (UV) parts of the spectrum, will pollute image files and cause unwanted color shifts and a loss of image sharpness, so the OLPF has both an IR-blocking and UV-blocking coat. These IR and UV blocking coatings are very efficient, consequently, the D60 cannot be recommended for any form of IR or UV light photography in the way that some earlier Nikon D-SLR cameras, such as the D1 and D100 can.

Note: In the analogue-to-digital conversion process, there is a specific frequency, known as the Nyquist frequency, which is related to the pitch of the photodiodes on the sensor. Input frequencies below the Nyquist frequency will be reproduced properly but those above it have an increased tendency to generate moiré and color fringing (also known as aliasing) effects. The OLPF of the D60 is designed to transmit frequencies below the Nyquist frequency for the pitch of the photodiodes on its sensor. The design of any OLPF is a compromise between reducing the potential for moiré and maintaining image sharpness; in this respect the OLPF of the D60 permits a relatively high level of acuity to produce images that look sharp straight from the camera without any need for further post-processing but the downside is an increased risk of moiré and color fringing effects.

File Formats

The D60 can record images as compressed files using the JPEG standard, and as files saved in Nikon's proprietary RAW format: Nikon Electronic File (NEF). The NEF files can only be saved in a compressed form; the D60 provides no option to record uncompressed NEF files.

The files using the JPEG standard can be saved at three different sizes: Fine (low compression 1:4), Normal (medium compression 1:8), and Low (high compression 1:16). Note as the level of compression is increased there is a greater loss of original image file data. Furthermore, all JPEG compressed files are ultimately saved to an 8-bit depth in camera.

The highest potential for quality files comes from recording files using the NEF format: These contain the values direct from the sensor's photosites without modification and virtually no other in-camera processing, apart from information concerning camera settings. The compression applied to the 12-bit NEF files is "visually lossless" (which is not quite the same as saying "lossless"), a claim that is due to the method of compression used by the camera, which averages

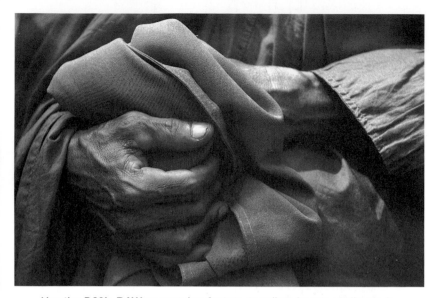

Use the D60's RAW processing feature to adjust image attributes in-camera as you shoot.

highlight data during the processing of the NEF file. To get the most out of NEF files you will need additional software such as Nikon Capture NX or a good quality third-party RAW file converter such as Adobe Camera RAW, see page 310 for full details.

In-Camera NEF RAW Processing

A new feature available in the Retouch menu of the D60 is the in-camera processing of NEF RAW files enabling adjustment of image quality, image size, white balance, exposure compensation, and optimize image options. Any copy of the original NEF RAW file, which must have been taken on the D60, can only be saved in the JPEG format.

The Viewfinder

The D60 has a fixed, optical pentaprism, eye-level viewfinder that offers a 0.8x magnification and shows approximately 95% (vertical and horizontal) of the full-frame coverage. It has an eye-point of 0.7 inches (18 mm), which provides a reasonably good view of the focusing screen and viewfinder information for users who wear eye-glasses, plus there is a built-in diopter adjustment. To set the diopter adjustment, mount a lens on the camera and leave the focus set to infinity. Point the camera at a plain surface that fills the frame and move the diopter adjustment switch (located to the right of viewfinder eyepiece) until the AF sensor brackets appear sharp. It is essential to do this to ensure you see the sharpest view of the focusing screen.

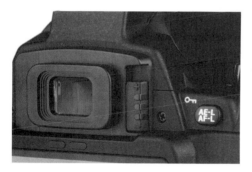

The diopter adjustment switch of the D60 is located beside the viewfinder eyepiece; to gain access to it I recommend you remove the DK-20 eyecup.

Nikon also produces a range of stronger optional eye-piece correction lenses. These are attached by slotting them on to the eyepiece frame (the DK-20 rubber eyecup must be removed first). The viewfinder eyepiece does not have an internal shutter to prevent light entering when the D60 is used remotely, so the camera is supplied with the DK-5 eye-piece cap that can be similarly fitted whenever the camera is operated this way in any of the Digital Vari-Program, P, S, or A, exposure modes.

The viewfinder display includes essential information about exposure and focus (see viewfinder information call-out). The focusing screen is marked with three pairs of

The Viewfinder

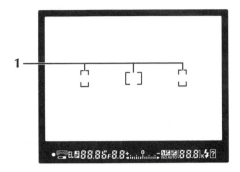

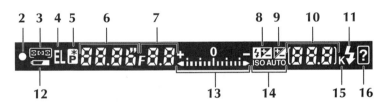

1. Focus points
2. Focus indicator
3. Focus point display
   AF-area mode
4. Autoexposure (AE) lock
5. Flexible program indicator
6. Shutter speed
7. Aperture (f-number)
   Noise reduction indicator
8. Flash compensation
   indicator
9. Exposure compensation
   indicator
10. Number of exposures
    remaining
    Number of shots remaining
    before memory buffer fills
    Preset white balance
    recording indicator

Exposure compensation
value
Flash compensation value
Active D-Lighting indicator
PC connection indicator
Dust off ref photo mode
indicator
11. Flash-ready indicator
12. Battery indicator
13. Electronic analog exposure
    display
    Exposure compensation
    Rangefinder
14. ISO auto indicator
15. "K" (appears when memory
    remains for over 1000
    exposures)
16. Warning indicator

square brackets to define the position of the autofocus sensing areas. The D60 employs conventional LED illumination for its focusing screen, so all three pairs of bracket markings are visible. To help distinguish the active focus area, its brackets are initially illuminated in red.

Shooting Information Display

To reduce the overall size of the D60 Nikon has chosen not to use a separate LCD display on the top of the camera to show the status of the principal camera controls, instead the D60 uses the same approach as the D40 and D40x cameras and displays these settings on the LCD monitor on the back of the camera, a feature that Nikon calls the Shooting Information Display. This color monitor enables "assist images," which are small picture files shown as examples for many of the main functions to help guide you in making a selection, or making an adjustment to the relevant setting. It is possible to choose one of three styles for the Shooting Information Display from the Setup menu: Classic, Graphic, and Wallpaper, each with a range of options as to the color of the background and font used. A new innovation on the D60 is the automatic rotation of the SID when the camera orientation is changed from horizontal to vertical (note this feature only applies to SID and does not function with either the Quick Settings Display, or image review). To gain access to the Shooting Information Display press the ◄𝐢► button. The LCD will show a wide range of camera control settings, including shutter speed, aperture, ISO, exposure and flash compensation, metering mode, shooting mode, active focus sensor and focus area mode, white balance, image quality and size, battery status, and audible warning.

Shooting Information Display

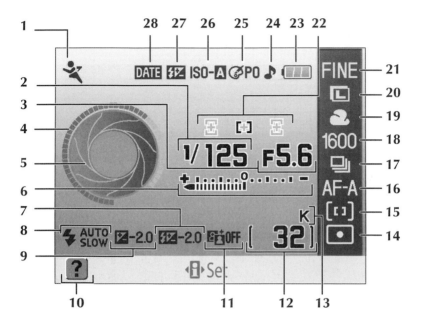

1. Shooting mode
2. Shutter speed
3. Aperture (f-number)
4. Shutter-speed display
5. Aperture display
6. Electronic analog exposure display
   Exposure compensation
7. Flash compensation value
8. Flash sync mode
9. Exposure compensation value
10. Help indicator
11. Active D-Lighting indicator
12. Number of exposures remaining
   Preset white balance recording indicator
   Capture mode indicator
13. "K" (appears when memory remains for over 1000 exposures)
14. Metering mode
15. AF-area mode
16. Focus mode
17. Release mode
18. ISO sensitivity
19. White balance mode

Shooting Information Display

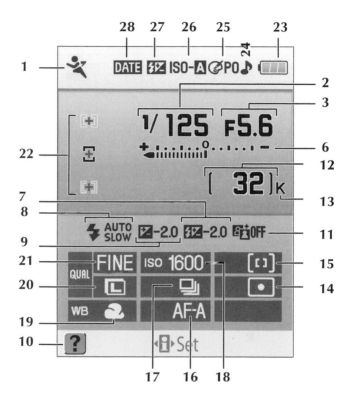

20. Image size
21. Image quality
22. Focus point display
    AF-area mode
23. Battery indicator
24. "Beep" indicator
25. Optimize image indicator

26. ISO auto indicator
27. Manual flash control
    indicator
    Flash compensation
    indicator for optional
    Speedlight
28. Date imprint indicator

37

Note: If you already understand the relationship between shutter speed and lens aperture, together with the concept of the lens aperture and its values, I recommend using the Classic display since it offers the greatest clarity and the presentation of the information will be familiar if you have used any other Nikon camera that has a control panel LCD display. The Graphic display is well intentioned and has been improved from the version used by the D40 / D40x models in as much as the effect of changes to shutter speed and lens aperture is much clearer but the scale of the information displayed is reduced compared with the Classic display. The Wallpaper option is in my opinion a gimmick and should be avoided; it often suffers from a lack of clarity, as the picture displayed in the background to the screen will often obscure information.

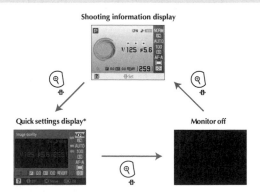

Use the ◄ᐅ button to scroll between the Shooting Information Display and the Quick Settings Display.

Quick Settings Display

To speed up adjustment to a range of camera settings by avoiding navigation of the menu system the D60 allows the user to make adjustments by displaying a range of camera settings in the Quick Settings Display; each setting is selected by using the multi selector button and the ⓞⓚ button (see page 95 for full details). To access the Quick Settings Display start by pressing ◄ᐅ to open the Shooting Information Display then press ◄ᐅ again.

Eye-Sensor Function

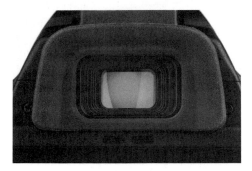

The optical sensors for the Eye Sensor function are located immediately below the viewfinder eyepiece.

Another new feature of the D60 is its Eye Sensor function that detects when a user's eye is close to the viewfinder eyepiece and turns the Shooting Information Display off to prevent it distracting the user and the viewfinder display on, automatically, which also helps to reduce battery drain; the monitor turns back on and the viewfinder display turns off again, as soon as the user moves their eye away from the viewfinder.

Note: The Eye Sensor function does not switch off the Quick Settings Display, or image review. If either of these is active, use the shutter release button to return the camera to the shooting mode.

Automatic Focus

The autofocus (AF) system is based on the Multi-CAM 530 AF module (up to 530 individual points are assessed in the process of focus acquisition, depending on the AF-area mode selected). It features three sensing areas arranged in a horizontal line across the viewfinder screen. The central sensor is a cross type that is sensitive to detail in both horizontal and vertical orientations, whereas the other two are single line sensors, sensitive to detail parallel to the short edge of the viewfinder frame.

The diagram shows the approximate coverage of the three autofocus sensing areas of the CAM530 AF module used in the D60; note only the central sensing area is a cross type sensitive to detail in both horizontal and vertical orientations.

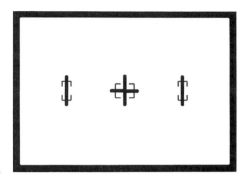

The detection range of the AF system is −1 to +19EV at an ISO100. An AF-assist lamp used in low light levels has an effective range from 1.67 to 9.83 feet (0.5 m to 3 m). The system has three focusing modes: Auto-servo focus (AF-A - the default setting), Continuous-servo focus (AF-C), and Single-servo focus (AF-S). In AF-A mode, the camera will activate AF-S automatically if the AF system determines that the subject is stationary; if the AF system determines that the subject is moving, AF-C mode will be activated. In the AF-C mode, the camera focuses continuously and if it detects that the subject is moving it will attempt to predict the position of the subject at the instant the shutter opens.

In addition, the D60 has three AF-area modes that not only determine which of the focus areas are used but also how the camera uses the selected focus area: Single-area AF, Dynamic-area AF, and Closest subject area AF. For more detailed information on autofocus, see pages 152-162.

AUTO and Digital Vari-Program Modes

The D60 is capable of operating in a fully automated way for point-and-shoot photography. The AUTO ᴬᵁᵀᴼ option relinquishes all control to the camera, and does not allow the user to apply any influence, or compensation to any of the settings selected by the camera pertaining to exposure or white balance. In additional to ᴬᵁᵀᴼ , there are seven Digital Vari-Program modes: ⚡ Auto (Flash off) cancels the operation of the built-in Speedlight flash, plus six scene / subject specific modes that Nikon refers to as, Portrait **Z** , Landscape **▲** , Child **☺** , Sports **⚲** , Close-up **✿** , and Night Portrait **▣** . For more detailed information on these modes, see pages 71-81.

Exposure Modes

The D60 offers four exposure modes that are partially or fully controlled by the user to determine how the lens aperture and shutter speed values are set when the exposure is adjusted: Programmed auto (P), Aperture-priority (A), Shutter-priority (S), and Manual (M):

P–Programmed auto selects a combination of shutter speed and aperture automatically but the photographer can override this using the Flexible program feature.

A–Aperture-priority allows the photographer to select the lens aperture while the camera assigns an appropriate shutter speed.

S–Shutter-priority allows the photographer to select the shutter speed while the camera assigns an appropriate lens aperture.

M–Manual mode places selection of both the shutter speed and lens aperture in the hands of the photographer.

For more detailed information about these exposure modes, see pages 136-141.

Exposure compensation can be set over a range of –5 to +5 stops in increments of 1/3EV; however, the D60 does not have an exposure, or flash-exposure bracketing feature. In P, S, A, and the automatic exposure modes, the exposure settings can be locked using the AE-L/AF-L button **AE-L/AF-L** **(○┓)** located on the rear of the camera.

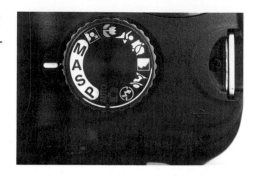

The exposure mode is selected via the mode dial; here aperture-priority auto (A) mode is set.

The D60 has an ISO sensitivity range (ISO equivalent) between ISO 100 and ISO 1600 that can be set in steps of 1EV. Additionally, the sensitivity can be increased by 1EV above ISO 1600, again in a single step, to Hi 1, which has an equivalent ISO rating of 3200. The camera also has a noise reduction feature that can operate at sensitivities over ISO 400.

Metering Exposure

The D60 offers three options within its TTL metering system, enabling the camera to cope with a variety of different lighting situations. The 3D Matrix and Center-weighted metering systems have an Exposure Value (EV) range of 0 to 20EV, and 2 to 20EV for Spot metering (ISO 100, lens aperture of f/1.4, 68°F/20°C). For more detailed information about metering modes, see pages 131-135.

▦ 3D Color Matrix Metering II

The D60 uses a 420-segment RGB sensor (the new camera uses the same sensor and processing algorithm as the D40, D40x, and D80 cameras), which is located within the camera's viewfinder head to assess the brightness, color, and contrast of light. Additional information from compatible D-type, and G-type Nikkor lenses, and the AF system is also taken in to account. Based on the focused distance and which focus area is active, the camera assumes the likely position of the subject within the frame area. The D60 then

uses a reference of over thirty thousand examples of photographed scenes, comparing these with the information
from the metering system to provide a final suggestion for
the exposure value.

Note: Standard Color Matrix Metering II is performed if CPU
lenses other than D or G-type are attached to the camera. If
you attach a non-CPU type lens (i.e. Ai, Ai-modified, Ai-s,
and E-series), the TTL metering system does not operate,
although it is still possible to use Manual exposure mode
(the shutter speed is set on the camera while the lens aperture is set via its aperture ring) and manual focus.

⊙ Center-Weighted Metering
The camera meters from the entire frame area, but assigns a
bias to a central, 0.31-inch (8 mm) diameter circle in a ratio
of 75:25.

⊡ Spot Metering
The camera meters a 0.13-inch (3.5 mm) circle, which represents approximately 2.5% of the full frame area, centered on
the selected (active) focus area brackets.

🔳 Active D-Lighting
A feature first introduced in the Nikon D300 camera the
Active D-Lighting feature (not to be confused with the D-
Lighting item in the Retouch menu) can be used to optimize
the exposure settings when using Matrix metering. It automatically detects situations of high contrast prior to exposure and modifies the exposure level to help retain detail in
the brightest highlights while preserving the shadow and
mid-tone values by adjusting in-camera processing, see page
133 for full details. Since the effects of Active D-Lighting are
applied during the processing of an image file it is not possible to reverse them when recording either JPEG files. The
effects of Active D-Lighting with an image recorded in the
NEF RAW format can be altered subsequently using appropriate Nikon software.

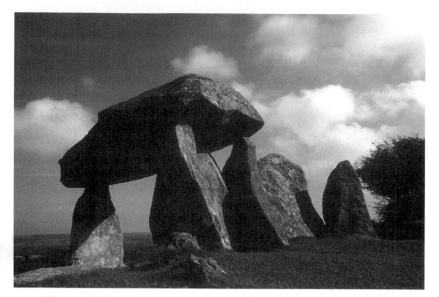

With the D60, you can choose to set the camera's white balance control to the option that is most appropriate for the kind of lighting you're shooting in, or you can take a custom reading of the light using the Preset option.

White Balance

The D60 offers several choices for white balance control, including a fully automatic option **AUTO** that uses the same 420-pixel RGB sensor in the viewfinder as the TTL metering system. There are another six user selectable manual options for specific lighting conditions: Incandescent ☀ (for typical tungsten type lighting), Fluorescent 🌠 (for fluorescent lighting – there are seven options for different types of fluorescent lighting), Direct Sunlight ☀ , Flash ⚡ (for lighting by both the internal and external flash units), Cloudy ☁ (for daylight under an overcast sky), and Shade 🏠 (for daylight in deep shade). Each of these settings can be fine-tuned to impart a slightly warmer (more red) or cooler (more blue) color.

In addition, the D60 has the ability to set the white balance using a Preset **PRE** option that can be set by assessing the color temperature of the prevailing light reflected from an appropriate test target. For more detailed information about white balance, see pages 106-117.

Note: Only one Preset white balance value can be stored in the camera and recalled as required; it is not possible to apply a fine-tuning white balance factor when using the Preset white balance option.

Optimizing Images

In the fully automated point-and-shoot and Digital Vari-Program modes, values for image attributes of sharpening, tone (contrast), color mode, saturation, and hue are assigned automatically; the user has no level of control over the settings used by the camera. In P, S, A, and M exposure modes, however, values for these image attributes are assigned by a number of options found by selecting Optimize Image in the Shooting menu, . This control allows an image to be processed by the camera according to the type of subject/scene being photographed, or to how the image will be used. The Optimize Image options include: Normal ⊘N , Softer ⊘SO , Vivid ⊘VI , More Vivid ⊘VI⁺ , Portrait ⊘PO , Black & White ⊘BW , or Custom ⊘⊘ . The camera sets values automatically for all options, with the exception of the Custom option, which allows the user to define their own settings. See pages 118-122 for more detailed information about the Optimize Image options.

The Shutter

The D60 uses a fully mechanical, electronically timed shutter unit, which Nikon tests to withstand at least 100,000 cycles. Providing a shutter speed range of 30 seconds to 1/4000-second, with a maximum flash synchronization speed of 1/200-second, it is the same unit used in the Nikon D80. The shutter release lag time is approximately 0.08 second, with a minimum viewfinder blackout time (from mirror up until down) that is approximately double the release lag time (note this is only achieved at shutter speeds of 1/250-second, or less. Apparently, a fully mechanical shutter was chosen for the D60 (in preference to a mechanical/ CCD shutter type as used in the D40 model, where briefer shutter speeds beyond 1/90th second are emulated by switching the CCD sensor on and off), in order to maintain image quality because the sensor in the D60 has many more photodiodes (pixels).

The shutter speed range runs from 30 seconds to 1/4000 second and can be set in steps of 1/3EV. There is a bulb option for exposures beyond 30 seconds. The D60 has a noise reduction option in the Shooting menu that helps reduce the effects of electronic noise in exposures of 8 seconds or longer (however the recording time for each exposure is extended by up to 100% as the camera performs a dark frame exposure as part of the long exposure noise reduction process). The maximum flash sync speed when using either the built-in Speedlight (flash unit), optional Speedlights, such as the SB-400, or any compatible off-brand flash unit, is 1/200th second.

Shooting Modes

The shooting mode determines when the camera makes an exposure. In Single frame mode $\boxed{S}$, the camera takes a single photograph each time the shutter release button is fully depressed. In Continuous mode $\boxed{\square}$, the camera shutter cycles up to a maximum rate of 3 frames per second (fps). However, the effective frame rate will be limited by a number of factors, including the camera functions that are active, the selected shutter speed, and the capacity of the remaining buffer memory.

⟳10s Self-Timer
The self-timer mode delays recording of the image after the shutter release button is depressed fully. It is useful for self-

portraits and for reducing the loss of sharpness caused by the effect of vibrations generated by touching the camera, in particular the shutter release button, especially when shooting at a high magnification or using a very long focal length. The default delay is 10 seconds, but you can use CS-16 in the Custom Setting menu to change the delay to 2, 5, or 20 seconds.

Remote Release

The shutter of the D60 can be released remotely using the ML-L3 infrared remote release, which allows the shutter release to be activated wirelessly. There are two options, quick response (immediate) release   **â** , or a delayed release **â** 2s that introduces a 2-second pause between the signal being sent to the camera and the shutter being released, which is helpful if you are shooting a self-portrait, see page 150 for a more detailed description of this accessory.

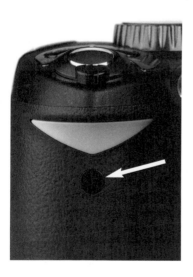

The shutter of the D60 can be released remotely using the ML-L3 release; the infrared receiver is located behind the small window on the front of the hand grip.

LCD Monitor

The 2.5 inch, 230,000 pixel, color LCD monitor screen located on the back of the camera offers a viewing angle of 170 degrees shows virtually 100% of the image file when it is reviewed. Pictures can be played back for review either as single images or in multiples. When used to display a single image, the review function has a zoom facility that enlarges images by up to twenty-five times for a large image (3,872 x 2,592 pixels), nineteen times for a medium image, and thirteen times for a small image.

By using the multi selector button   ◉   located on back of the camera, you can scroll through a range of six pages containing shooting/image information about any image reviewed in single-image playback. These include a page of basic information, two pages of shooting data, a page that shows settings for Active D-Lighting and any alterations made using the retouch menu, a page that displays a highlight warning (to indicate potentially over exposed areas of the image, which will blink), and a page showing a composite histogram of the color channels (red, green, and blue).

You have the option to delete your image files while they are still in the camera or protect them from unintentional erasure while reviewing them on the LCD monitor. Also use the LCD to view the Shooting Information Display, as described above, as well as the various camera menus, from which you can activate or deactivate a wide range of camera features and functions. The brightness of the LCD monitor screen can be adjusted via the Setup menu.

Menus

Although most of the principal controls of the D60 can be accessed and easily operated by buttons or dials located on the camera body in conjunction with the Shooting Information Display and Quick Settings Display, there are some core functions and features that must be applied through the camera's five menus: Playback , Shooting 📷 , Custom Settings ✐ , Setup ⓨ , and Retouch ☑ . To facilitate access to items in any of these, a feature known as "My menu" in the Setup menu allows you to display only items that you choose. To open a menu display, press the menu button ⓜ located in the row of buttons on the back left of the camera. Select the appropriate menu by scrolling with the multi selector. The various options and sub-options are color coded to facilitate navigation and selection of the required setting.

Built-In Speedlight (Flash)

Nikon always refers to its flash units, built-in or external, as Speedlights. The D60 has a built-in Speedlight housed above the viewfinder. In Auto ᴬᵁᵀᴼ📷 and in the Digital Vari-Programs for Portrait, Child, Close-up, and Night Portrait, the built-in flash will raise automatically if the camera determines the light level is sufficiently low to require additional illumination from the flash. The built-in Speedlight will not pop up automatically in P, A, S, or M exposure modes, but must be activated manually by pressing the Speedlight flash mode button ⚡ on the front of the camera to the left of the viewfinder head.

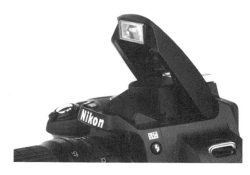

The built-in Speedlight of the D60 can be useful for providing fill-in flash, as well as acting as the main source of illumination.

At full output, the Guide Number (GN) of the built-in Speedlight is GN 39 feet (12 m) at ISO 100 when TTL control is used, and GN 43 feet (13 m) at ISO 100 with manual flash control. It is fully compatible with the latest i-TTL flash exposure control system for balanced fill-flash, but defaults to standard i-TTL flash when spot metering is selected. The D60 also supports the Advanced Wireless Lighting system when it is used with either an SB-800 (in Commander mode) Speedlight, or the SU-800 to control a number of remote flash units (currently the SB-800, SB-600, or SB-R200).

The built-in flash can be used with any CPU-type lens with a focal length of 18–300mm. The minimum distance at which the Speedlight can be used is 2 feet (0.6 m). However, with certain lenses the minimum distance must be greater due to the proximity of the flash tube to the central axis of the lens, otherwise light from the flash is prevented from illuminating the entire frame area (see pages 239-268 for full details on using the D60 for flash photography).

External Ports

On the left side of the D60 is a rubber cover that houses two ports, one for connecting the camera to a computer or printer (the D60 supports High-speed USB 2.0 for data transfer), and another for connecting the camera to a Video monitor for image playback. Located between these two ports is the camera's reset switch that is used to rectify problems that can occur due to the build up of static charge within the camera.

Basic Camera Care

Regardless of how meticulous you are about keeping your camera clean, dust and dirt are sure to accumulate inside it eventually. Since prevention is better than cure, always keep body and lens caps in place when not using your equipment. Be sure to switch the D40x off before attaching or detaching a lens to prevent particles from being attracted to the low-pass filter by the electrical charge of the sensor. Hold the camera body with the lens mount facing downwards whenever you change lenses. You should also vacuum the interior of your camera bag periodically.

It is a good idea to put a basic cleaning kit together for shooting in the field. It should consist of a soft ?-inch (12 mm) artist's paintbrush, a micro-fiber lens cloth, a micro-fiber towel (available from a good outdoors store) for absorbing moisture when working in damp conditions, and a rubber bulb blower (either from a traditional blower brush or made specifically for use in cleaning lenses and the low-pass filter).

Always brush or blow material off equipment before wiping it with a cloth. For lens elements and filters, use a micro-fiber cloth and wipe surfaces in short strokes, not a sweeping circular motion, turning the cloth frequently. For residue that cannot be removed with a dry cloth, use a lens cleaning fluid suitable for photographic lenses. Apply the fluid sparingly to the cloth, not directly to the lens (it may seep inside and cause damage). Wipe the residue and buff with a dry cloth. Any lens cloth should be washed on a regular basis to keep it clean.

Self-Cleaning

The presence of dust and other similar unwanted particulate material on the front surface of the optical low-pass filter (OLPF, the surface closest to the rear of the lens mounted on the camera) is the bane of all digital photographers, as it results in dark shadow spots appearing in the final image. The definition of such spots will to some extent be dependent on the lens aperture used; at very wide aperture settings (low f/number) these shadow spots will appear less well defined and in some instances may not even be apparent but at moderate to small aperture settings (high f/number) they will mar the image. This will require extra effort to remove them using software cloning tools in post-processing.

Regardless of how careful you are dust and other foreign material will eventually find its way into a camera. The action of focusing, or adjusting the zoom ring of a lens causes groups of lens elements to be shifted inside the lens barrel creating very slight changes in air pressure, which causes dust in the atmosphere to be drawn through the lens into the camera. A visual inspection of OLPF is often fruitless due to the extremely small size of the offending dust particles, which can be just a few microns across, so they are beyond the resolution of our eyes.

In an effort to help reduce the effects of such deposits on the OLPF and reduce the frequency with which external cleaning measures need be applied, Nikon has incorporated a self-cleaning mechanism into the D60 that vibrates the OLPF at four different frequencies using a piezo-electric oscillator. The cleaning process can be set to activate automatically when the camera is turned on, turned off, or both. Alternatively, it can be activated at anytime the user deems it necessary.

The Air Control System
The self-cleaning function is supplemented by a new feature, which is seen for the first time in the D60. Nikon's innovative Airflow Control System is designed to use changes in air pressure caused by the movement of the reflex mirror to direct air inside the mirror box toward ducts set into its base, which helps to draw dust particles away from the low-pass filter located in front of the camera's CCD sensor. Below the bottom edge of the OLPF and the ducts in the base of the mirror box are areas covered with a tenacious adhesive material that is design to capture dust and other particulate matter dislodged by the self-cleaning processes.

Beyond the self-cleaning function of vibrating the OLPF and the effects of the Air Control System, Nikon implements a comprehensive regime, which spans camera production through to using software during post-processing of an image, to reduce the risk of dust affecting images recorded by the camera. This includes the following:

- All internal mechanisms with moving parts such as the shutter unit are designed to minimize the generation of dust, or other particles.

- During manufacture of the D60 its shutter unit is activated 500 times before being installed in the camera as part of a running-in process. A similar procedure is performed once the camera is assembled.

- An anti-static coating is applied around the image sensor and OLPF assembly, while a border area surrounding the OLPF is specially treated with a tenacious adhesive material, so any dust particles dislodged from the OLPF by the self-cleaning process adhere to it and prevent them from migrating elsewhere inside the camera.

- In the D60 the space between the OLPF and image sensor has been increased, so that dust is less likely to affect the final image and the gap between the two is sealed to prevent dust particles from entering the senor assembly.

- The camera can record a reference frame that shows the location of dust spots, which can be applied using a feature in Nikon Capture NX software to reduce the effects of dust in images shot using the NFF (RAW) format.

Manual Cleaning of the OLPF

The self-cleaning and Airflow Control systems can be effective at removing loose, dry material that settles on the surface of the OLPF, but if moisture condenses on it and residues are left behind once it has evaporated, or the OLPF has smear marks on it, an alternative method of cleaning will be required. Despite their recommendation concerning cleaning of the OLPF (see the note below), Nikon realizes this may be impractical for a variety of reasons; therefore they have provided the D60 with a function to help users clean it themselves.

Note: In all cases Nikon recommends the optical low-pass filter (OLPF) should be cleaned by an authorized service center. In the Nikon instruction manual to the D60 it states that under no circumstances should you touch or wipe the OLPF.

Caution: It must be stressed that you clean the OLPF entirely at your own risk, regardless of the method employed. Any damage caused to the low-pass filter, or any other part of your camera as a result of manual cleaning by the user will not be covered by warranties provided by Nikon.

Go to the Setup menu and scroll to [Mirror lock-up]. Then press ⊚ to select [On] (highlighted as the default). Press ⊚ again and a dialog box will appear with the following instruction: "When shutter button is pressed, mirror lifts and shutter opens. To lower mirror, turn camera off." Once the shutter is pressed, the mirror will lift and remain in its raised position. Keep the camera facing down so any debris falls away from the filter; look into the lens mount to inspect the low-pass filter surface (it is probably helpful to shine a light on to it – a head torch is ideal for this purpose), but remember that offending particles will be very small, making it unlikely you will be able to resolve them by eye.

Keep the camera facing down and use a rubber bulb blower to gently puff air towards the filter array surface. Take care that you do not enter any part of the blower into the camera. Under no circumstances should you touch or wipe the filter array. Never use an ordinary brush with bristles or compressed air to clean the filter array (they can leave residue or damage its surface). Once you have finished cleaning, switch the camera off to return the mirror to its down position. If the blower bulb method fails to remove stubborn material, I recommend you have the sensor cleaned professionally.

For users with plenty of confidence there is a range of proprietary sensor cleaning materials, including brushes, swabs and fluids available from a number of manufacturers (see the list of resources on page 288) that can be used to clean stubborn and tenacious material from the low-pass filter. Again I must stress that you do use any such materials, or implements entirely at your own risk. If you have Nikon Capture NX software, you can use the Dust Reference Photo feature with NEF RAW files shot using the D60 to help remove the effects of dust particles on the low-pass filter by masking their shadows electronically.

Caution: The Indium Tin Oxide anti-static coating applied to the surface of the OLPF is more susceptible to being damaged by physical contact or use of alcohol based cleaning fluids compared with the Lithium Niobate coating used in other Nikon D-SLR cameras, such as the D200 and D300. Take extra care if you decide to clean the OLPF of your D60 yourself, and always check on the compatibility of any cleaning materials you use.

Caution: It is essential that the camera's battery be fully charged before you attempt any of these procedures (preferably use the EH-5 / EH-5a AC adapter with the EP-5 adapter connector to ensure a continuous power supply). If the power supply fails during the cleaning process, the shutter will close and the mirror will return to its down position, with potentially dire consequences if you have any cleaning utensils in the camera!

Note: If the battery level of the camera drops too low, it will not be possible to access [Mirror lock-up] in the Setup menu. Also, if the battery power becomes too low while the mirror is locked-up, the camera will emit an audible alert and the AF-assist lamp will begin to flash, warning that the mirror will lower automatically in approximately two minutes.

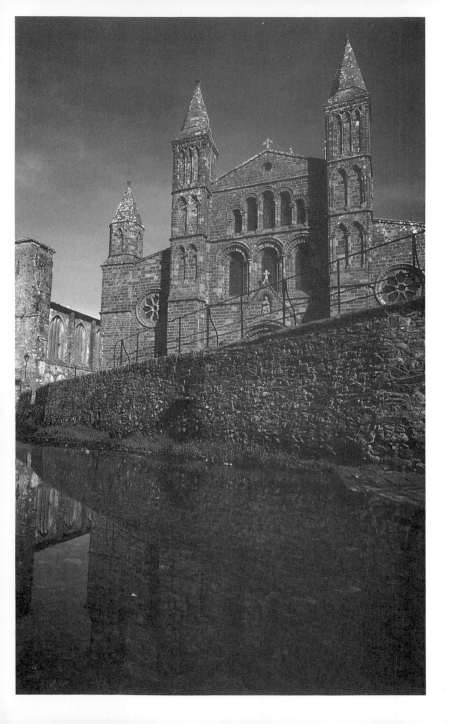

Quick Start Guide

It is only natural to want to start using your new D60 camera as soon as you remove it from its box. However, there are a few basic steps that you should take before you start shooting your first pictures. Spend a little time with your new camera to acquaint yourself with the principal controls and functions.

Charging/Inserting the Battery

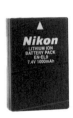
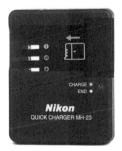

The EN-EL9 battery is charged in its dedicated AC charger the MH-23.

Since the D60 is entirely dependent on electrical power, it is essential to fully charge the EN-EL9 battery supplied with the camera (it is only partially charged when shipped). There is no need to pre-condition the battery, but for its first charge leave it connected to the MH-23 charger until it is cool to the touch. Do not be tempted to remove it as soon as the charge indicator lamp on the MH-23 has stopped flashing.

The following chapter covers the basics of camera handling and shooting so that you can get started quickly shooting great pictures with your Nikon D60.

Make sure the camera's power switch is OFF. Slide the battery-chamber cover lock (on bottom of camera) toward the center of the D60 to open. Insert the battery so its three contacts enter first. Close the chamber cover by pressing it down until it clicks into place to lock. Turn the camera ON and check the battery-status indicator in the Shooting Information Display shown on the LCD monitor to confirm the battery is fully charged; **IIII** should be displayed.

The battery chamber of the D60 accommodates a single EL-EN9 battery; access is via the base of the camera; note the diagram on the inside of the chamber door indicating the orientation of the battery

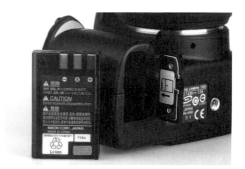

Attaching the Camera Strap

The camera strap is not only useful to prevent the camera from being dropped accidentally, it also helps you brace the camera to reduce camera shake that can spoil your pictures. You can aid support of the camera if you adjust the strap to a length that is taut when wound around your arm.

To attach the strap, start by threading it from the outside of the left camera strap eyelet and feed it back through the keeper-loop. Then pass it through the inside of the buckle, under the section of the strap that already passes through the buckle, before pulling it tight. Repeat this process with the other end of the strap, working it through the right strap eyelet. Finally adjust the strap to your preferred length.

Choosing a Language

Once you have inserted a fully charged battery and turned the camera on for the first time by rotating the power switch set around the shutter release button, there are a couple of steps you need to take to set up the D60. No pictures can be taken until these have been completed.

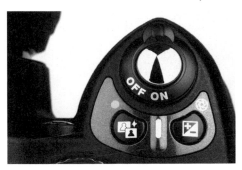

The main power switch is located on a collar around the shutter release button.

After switching the camera on for the first time, the [Language] option from the Setup menu is displayed. Press the multi selector arrows (on back of camera) up or down until the required language is highlighted, and press the 🆗 button to confirm and lock your selection.

Note: If you wish to change the language at any time, open the Setup menu and highlight the [Language] option, then repeat the procedure just described.

Setting the Internal Clock

After you have selected the language, the [Time Zone] option in the [World Time] menu will be displayed; press the multi selector to the left or right to highlight the appropriate local time zone, and press the 🆗 button to confirm and lock your selection. The [Daylight Saving Time] page will now open. Use the multi selector to highlight either [ON] or [OFF] as required for your local time zone, and press the 🆗 button to confirm and lock. The last page to open is the [Date] page; press the multi selector to the left or right to highlighted each box and press it up or down to adjust the setting as required. Once you have completed setting the date and time, press the ⓞⓚ button to confirm and lock your selections. The monitor will turn off and the camera is returned to the shooting mode.

Note: The D60 has an internal clock powered by an independent rechargeable battery that is charged from the camera's principal power source, either the main EN-EL9 battery or the EH-5 /EH-5a AC adapter with the EP-5 power connector. The clock battery is not accessible by the user. It requires approximately 72 hours of charging to power the clock for about one month. Should the clock battery become exhausted the "Clock not set" warning message is displayed on the monitor screen. It will be necessary to reset the clock to the correct date and time should this occur.

Hint: The internal clock is not as accurate as many wristwatches and domestic clocks, so it is important to check it regularly, particularly if the camera has not been used for a few weeks.

Lens Compatibility

Either an AF-S or AF-I Nikkor lens is required to access all the functions and features of the D60, including autofocus; other types of Nikkor lenses can only be used with manual focus and provide lesser degrees of compatibility (see table on right).

Mounting a Lens

Align the mounting index-mark (white dot) on the lens with the mounting index-mark (white dot) next to the bayonet ring of the camera's lens mount. Enter the lens bayonet into the camera and rotate the lens counter-clockwise until it locks into place with a positive click.

D60 Lens Compatibility Table

Lens Type	Focus Mode		Exposure modes	Metering	
	AF	**Manual**	**D V-P + P, S, and A modes**	**Matrix**	**C-W & Spot**
AF-S, AF-I	OK	OK	OK	OK	OK
AF-D and AF-G (without AF-S)	-	OK	OK	OK	OK
AF lenses	-	OK	OK	OK [1]	OK
Ai-P	-	OK	OK	OK [1]	OK
PC-Micro Nikkor 85mm f/2.8D [2]	-	OK	-	OK	OK
Ai and Ai-S compatible manual focus lenses [3]	-	OK	-	-	-

1   *Color Matrix metering is used instead of 3D Color Matrix metering II.*

2   *Exposure metering and flash control may not function properly when lens is shifted and/or tilted, or aperture is not at its maximum.*

3   *Non-CPU lenses (such as manual focus Ai and Ai-S type lenses) can be used but only in manual (M) exposure mode. Selecting another mode disables the shutter release. Aperture must be manually adjusted using the lens aperture ring; the autofocus system, exposure metering, electronic analog exposure display, and TTL flash control are not available. If another exposure mode is selected, the shutter release will be disabled and "F—" will appear in the monitor display, blinking. The electronic rangefinder can be used with most lenses that have a maximum aperture of f/5.6 or faster (see page 230 for more details).*

Mounting a lens on the D60 requires the two white index dots, one on the lens and the other on the edge of the camera's lens mount, to be aligned.

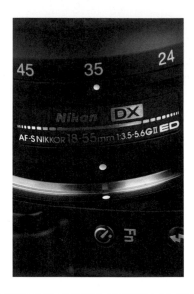

Hint: Whenever you attach or detach a CPU-type lens (these have a series of electrical contact pins set around the lens mount bayonet) to or from the D60, ensure that the camera is turned off. If the camera is on while a lens is being rotated, there is a risk that the electrical contact pins on the lens mount could cause an improper connection with the contact plates in the camera, causing the electronics of the camera to malfunction.

Apart from G-type lenses that lack a conventional aperture ring, it is necessary to set the aperture ring of all other CPU-type Nikkor lenses to the minimum aperture value (highest f/number), and I recommend you use the small locking switch to ensure the aperture ring is secured in this position.

Hint: If you turn the camera on after mounting a lens and **FE E** blinks in the viewfinder, the lens has not been set to its minimum aperture (highest f/number). When this happens, the shutter release is disabled and the camera will not operate.

To remove a lens from the camera, press and hold the lens release button, then turn the lens clockwise until the white mounting index-mark on the lens is aligned with the mounting index-mark next to the bayonet ring of the camera's lens mount. Now lift the lens clear of the camera body. If you do not intend to mount another lens, always replace the BF-1A body cap to help prevent unwanted material from entering the camera.

Adjusting Viewfinder Focus

The viewfinder eyepiece lens has a diopter adjustment so that the camera can be used regardless of whether or not you normally wear eyeglasses. To check and set the viewfinder focus, turn the camera on with a lens attached and use the multi selector to select the central focus sensor area. Look through the viewfinder and slide the diopter control button up and down until the focus area brackets appear sharp. If the viewfinder display turns off as you make adjustments, press the shutter release button halfway to re-activate the displays.

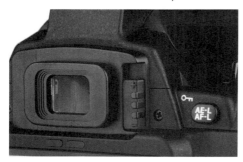

The viewfinder eyepiece has a diopter adjustment set by sliding the small button to the right of the viewfinder eyepiece; to improve access the eyecup can be removed by sliding it upwards.

Note: It is usually easier to judge the viewfinder focus if the camera is pointed at a plain pale surface. To prevent the focusing system from hunting when pointed at such a featureless subject, select manual focus by setting the focus mode switch on the lens to M (not A, or M/A). Alternatively, select Focus mode from the camera's Quick Settings Display and set it to MF (manual focus). Finally, assuming the lens has one, set the focus to the infinity mark on the lens distance scale, or, if the lens does not have an infinity mark, focus on a distant object.

Using Your SD Memory Card

The D60 records pictures to Secure Digital (SD) memory cards, which use solid-state flash memory (i.e. no moving parts). The card slot of the D60 can accommodate one card at a time (a list of memory cards tested and approved by Nikon is shown on page 294).

Installing the Memory Card

Turn the camera OFF before opening the card slot cover by sliding it in the direction of the small arrow marked on the door. The door will swing open to reveal the memory card port. Insert the card with its contacts pointing toward the cover; the small write-protect switch should be at the bottom with the main (top) label on the memory card facing you. The card will slide easily until you feel slight resistance, then keep pushing gently until it clicks in to place (the green memory card access lamp illuminates briefly as confirmation that the card is installed properly). Finally, close the cover.

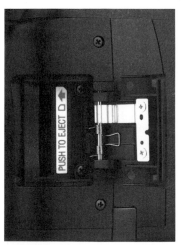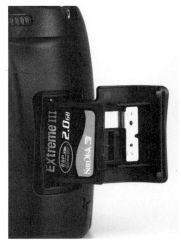

The card port door of the D60 is simply slid backwards and it will swing open under tension of a spring to reveal the memory card port. Pay attention to the orientation of the memory card when you insert it in the D60. The main (top) label of the card must face you (i.e. face toward the back of the camera), and the beveled corner should be to the top left as you look at the card.

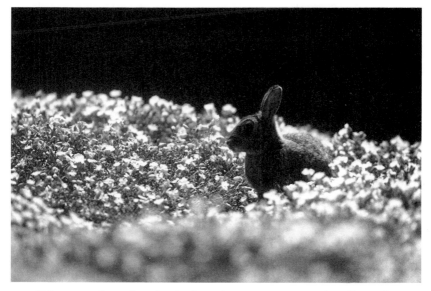

Take care when choosing to format your memory card as the paths to any image files remaining on the card will be erased, making it very difficult to recover them. Be sure you have downloaded and saved your files to another location before formatting the card.

Formatting the Memory Card

All new memory cards must be formatted before first use. To format a memory card, first ensure the write-protection switch on the card is not set to Lock, then install the card and turn the camera ON. Press the ⊙ button, then navigate to the Setup menu ⵑ and open it. Now highlight Format memory card and press the multi selector to the right. The next menu page carries the warning: "All pictures on memory card will be deleted. OK?" To proceed with the formatting process, highlight [Yes] and press the ⊙ button (if you wish to cancel the formatting process highlight No and press the multi selector to the right). During formatting, the message "Formatting memory card" appears on the monitor screen. Once formatting is finished, a further message, "Formatting complete" appears briefly on the monitor screen before the camera returns to the Setup menu display.

Note: You should never switch the camera OFF, interrupt the power supply to the camera, or remove the memory card during the formatting process.

Hint: It is good practice to format any memory card each time you install it in your D60, even if you have deleted its contents using a computer. If you do not get into the habit doing this, there is an increased risk of communication problems occurring between the card and the camera, particularly if the memory card is used in different camera bodies.

After formatting the memory card, check the Shooting Information Display on the LCD monitor to verify the number of exposures available in the frame counter. When the installed memory card reaches its capacity, the viewfinder display will change; the figure "0" will flash in the frame counter brackets of the viewfinder display, and **FuL** will replace the shutter speed value and blink. The camera cannot take more pictures until one or more files are deleted from the card, or a different memory card is installed. However, it may be possible to take additional pictures if you reduce the image quality and size settings.

Removing the Memory Card
Before removing your memory card, make sure the green memory card access lamp has gone out. Then switch the camera OFF and open the card slot cover to push the exposed edge of the SD memory card gently towards the center of the camera, and then release it. The memory card will be partially ejected, and it can then be pulled out by hand.

Note: You should be aware that memory cards can become warm during use; this is normal and not an indication of a problem.

If the D60 has no memory card inserted when a charged battery is installed, or it is connected to a AC supply via the EH-5 / EH-5a AC adapter and EP-5 power connector, [**-E -**] appears in the exposure counter brackets within the Shooting Information Display on the monitor screen.

Holding the Camera

Proper hand-holding technique reduces the risk of camera shake, which is a principal cause of pictures that appear blurred. Regardless of whether you shoot with the camera held horizontally or vertically, it should be grasped firmly but not overly tight. The fingers of your right hand should wrap around the handgrip so that your index finger is free to operate the shutter release. Cup your left hand under the camera to cradle the camera and lens for support; your left thumb and index finger should be able to rotate either the focus or zoom ring of a lens. Keep you elbows tucked in towards your body while standing with your feet shoulder-width apart with one foot half a pace in front of the other.

Point-and-Shoot Photography with the D60

Though the Nikon D60 is a sophisticated digital SLR, it can also be used for straightforward "point-and-shoot" photography, in which the camera controls most of the settings according to the prevailing shooting conditions. As well as its fully automatic Auto $\overset{\text{AUTO}}{\blacksquare}$ mode, there are six other scene-specific automatic modes in which the camera attempts to tailor its settings to suit the nature of the subject. Nikon calls these Digital Vari-Programs (you may be more familiar with the expression "scene modes"). Though they may appear tempting to less experienced photographers, it is important to remember a camera cannot think for itself–only photographers can do that!

Note: There is a Digital Vari-Program called Auto (Flash off), which cancels flash operation. See page 73 for more details.

By using one of these modes, you not only relinquish all exposure control to the camera, but you are also locked out of the ability to adjust several key functions, including white balance, metering mode, exposure compensation, and flash output compensation. In my opinion the Digital Vari-Program modes can be more of a hindrance than a help to photographers seeking to develop their photographic skills; you can never be sure what settings the camera is using. Still, Nikon has included these options because the D60 is designed with less experienced photographers in mind, many of whom will be content to rely on the automation offered by the camera.

Select a Digital Vari-Program

Once you are ready to take pictures, rotate the mode dial (on top left of camera) to ᴬᵁᵀᴼ📷 , or choose one of the other Digital Vari-Programs by turning the mode dial so that the desired icon is aligned with the white index mark on the side of the viewfinder head.

Hint: All the Digital Vari-Programs, including ᴬᵁᵀᴼ📷 , require a lens with a CPU to be fitted to the D60. If you attach a non-CPU lens the shutter release will be disabled.

The D60 lends itself to simple point-and-shoot type photography due to its fully automated options, such as the Auto mode.

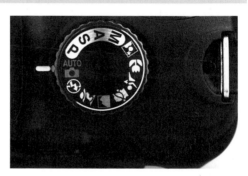

ᴬᵁᵀᴼ📷 AUTO Mode – Default Settings

At the default settings for ᴬᵁᵀᴼ📷 mode, the camera is set to the following:

- **Image Quality:** Normal - pictures are compressed (1:8) using the JPEG standard.

- **Image size:** Large (L) - images are 3,872 x 2,592 pixels in size.

- **Shooting mode:** Single frame - one exposure is made each time you press the shutter release.

- **Flash sync mode:** Auto - standard front curtain flash sync is performed.
- **Autofocus mode:** AF-A - automatic selection of either single-servo or continuous servo modes.
- **Autofocus-area mode:** Closest subject all focus points selected, and the camera will determine which one to use automatically.
- **Metering mode:** TTL metering is locked to Matrix metering mode; center-weighted and spot metering are not available.
- **Sensitivity (ISO):** ISO AUTO - the camera will adjust the sensitivity setting automatically if required to maintain a proper exposure.

It is possible to change the default settings of AUTO mode, and regardless of whether you turn the camera off or switch to another mode and return to AUTO mode subsequently, most of the adjusted settings remain. Press the i button to open the Shooting Information Display, and then press i button again to open the Quick Settings Display. Now use the multi selector button to highlight the required setting and press OK button to open a display of the available options. Highlight the required setting and press OK button to confirm the selection.

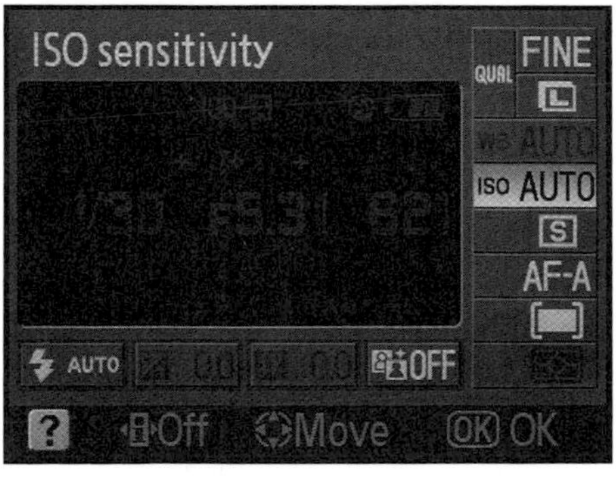

The Quick Settings Display can be used to alter the default settings of the AUTO mode.

Note: To restore the 📷^{AUTO} mode default settings, use the two-button reset option by pressing and holding the 🔳 button (top right of camera) together with the 🔘 button (back lower left corner) for approximately two seconds (there is a small green dot beside each button as a reminder of this dual button function); to reset the options in the Custom menu to their default values you must select Custom Setting R (Reset).

Composing, Focusing, and Shooting

Since all three autofocus areas are active in closest-subject AF area mode (the default setting in Auto 📷^{AUTO} mode), compose each shot so that the main subject is completely covered by one of the three bracket pairs on the focusing screen in the viewfinder. Press the shutter release halfway to activate the focusing system. If the camera can acquire focus, one or more of the autofocus sensing area bracket pairs illuminate and a beep will sound (assuming CS-01 is set to On). The in-focus indicator, a solid green dot, will appear in the viewfinder display.

If the in-focus indicator blinks, the camera has not been able to acquire sharp focus. Recompose and place the autofocus brackets over a different part of the subject and press the shutter release halfway again. If you still have difficulty focusing, try rotating the camera slightly toward a more vertical orientation and re-focus. Once acquired, the focus will lock at the current camera-to-subject distance.

Note: If the subject moves closer or farther from the camera before you release the shutter, and assuming the camera is set to the default AF-A autofocus mode (automatic selection of autofocus mode) the camera should select AF-C (continuous-servo autofocus mode) and begin tracking the moving subject.

Hint: The D60 shows approximately 95% (vertically and horizontally) of the full frame in its viewfinder. There is a narrow border around all sides that you cannot see but will be included in the final picture, so take care when composing a picture, especially if there is a subject at the very edge of the viewfinder frame area.

AUTO and Digital Vari-Program Modes

AUTO: The mode is designed as a universal point-and-shoot mode. The camera attempts to select a combination of shutter speed and aperture that will be appropriate for the current scene. It does this by using information from the through-the-lens (TTL) metering system in the camera, which assesses the overall level of illumination, contrast, and color quality of the prevailing light, together with information from the autofocus system used to estimate the location of the subject in the frame area and its distance from the camera. This mode is most effective for general-purpose snapshot photography, such as family events or vacations.

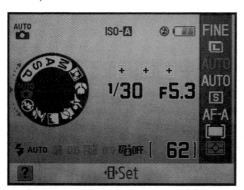

When the Shooting Information Display is active it will show the position of the mode dial as it is rotated; here it is positioned at .

In this mode the D60 uses its 3D Color Matrix Metering II system with D-type or G-type lenses. Using an AF-S or AF-I type lens, the camera's default AF settings are closest subject for AF-area mode (the camera will focus on the subject it determines to be closest) and AF-A (Auto-servo AF) for

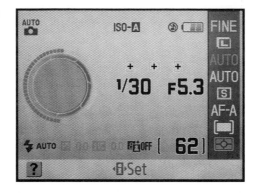

At the default settings of the D60 the Shooting Information Display is shown in the graphic style with a white background.

focus mode; the latter option cannot be overridden. Using any other type of lens will cause the camera to select Manual focusing, with the central AF sensing area supporting the electronic rangefinder to assist focusing (only with compatible lenses; see pages 61 and 275).

Note: If you alter the default setting for the AF-area mode, the selected AF-area option is only retained while the camera remains in 🔲 mode. If you turn the mode dial to an alternative Digital Vari-Program mode, the default settings for autofocus operation (AF-area mode & AF mode) are restored.

The built-in Speedlight will activate automatically if the camera determines that additional illumination is required. The camera automatically selects standard front curtain flash sync mode **⚡ AUTO** and an appropriate shutter speed between 1/60 and 1/200 second. Alternatively, you can select Auto flash with red-eye reduction **⚡ AUTO ◉** , or Auto (flash off) **⚡** ; other flash modes are not available.

Hint: It is important to make sure your subject is within the shooting range of the flash. The built-in Speedlight has a Guide Number (GN) of 39 feet (12 m) at ISO 100. For example, at an aperture of f/5.6 and the base ISO sensitivity of the D60, which is equivalent to ISO 100, the maximum effective range of the flash unit is approximately 7 feet (2.1 m). If the **⚡** flash symbol in the viewfinder blinks for approximately three seconds after the flash has fired, it indicates that the flash discharged at its maximum output; therefore the shot may be underexposed. In this case, either set a higher ISO sensitivity, select a wider aperture (lower f/number), or move closer to the subject.

⑨ **Auto (Flash off):** This mode is essentially the same as the AUTO mode, with the exception that the built-in flash is turned off and will not operate regardless of the level of ambient illumination, even if it is very low.

⑨ is useful in situations where the use of flash is undesirable; for example when shooting in a museum where flash may be prohibited, or in natural low-light conditions where you do not want to spoil the atmosphere by using flash. Although the operation of the built-in flash is cancelled, the AF-assist illuminator lamp will still function to assist autofocus operation in poor lighting conditions.

In this mode the D60 uses its 3D Color Matrix Metering II system with D-type or G-type lenses. Using an AF-S or AF-I type lens, the camera's default AF settings are closest subject [■] for AF-area mode (the camera will focus on the subject it determines to be closest) and AF-A (Auto-servo AF) for focus mode; the latter option cannot be overridden. Using any other type of lens will cause the camera to select Manual focusing, with the central AF sensing area supporting the electronic rangefinder to assist focusing (only with compatible lenses; see pages 61 and 275).

Note: If you alter the default setting for the AF-area mode, the selected AF-area option is retained only while the camera remains in ⑨ mode. If you turn the mode dial to an alternative Digital Vari-Program mode, the default settings for autofocus operation (AF-area mode and AF mode) are restored.

Hint: Since the camera can set slow shutter speeds in this mode, always check the viewfinder information to ensure that the selected shutter speed will allow the camera to be held without risk of camera shake affecting the picture. At slow shutter speeds consider using a camera support, such as a tripod.

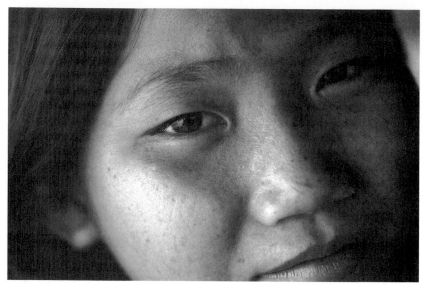

Use the D60's Portrait mode to automatically select a wide aperture to minimize depth of field.

Z̆ Portrait: The Z̆ mode is designed to select a wide aperture (low f/number) in order to produce a picture with a shallow depth of field. Generally this renders the background out-of-focus so it does not detract from the subject, although the effect is also dependent on the distance between the subject and the background, and the focal length of the lens used. This mode is most effective with focal lengths of 100mm, or more when the subject is relatively far away from the background.

Again, in this mode the D60 uses its 3D Color Matrix Metering II system with D-type or G-type lenses. Using an AF-S or AF-I type lens, the camera's default AF settings are closest subject [■] for AF-area mode (the camera will focus on the subject it determines to be closest) and AF-A for focus mode; the latter option cannot be overridden. Using any other type of lens causes the camera to select manual focus and the central AF area (focus bracket), which supports the electronic rangefinder (only with compatible lenses) to assist focusing.

Note: If you alter the default setting for the AF-area mode, the selected AF-area option is retained only while the camera remains in ⚡ mode. If you turn the mode dial to an alternative Digital Vari-Program mode, the default settings for autofocus operation (AF-area mode & AF mode) are restored.

The built-in Speedlight will activate automatically if the camera determines that additional illumination is required. The camera automatically selects standard front curtain flash sync mode ⚡ **AUTO** and an appropriate shutter speed between 1/60 and 1/200 second. Alternatively, you can select Auto flash with red-eye reduction ⚡ **AUTO** 👁 , or Auto (flash off) ⚟ ; other flash modes are not available. If using flash, it is important to make sure your subject is within the shooting range of the flash (see the Hint about Guide Numbers on page 72).

Hint: Best results for portraits are often achieved when the subject nearly fills the frame. Since the autofocus area is set automatically to the closest-subject ▣ AF area mode, there is no guarantee that the camera will focus on at least one of the subject's eyes. Therefore I strongly recommend that you override the default option and use Single area AF [⊡] , and choose a focus area that covers one of the subject's eyes to ensure it is focused sharply. To select Single area AF, press the ◄⎈► button to open the Shooting Information Display, then press the ◄⎈► button again to open the Quick Settings Display; use the multi selector to highlight the AF-area mode option and press ⊙ . Use the multi selector to highlight [⊡] , and confirm the selection by pressing ⊙ .

▰ **Landscape:** The ▰ mode is designed to select a small aperture in order to produce a picture with an extended depth of field. Generally, this renders everything from the foreground to the horizon in-focus, although this will depend to some degree how close the lens is to the nearest subject. This mode is most effective with wide-angle or wide-angle zoom lenses, and when the scene is well lit.

Again, in this mode the D60 uses its 3D Color Matrix Metering II system with D-type or G-type lenses. Using an AF-S or AF-I type lens, the camera's default AF settings are closest subject [■] for AF-area mode (the camera will focus on the subject it determines to be closest) and AF-A for focus mode; the latter option cannot be overridden. Using any other type of lens will cause the camera to select Manual focusing, with the central AF sensing area supporting the electronic rangefinder to assist focusing (only with compatible lenses; see pages 61 and 275). Operation of the built-in Speedlight and AF-assist lamp is cancelled in [▲] mode; there are no flash modes available in the Landscape mode.

Note: If you alter the default setting for the AF-area mode, the selected AF-area option is only retained while the camera remains in [▲] mode. If you turn the mode dial to an alternative Digital Vari-Program mode, the default settings for autofocus operation (AF-area mode & AF mode) are restored.

Hint: It is important to ensure the main area of interest in your composition is in sharp focus. Since selection of the focusing area is fully automatic at the default setting, the camera may not focus where you expect it to; in [▲] mode you may prefer to override the default option by selecting Single area AF [ɛ] to ensure you know which part of the scene the camera is focusing on. To select Single area AF, press the ◄⊞► button to open the Shooting Information Display, then press the ◄⊞► button again to open the Quick Settings Display; use the multi selector to highlight the AF-area mode option and press ⊙⃝ . Use the multi selector to highlight [ɛ] , and confirm the selection by pressing ⊙⃝ .

Hint: When using a wide-angle focal length (i.e. a focal length less than 35mm), try to include an element of interest in the foreground of the scene, as well as the middle distance, to help produce a balanced composition and a way of leading the viewer's eye into the picture.

Child: The ⚘ mode sets a bias toward a wide aperture (low f/number) to reduce the depth of field; although the effect is also dependent on the distance between the subject and the background, together with the focal length of the lens used. This mode is most effective with telephoto focal lengths and when the subject is relatively far away from the background. Image processing in camera is designed to render soft, natural skin tones without affecting the vividness of other colors.

Once again, in this mode the D60 uses its 3D Color Matrix Metering II system with D-type or G-type lenses. Using an AF-S or AF-I type lens, the camera's default AF settings are closest subject for AF-area mode (the camera will focus on the subject it determines to be closest) and AF-A [■] for focus mode; the latter option cannot be overridden. Using any other type of lens will cause the camera to select Manual focusing, with the central AF sensing area supporting the electronic rangefinder to assist focusing (only with compatible lenses, see pages 61 and 275).

Note: If you alter the default setting for the AF-area mode, the selected AF-area option is only retained while the camera remains in ⚘ mode. If you turn the mode dial to an alternative Digital Vari-Program mode, the default settings for autofocus operation (AF-area mode & AF mode) are restored.

The built-in Speedlight will activate automatically if the camera determines that additional illumination is required. The camera automatically selects standard front curtain flash sync mode ⚡ AUTO and an appropriate shutter speed between 1/60 and 1/200 second. Alternatively, you can select Auto flash with red-eye reduction ⚡ AUTO ⊙ , or Auto (flash off) ⚡ ; other flash modes are not available.

Hint: Like shooting portraits, best results for pictures of children are often achieved when the subject nearly fills the frame. Since the autofocus area is set automatically to the closest subject [■] AF area mode, there is no guarantee that the camera will focus on at least one of the subject's eyes. Therefore I strongly recommend that you override the default option and use Single area AF [⊡] , and choose a focus area that covers one of the subject's eyes to ensure it is focused sharply. To select Single area AF, press the ◄⚑► button to open the Shooting Information Display, then press the ◄⚑► button again to open the Quick Settings Display; use the multi selector to highlight the AF-area mode option and press ⊙ . Use the multi selector to highlight [⊡] , and confirm the selection by pressing ⊙ . If the child you are photographing is particularly active I recommend using the Dynamic-area AF mode; in this case follow the same procedure but select [⊡] in place of [⊡] .

When photographing children it is often preferable to lower the camera so the lens is at the child's eye level because this helps to produce a more pleasing perspective. Using a focal length in the range of 70–105mm will allow you to maintain a comfortable working distance from your subject(s) reducing the risk of disturbing them and increasing the chances of capturing some candid moments. If using flash, it is important to make sure your subject is within the shooting range of the flash (see the Hint about Guide Numbers on page 72).

🏃 **Sports:** The 🏃 mode is designed to select a wide aperture in order to maintain the highest possible shutter speed to "freeze" motion in fast–paced action, such as sports or children on the go. It also has a beneficial side effect, since this combination produces a picture with a very shallow depth of field that helps to isolate the subject from the background. This mode is most effective with telephoto or telephoto-zoom lenses, and when there are no obstructions between the camera and the subject that may cause the autofocus function to focus on something other than the subject.

In 🏃 mode the D60 uses its 3D Color Matrix Metering II system with D-type or G-type lenses. Using an AF-S or AF-I type lens, the camera's default AF-area setting is Dynamic-area [⊡] . The camera will use the central focus area, but if the subject leaves the coverage of the central AF-area, the camera will continue to perform autofocus, tracking a moving subject using information from the two other focus areas, provided the shutter release button is kept half depressed. The focus mode is always set to AF-A and cannot be overridden. Using any other type of lens will cause the camera to select Manual focusing, with the central AF sensing area supporting the electronic rangefinder to assist focusing (only with compatible lenses; see pages 61 and 275). Operation of the built-in Speedlight and AF-assist lamp is cancelled in ⚡ mode; there are no flash modes available in the Sports mode.

Note: If you alter the default setting for the AF-area mode, the newly selected AF-area option will be retained while the camera remains in ⚡ mode. If you turn the mode dial to an alternative Digital Vari-Program mode, the default settings for autofocus operation (AF-area mode & AF mode) are restored.

Hint: There is always a slight delay between pressing the shutter release button and the shutter opening; therefore, it is important to anticipate the peak moment of the action and press the shutter just before it occurs. The decisive moment will be missed if you wait to see it in the viewfinder before pressing the shutter release.

🌷 **Close-Up:** The 🌷 mode is for taking pictures at short shooting distances of subjects such as flowers, insects, and other small objects. It is designed to select a small aperture (high f/number) in order to produce a picture with an extended depth of field. Generally, depth of field is limited when working at very short focus distances, even when using small apertures, so this program tries to render as much of the subject in focus as possible. The final effect will also be dependent on how close the camera is to the subject and the focal length of the lens used. This mode is most effective with lenses that have a close-focusing feature, or dedicated Micro-Nikkor lenses.

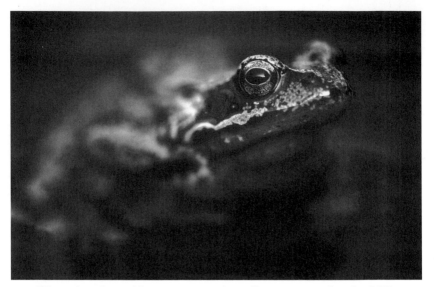

When shooting subjects at a very close distance, try using the D60's Close-Up mode, which automatically chooses a small aperture to maximize depth of field.

In this mode the D60 uses its 3D Color Matrix Metering II system with D-type or G-type lenses. Using an AF-S or AF-I type lens, the camera's default AF-area setting is Single-area [⌑] , using the central focus area to focus on the subject (either of the two other focus areas can be selected by pressing the multi selector). The focus mode is always set to AF-A, which you will not be able to override. Using any other type of lens will cause the camera to select Manual focusing, with the central AF sensing area supporting the electronic rangefinder to assist focusing (only with compatible lenses; see pages 61 and 275).

Note: If you alter the default setting for the AF-area mode, the selected AF-area option will be in effect while the camera remains in ✿ mode. If you turn the mode dial to an alternative Digital Vari-Program mode, the default settings for autofocus operation (AF-area mode & AF mode) are restored.

The built-in Speedlight will activate automatically if the camera determines that additional illumination is required. The camera selects standard front curtain flash sync mode ⚡ AUTO and an appropriate shutter speed between 1/125 and 1/200 second. Alternatively, you can select Auto flash with red-eye reduction ⚡ AUTO ⊙ , or Auto (flash off) ⊛ ; other flash modes are not available.

Hint: Due to the emphasis this mode places on using a small aperture, the shutter-speed can quite often be relatively slow. To prevent image blur caused by camera shake, use a tripod or some other form of camera support.

▣ **Night Portrait:** The ▣ mode is designed to capture properly exposed pictures of people against a background that is dimly lit. It is useful when the photographer wants to include background detail, such as a cityscape or sunset, in the photo and is most effective when the background is in low light, as opposed to near dark or totally dark conditions. The built-in Speedlight will activate automatically in low-light; alternatively, an external Speedlight such as the SB-400, or SB-600, can be used to supplement the ambient light.

The camera automatically selects standard front curtain flash sync mode ⚡ AUTO and an appropriate shutter speed between one second and 1/200 second. Alternatively, you can select Auto flash with red-eye reduction ⚡ AUTO ⊙ , or Auto (flash off) ⊛ ; other flash modes are not available.

In this mode the D60 uses its 3D Color Matrix Metering II system with D-type or G-type lenses. Using an AF-S or AF-I type lens, the camera's default AF settings are closest subject [▦] for AF-area mode (the camera will focus on the subject it determines to be closest) and AF-A for focus mode; the latter option cannot be overridden. Using any other type of lens will cause the camera to select Manual focusing, with the central AF sensing area supporting the electronic rangefinder to assist focusing (only with compatible lenses; see pages 61 and 275).

Note: If you alter the default setting for the AF-area mode, the selected AF-area option is only retained while the camera remains in 🅰 mode. If you turn the mode dial to an alternative Digital Vari-Program mode, the default settings for autofocus operation (AF-area mode & AF mode) are restored.

Hint: It is important to ensure the main area of interest in your composition is in sharp focus.

Since focus area selection is fully automatic at the default setting, there is no guarantee that the camera will focus where you expect it to in 🅰 mode. Therefore I strongly recommend that you override the default option. Use Single-area AF [⑴] , and choose a focus area that covers the subject to ensure it is focused sharply. To select Single area AF, press the 🔘 button to open the Shooting Information Display, then press the 🔘 button again to open the Quick Settings Display; use the multi selector to highlight the AF-area mode option and press 🆗 . Use the multi selector to highlight [⑴] , and confirm the selection by pressing 🆗 .

Common Settings
The following are shared between 🅰 and all Digital Vari-Program Modes:

• All photographs are recorded in the sRGB color space.

• All shooting modes (Single, Continuous, Self-timer, Remote, and Remote-delay) can be used.

• If the light levels exceed the sensitivity of the TTL metering system in the D60, 𝗛𝗶 will be displayed in the viewfinder and 𝗟𝗼 will be displayed if the overall illumination is too low.

The D60 applies the values in the following table when either 🅰 or one of the Digital Vari-program modes is selected. The user has no control over these settings, which are applied automatically by the camera.

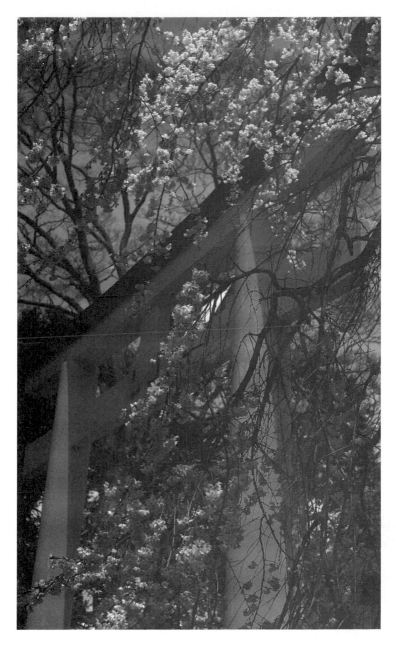

Optimizing Image Settings

	Sharpening	Tone	Color Mode/ Space	Saturation	Hue
Auto	Auto	Auto	IIIa / sRGB	Auto	0
Auto (Flash off)	Auto	Auto	IIIa / sRGB	Auto	0
Portrait	Auto	Auto	Ia / sRGB	Auto	0
Landscape	Auto	Auto	IIIa / sRGB	Auto	0
Child	Auto	Auto	Ia / sRGB	Auto	0
Sport	Auto	Auto	IIIa / sRGB	Auto	0
Close-up	Auto	Auto	IIIa / sRGB	Auto	0
Night Portrait	Auto	Auto	Ia / sRGB	Auto	0

Basic Image Review

Assuming CS-07 is set to its default setting of [On], a photograph will be displayed on the LCD monitor almost as soon as the exposure is made. If no picture is displayed, the most recent picture recorded by the D60 can be displayed by pressing the ▶ button (located on back upper left of camera). To review other pictures, use the multi selector to scroll through the pictures stored on the memory card by pressing it to the left or right. To return to the shooting mode at any time, simply press the shutter release button halfway.

If you want to delete the displayed picture, press the 🗑 button (located on back lower right of camera). A message will be shown over the displayed picture asking for confirmation of the delete action, with an option to cancel. Press the 🗑 button again to proceed and delete the picture. To stop the delete operation, either press ▶ , or press the shutter release button halfway.

To protect an image from accidental deletion, display it on the monitor screen by pressing ▶ and press the AE-L/AF-L button (on the back of camera to the right of

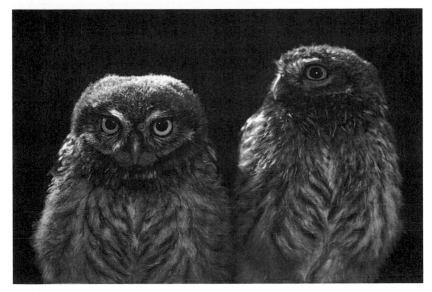

One of the best things about digital photography is the ability to review a photo right after it is taken. This is an amazing advantage over film photography, but it does use battery power so try to keep image review to a minimum.

viewfinder eyepiece). A key icon will appear in the top left corner of the displayed image to indicate its protected status. To remove the protection, display the image and press the 🔘 button again; the key icon will disappear.

Note: Never be in too much of a hurry to delete pictures unless they are obvious failures; it is better to leave the editing process to a later stage, as your opinions about a particular picture can, and often do, change. Also, any image file marked as protected will maintain this status as a read-only file even when the image file is transferred to the computer or other data storage device.

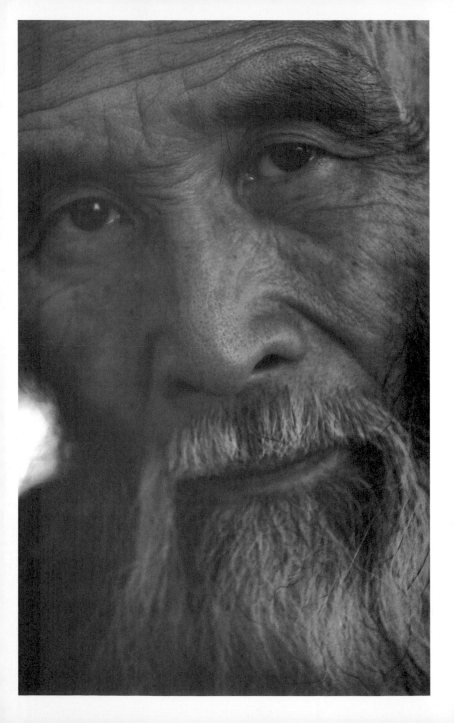

Detailed Shooting Operations

Powering the D60

The D60 uses the Nikon EN-EL9, a rechargeable lithium-ion cell; it cannot accept any other battery. The EN-EL9 can only be inserted the correct way into the camera and is charged with the dedicated MH-23 Quick Charger (supplied with the camera). This battery is rated at AC 100-240V (50/60Hz) so it can be used worldwide. A fully discharged EN-EL9 can be completely recharged in approximately 90 minutes using the MH-23. Unlike some other types of rechargeable batteries, the EN-EL9 does not require conditioning prior to its first use. However, the battery supplied with the camera is only partially charged. It is advisable to allow the initial charge cycle for a new battery to continue until the battery cools down while still in the charger before removing it. Do not be tempted to remove it as soon as the charging/charged indicator lamp on the MH-23 stops flashing, as the battery is unlikely to have reached full charge.

Note: Do not leave the EN-EL9 battery charging in the MH-23 for protracted periods as this may cause damage to the battery.

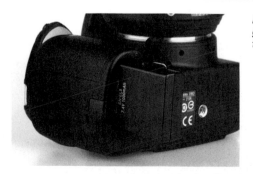

Housed in the hand-grip, the EN-EL9 battery powers the D60.

◁ *It is important to turn the D60's power switch to the OFF position whenever you change batteries, memory cards, or lenses. This prevents problems that could be caused by static charges and dust.*

The profile of the EN-EL9 battery ensures that it can only be inserted in the camera in the correct orientation; note the diagram on the inside of the battery chamber door.

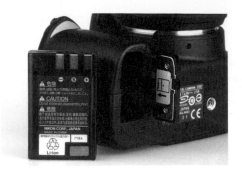

Using the EN-EL9 Battery

To insert an EN-EL9 into the D60:

1. Push the small button on the battery chamber cover (on bottom of camera) toward the tripod socket. The cover should swing open.

2. Open the cover fully and slide the battery into the camera observing the diagram on the inside of the chamber cover.

3. Press the cover down (you will feel a slight resistance) until it locks (you will hear a slight click as the latch closes).

To remove an EN-EL9 from the D60:

1. Repeat Step 1 (above).

2. Hold the cover open, turn the camera upright, and allow the battery to slide out taking care that it does not drop.

Whenever you insert or remove an EN-EL9, it is essential that you power the camera off. If you are in the process of making changes to the camera settings and the battery is removed while the power switch is still set to the ON position, the camera will not retain the new settings. Likewise, if the camera is still in the process of transferring data from the buffer memory to the storage medium when the battery is removed, image files are likely to be corrupted, or data lost.

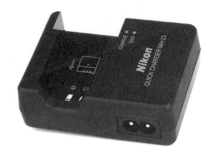

The MH-23 is the dedicated AC charger for the EN-EL9 battery.

To charge an EN-EL9:

1. Connect the MH-23 to an AC power supply.

2. Align the white arrowhead on the EN-EL9 with that in the MH-23 slot, and then slide the battery toward the contact plates of the charger until it locks in place. The charge lamp should begin to flash immediately.

3. To ensure the battery has recharged fully, leave it in place until it has cooled to the ambient room temperature.

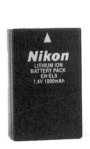
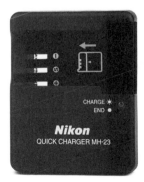

The profile of the slot in the MH-23 ensures that the battery can only be inserted in the correct orientation; note the arrowhead symbol on the battery and diagram in the battery slot of the charger.

Hint: Partially discharged lithium batteries, like the EN-EL9, can take a "top-off" charge without adverse consequences to battery life or performance. However, I recommend buying a spare EN-EL9. Whenever the battery is not in the camera or charger, always place the semi-opaque plastic terminal cover in place on the battery. Without it there is a risk that the terminals may short and cause damage to the battery.

D60 Battery Status

Monitor	Viewfinder	Battery Status
▭	—	Fully charged
▭	—	Partially discharged
▭		Low – charge battery
▭ (blinks)		Discharged – charge battery; shutter disabled.

The EN-EL9 battery has an electronic chip in its circuitry that enables it to report detailed status information. To check this press the ◄❸► button to open the Shooting Information Display on the monitor screen. When the battery power reaches a low level ▭ will be displayed in the viewfinder as a warning.

EH-5 / EH-5a AC Adapter and EP-5 DC Power Connector

The Nikon EH-5 / EH-5a AC adapters, which are available separately, can also power the D60 via the EP-5 DC power connector. These accessories are particularly useful for extended periods of shooting, or camera use such as image playback through a TV set, to prevent the camera from powering off while the reflex mirror is raised (using the mirror lock-up facility in the setup menu) when inspecting or cleaning the low pass filter, and when shooting with the D60 tethered to a computer and operated by Nikon Camera Control Pro 2, or for direct transfer of pictures to the computer hard drive. The EH-5 or EH-5a cannot be connected directly to the D60; it

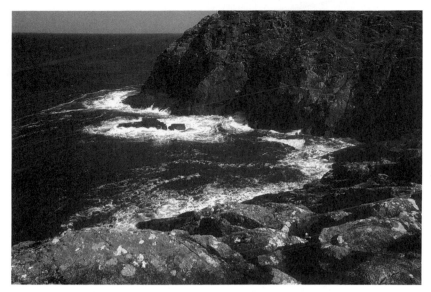

While the EN-EL9 battery can take a "top up" charge, I recommend you purchase one or two spares to ensure you have enough power to handle all of your shooting requirements.

requires the EP-5 DC power connector to be inserted in the camera's main battery chamber, substituting for the EN-EL9 battery (ensure the + and − terminals of the EP-5 are in the correct orientation). The cord from the EP-5 should be laid in the small notch in the edge of the battery chamber before closing the chamber cover. Connect the DC plug of the EH-5 / EH-5a to the DC terminal of the EP-5. Finally, connect the EH-5 / EH-5a AC plug of the AC cord to the EH-5 / EH-5a AC terminal, and connect the other end to the AC supply. When powered from an AC supply, the battery indicator of the D60 will show ◀▣ in the Shooting Information Display.

Note: Always ensure that the power switch on the D60 is set to OFF before connecting/disconnecting the EH-5 / EH-5a and EP-5. There is a risk that the camera's circuitry could be damaged if you plug/unplug the EH-5 / EH-5a and EP-5 while the power switch is set to ON.

Internal Clock/Calendar Battery

The D60 has an internal clock/calendar that is powered by a rechargeable battery that, when fully charged, will power the clock/calendar for approximately one month. It requires charging for approximately 72 hours by the camera's main power supply, either the EN-EL9 battery or the EH-5 / EH-5a and EP-5 AC adapter. Should the clock battery become exhausted, the message "Clock not set" will be displayed on the LCD, and the clock is reset to a date and time of 2008.01.01 00:00:00. If this occurs, the clock/calendar will need to be reset via the World Time option in the setup menu.

Note: Since the clock/calendar battery is not changeable by the user, when it no longer recharges, the camera must be returned to a service center for a replacement battery to be installed.

Battery Performance

Obviously the more functions the camera has to perform the greater the demand for power. Reducing the number of functions and the duration for which they are active is fundamental to reducing power consumption. Here are a few suggestions that will help preserve battery power.

• The EN-EL9 will lose some of its charge if left dormant for a month or more, so recharge it fully before use.

• Using the camera's LCD monitor increases power consumption significantly. Unless you need it, turn the monitor off by pressing the shutter release button down halfway. Consider setting CS-07 (Image review) to Off (the default setting is On). You can use CS-15 (Auto off timers) to limit the time the monitor remains on for Shooting Information Display, Image review, and the delay before Auto meter off.

Hint: When the camera is powered by the EN-EL9 battery you can switch the monitor display off at anytime by pressing the shutter release lightly to return the camera to its shooting mode.

The Vibration Reduction (VR) feature available with some Nikkor lenses remains active as long as the shutter release button is depressed, thereby reducing battery life by approximately 10% to 15%.

Maintaining a connection to either a computer or Pict-Bridge compatible printer will have a significant affect on battery charge since both functions draw a considerable level of power. Always disconnect the D60 from these devices as soon as you have finished using it.

Low temperatures cause a change to the battery's internal resistance, which impairs performance. Though Lithium batteries are fairly resilient to cold conditions, to ensure continued shooting in such conditions keep a spare battery in a warm place (such as an inside pocket). As the performance of the battery in the camera dwindles, exchange it with the warm one. Allow the used battery time to warm-up again, and keep rotating the two batteries to maximize their shooting capacity.

Finally, if you expect to store the camera for more than four weeks, always remove the battery. Never store a battery that is discharged; if left in this condition for any period of time there is a risk it may be damaged permanently.

Battery Storage

A fully charged Nikon Lithium-ion EN-EL9 battery, in good condition, will retain its full capacity over a period of a few days. However, if it left dormant for four weeks, or more, regardless of whether it is installed in a camera or not, expect it to suffer a noticeable loss of charge, so ensure it is recharged fully before use (see comments concerning top-up charging above). If you expect to store a camera battery for an extended period avoid leaving it fully charged, or heavily discharged. Storing a fully charged battery can have a long-term affect on its overall capacity, while storing a heavily discharged battery can risk it shifting to a deeply discharged state, which can damage it. The optimum charge level for a battery that will be stored for four weeks, or more is between 20 – 80%. Always store your camera and batteries in a well-ventilated, cool, dry place.

Secure Digital (SD) Memory Cards

These small solid-state cards measure 1.3 x 0.9 x 0.08 inches (34 x 22 x 2 mm) and have a capacity of up to 2GB. While you should treat any memory card with the same care you would give your camera equipment, SD cards have no moving parts and are reasonably robust. They have a small, sliding write-protection switch on one edge that can be set to prevent data from being written to the card by the camera, or prevent deletion of data from the card by either a camera or computer (if you insert a locked SD card in to the D60 the camera will display a warning message). Finally, they are not affected by radiation from X-ray security equipment.

Secure Digital High Capacity (SDHC) Memory Cards

To support the larger file sizes now generated by digital cameras and other devices, there is a growing need for SD cards with a capacity in excess of 2GB. To meet this demand, a new design of SD card has been introduced that retains the same physical dimensions and write-protect feature of standard SD cards. The new card type complies with the SD specification version 2.0, which supports card capacities of 4GB and over, and is called Secure Digital High Capacity (SDHC). Manufacturers within the industry are now marketing these higher-capacity memory cards.

The D60 is fully compatible with SDHC memory card format that conforms to the SD version 2.0, design specification. Already, at the time of writing, there are a number of

8GB cards available but this is nowhere near the theoretical maximum capacity, and card capacities up to 32GB are likely in the future.

Note: The D60 accepts standard SD cards and SDHC cards; it is important to remember that many devices that are only SD compliant do not support SDHC cards. This will affect your ability to use SDHC cards with some card readers and other non-SDHC compliant devices.

Formatting

As data is written to and erased from SD and SDHC cards, small areas of its memory can become corrupt; these are known as "bad sectors". Files can also become fragmented, particularly if you delete individual image files from the card. By formatting the card in the camera, the worst consequences of these effects are generally avoided.

It is a misconception that formatting a memory card permanently deletes the data on the card. Actually, the process of formatting causes the existing file directory information to be over-written, so that it no longer "points" to the image data held on the card. It is therefore difficult, although far from impossible, to recover previously written data from the card. If you should format a card inadvertently, it can be possible to retrieve the image files using software designed to recover data. To maximize your chances of recovering the data successfully, ensure no new data is written to the card before carrying out the recovery process. Since prevention is better than cure, always save your images to a computer or other storage device (and make a back up copy) before formatting a card.

Quick Settings Display

To speed up adjustment of a range of camera controls and avoid navigation of the menu system the D60 allows the user to make adjustments via the Quick Settings Display. Each time the **⊞** button is pressed the monitor display changes in the following order: Shooting Information Display - Quick Settings Display - monitor off - Shooting Information Display. Assuming the monitor is currently off, pressing the ◀️⃞▶ button once will open the Shooting Information Display, pressing the ◀️⃞▶ button again will open the Quick Settings Display.

The Shooting Information Display shows the current settings for most of the principal shooting controls of the D60.

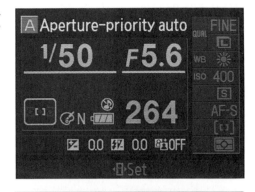

The Quick Settings Display enables twelve different shooting controls to be adjusted swiftly and efficiently obviating the need to navigate through the menu system of the D60.

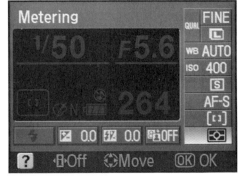

From the Quick Settings Display twelve different shooting controls to be adjusted. Eight controls are shown in a column down the right edge of the display. Starting from the top and moving downwards they are: Image quality, Image Size, White balance, ISO sensitivity, Release mode, Focus mode, AF-area mode, and Metering. The remaining four controls are shown along the bottom edge of the display. Moving from left to right they are: Flash mode, Exposure compensation, Flash compensation, and Active D-Lighting.

To select a shooting control, press the multi selector up/down, or left/right to highlight it; if a particular control is grayed out it cannot be selected in the current shooting mode. To open the options for the selected shooting control press the ⊛ button. Press ⊚ to highlight the required option (to return to the Quick Settings Display press the multi selector to the right, alternatively press the ◀️ button to exit the Quick Settings Display without adjusting any settings), and then press the ⊛ button to apply the option. Finally, either press the ◀️ button, or press the shutter release button down halfway to complete the process.

File Formats

The D60 saves images to the memory card in two file formats, Joint Photographic Experts Group (JPEG) and Nikon Electronic File (NEF), Nikon's proprietary RAW files. Strictly speaking, JPEG is not a file format but a standard of compression established by the Joint Photographic Experts Group (JPEG), but these days the term "JPEG format" is ubiquitous.

The Charge Coupled Device (CCD) sensor used in the D60 has a two-channel output to an analogue-to-digital converter (ADC), which processes the analogue electrical signal from the sensor at a 12-bit depth, there after all further internal camera processing is handled at a 12-bit depth by a single ASIC, prior to the final stage when the data is saved in the selected file format as determined by the selected option for image quality. The data processing engine is one element of what Nikon refer to as their new "Expeed" internal processing regime; it involves a range of different components designed to enable the D60 to produce images with the same basic color characteristics as all other images recorded by Nikon D-SLR cameras that use "Expeed" processing.

Image data destined to be saved as a JPEG file is processed at a 12-bit depth and is only reduced to an 8-bit depth at the very last stage of processing when the JPEG compression encoding is performed. In many earlier Nikon D-SLR cameras, the application of image attributes such as sharpening, tone (contrast), and color adjustments is performed at an 8-bit level, which can result in posterization (abrupt shifts in color and/or contrast), as a result of the loss of certain tonal values. In shadow tones, this can result in an uneven appearance; and in highlight tones it can result in areas that lack detail. By maintaining the image data at a 12-bit depth when performing in-camera modifications, the D60 produces far better looking JPEG files compared with previous Nikon D-SLR models, particularly in the shadow areas. To prevent a build up of contrast and loss of acuity, I recommend you use the lowest level of compression when saving images in the JPEG format by selecting an image quality of JPEG Fine.

Using the NEF (RAW) format, the camera deals with sensor data in a different way. The D60 records compressed NEF (RAW) files, so some of the 12-bit data from the sensor is discarded in a process that Nikon describes as being "visually lossless" (see below for the explanation of what actually occurs). The camera settings in use at the time an image is taken are recorded and saved as a set of instructions in the relevant metadata fields of the image file. The camera also creates and stores a thumbnail image, akin to a JPEG file, alongside the NEF (RAW) file.

Note: There is no option to record uncompressed, or lossless compressed NEF (RAW) files with the D60.

Using the JPEG format the camera produces a "finished" image from the sensor data and the settings in use at the time of the exposure. I put finished in quotation marks because these files can still be enhanced, if you want, after they have been imported to a computer. However, shooting in the NEF (RAW) format requires the user to do much of the work, using appropriate software and a computer, performed by the internal camera processing in producing a "finished" JPEG image.

If you are beginning to form the impression that to eek out every last ounce of quality the D60 has to offer you should shoot in the NEF (RAW) format, you are not wrong. However, while many photographers refer to RAW files as being "better" than JPEG, I prefer to consider the issue in terms of the relative flexibility and benefits each offers, and recommend that you use the one that is best suited to your specific requirements. It is worth taking a look at the attributes of each format so you can make an informed decision.

JPEG Format

JPEG files have three attributes that can influence image quality in an adverse manner:

- In-camera processing reduces 12-bit data from the sensor to 8-bit values when it creates a JPEG file. The D60 does have an advantage in that all in-camera adjustments are made at a 12-bit level before the data is reduced to an 8-bit level, so the reduction to 8-bits is of little consequence if you have no intention of applying image processing with computer software. However, if you make significant changes to an image using software in post-processing, the 8-bit data of a JPEG file can impose limits on the degree of manipulation that can be applied.

- When the camera saves an image using JPEG, it encodes most of the camera settings for attributes such as white balance, sharpening, contrast, saturation, and hue into the image data. If you make an error and select a wrong setting, you will need to correct your mistake in post-processing using a computer. Inevitably this is time consuming time and there is no guarantee it will be successful.

- The technology of digital imaging is fast paced and the electronics used in any particular camera are only as good as the day the manufacturer decided on their specification and finalized the design of the camera. Granted, updated firmware may help to offset some obsolescence, but updates eventually stop being produced. By processing images in software on a computer, you can often take advantage of the latest advances in image processing, which are unavailable to the camera.

NEF (RAW)

Using NEF RAW has only one real disadvantage to my mind, and that is the extra time it takes to process each image, using compatible imaging software to produce a finished picture. The larger file size of the NEF RAW format can also be an issue in terms of the amount of available storage needed on your memory card and external storage facilities for archiving pictures. Equally, there can be limitations with some third party software applications when it comes to their ability to read and interpret Nikon's proprietary NEF (RAW) files. The benefits of NEF include:

• More consistent and smoother tonal graduations

• Color that is more subtle and accurate to the original subject or scene

• A slight increase in the level of detail that is resolved.

• The ability (within fairly limited parameters of ±1EV) to adjust exposure in post-processing to correct for slight exposure errors

• The ability, in post processing, to correct and/or alter image attributes such as the white balance value, sharpening level, contrast, saturation, and hue.

Note: Most modern software is capable of reading NEF (RAW) files generated by a D60; there is a wide variety of third party raw file converters that enable a NEF (RAW) file to be opened in most popular digital imaging software applications. For compatibility between NEF (RAW) files from the D60 and Nikon software, you will require the following, or later versions of: Nikon Transfer (version 1.0.2), Nikon View NX (version 1.0.4), Capture NX (version 1.3.3), and Nikon Camera Control Pro (version 2.1.0).

Nikon describes the compression applied to NEF files as being "visually lossless," by which they mean it is impossible to see the difference between compressed and uncompressed NEF files. This compression process used by Nikon is selective, working on certain image data while leaving other data unaffected. It works in two phases: the first phase groups and rounds certain tonal values while the second is where conventional lossless compression is applied.

To begin, the analog signal from each pixel site on the sensor is converted to one of 4,096 possible values (i.e. a 12-bit depth). A value of 0 represents pure black (no data), and a value of 4,095 represents pure white (total saturation). During the first phase, the values that represent the very dark tones are separated from the rest of the data. Then the data with values that represent the remaining tones is divided into groups, but this process is not linear. As the tones become lighter the size of the group increases, so the group with the lightest tones is larger than a group containing mid-tone values. A lossless compression is then applied to each individual dark tone value and the rounded value of each group in the mid and light tones.

When an imaging application such as Nikon Capture NX opens a NEF (RAW) file, it reverses the lossless compression process. The individual dark tone values are unaffected (remember the compression is lossless) but – and here is the twist – each of the grouped values for the mid and light tones must be expanded to its appropriate range on a 12-bit scale. Since the rounding error in each group becomes progressively larger as the tonal values become lighter, the gaps in the data caused by the rounding process also become progressively larger at lighter tonal values.

However, the human eye does not respond in a linear way to increased levels of brightness, so it is incapable of resolving the very minor changes that take place, even in the lightest tones where the rounding error is greatest and therefore the data "gap" is largest (remember Nikon's phrase – "visually lossless"). Furthermore, our eyes are generally only

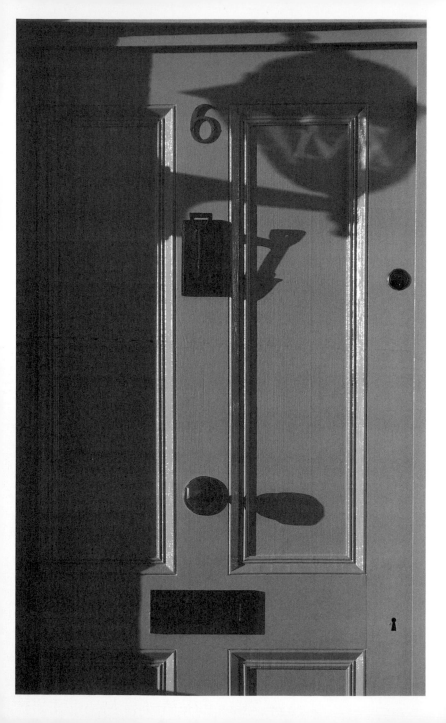

capable of detecting tonal variations equivalent to those produced by 8-bit data, and even a compressed NEF (raw) file has more than that. Consequently the data gaps caused by Nikon's compression process are of no consequence.

Note: There is a small risk that the data loss caused by compression of NEF (RAW) files might manifest in the highlight areas of an image that is highly altered during image processing (e.g., considerable color shift, significant modification of tone, or excessive sharpening).

Which Format?

In considering the attributes of JPEG and NEF, many photographers make an analogy with film photography; they compare the NEF file to an original film negative and the JPEG file to a machine-processed print. I do not disagree, but not every photographer has the desire, ability, or time to process NEF files with imaging software, so JPEGs are fine for them. The good news is that we have a choice. If you have sufficient storage capacity, you could select NEF (RAW) + JPEG from the options for image quality. That way the D60 can save a copy of an image in both formats, but this setting uses the highest level of compression for the JPEG file.

Image Quality and Size

The D60 allows you to save JPEG files at three different levels of quality:

- **FINE** – Uses a low compression of approximately 1:4
- **NORMAL** – The default uses a moderate compression ratio of approximately 1:8
- **BASIC** – Uses a high compression ratio of approximately 1:16

JPEG quality settings control the amount of lossy compression applied to the image file. For the highest quality/lowest compression level, choose FINE—the setting I recommend for almost all types of shooting.

103

Each JPEG file can also be saved by the D60 at one of three different sizes:

- **L – Large** (3,872 x 2,592 pixels)
- **M – Medium** (2,896 x 1,944 pixels)
- **S – Small** (1,936 x 1,296 pixels)

You should select the lowest level of compression to maintain the highest image quality possible; a file saved at the FINE setting will be visually superior to a file saved at the BASIC setting. It is also true that JPEG compression can generate visual artifacts, and the higher the compression ratio the more apparent these become. If you are shooting for web publication, this is unlikely to be an issue. But if you intend to make prints from your JPEG images, you will probably want to use the Large/FINE settings.

There is no size option with NEF (RAW) files since the D60 always uses the full 3,872 x 2,592 resolution of the sensor. NEF (RAW) files can only be saved in a compressed form, quoted at a size of approximately 9.0MB in the Nikon manual. However, the degree of compression in a NEF as well as a JPEG will vary slightly depending on the nature of the scene photographed, meaning the file size will also vary. Hence it is possible the camera will record more pictures than the quantity initially displayed as the number of exposures remaining when the card is formatted in the camera.

Note: The make of memory card can also influence the total number of pictures that an individual card can store, so do not be surprised if you see slight differences in card capacity between cards from different manufacturers.

Setting Image Quality and Size

To set image quality (JPEG or RAW) on the D60, open the ⬛ Shooting menu and use the multi selector to highlight Image quality; press the multi selector to the right to open a list of options and scroll up or down to highlight the desired one. Finally, press the 🆗 button to confirm your selection.

Alternatively, and in my opinion far more convenient and quicker, is to use the button method, which obviates the need to open the menu system. Press the ◀🅘▶ button to open the Shooting Information Display, and then press it again to open the Quick Settings Display, now use the multi selector to highlight Image quality. Press the 🆗 button to open the list of quality settings, and use the multi selector to highlight the required option; there are five available:

- **RAW** (NEF)
- **FINE** (JPEG)
- **NORM** (JPEG)
- **BASIC** (JPEG)
- **RAW + B** (NEF + JPEG Basic)

Finally, press the 🆗 button to confirm the selection.

To set image size for JPEGs on the D60, start by opening the ⬛ Shooting menu and use the multi selector to highlight Image size. Press the multi selector to the right to open the list of options and press it up or down to highlight the desired setting: Large, Medium, and Small. Finally, press the 🆗 button to confirm your selection.

You can also use the more convenient and quicker button method to set the image size. Press the ◀🅘▶ button to open the Shooting Information Display, and then press it again to open the Quick Settings Display, now use the multi selector to highlight Image size. Press the 🆗 button to open the list of quality settings, and use the multi selector to highlight the required option

- **L** (Large – 3,872 x 2,592 pixels) – this is the default setting.
- **M** (Medium – 2,896 x 1,944 pixels)
- **S** (Small – 1,936 x 1,296 pixels)

Press the ⊛ button to confirm your selection.

White Balance

We are all familiar with the way the color of daylight changes during the course of a day, from the orange/yellow colors immediately after sunrise, through the cooler look of light around midday, to the red/orange colors that appear as the sun sets. However, the color of light, not to be confused with the color of the objects from which it is reflected, changes in subtle ways at other times of the day and in different climatic conditions. Furthermore, different types of light sources, such a household bulb or camera flash unit, emit different colored light. The color of light is defined by a color temperature and measured in degrees on the Kelvin (K) scale. Our eyes and brain are remarkably good at adapting to light with different color temperatures, so subtle changes are not always apparent to us.

Digital sensors, however, have an objective, fixed response to light with a specific color temperature. The electronics of digital cameras such as the D60 permit flexibility with regard to recording the color temperature of light, processing the picture data to equate to a variety of specific color temperatures, either automatically, or by selecting the color temperature manually. This function is known as the white balance (WB) control.

White Balance Options

The D60 offers a number of white balance options that are only available when shooting in the P, A, S, and M exposure modes. In ᴬᵁᵀᴼ🄰 Auto and the Digital Vari-Program modes, the white balance value is always selected automatically using the **AUTO** option. The approximate color temperature

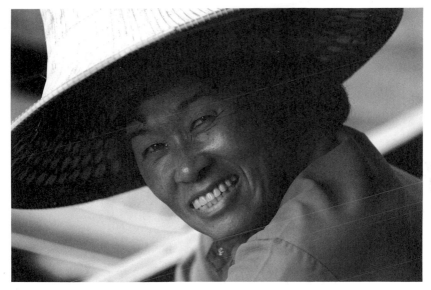

For average outdoor snapshots, AUTO white balance works surprisingly well or for more accuracy, you can choose one of the options in the Quick Setting Display.

for each option, except **PRE** , is in parentheses in the following list of descriptions:

AUTO **Auto (3500 – 8000K):** Nikon suggests that the D60 will measure light with a color temperature between 3500K and 8000K automatically. For average middle of the day daylight conditions the automatic white balance works well enough but under any other lighting conditions, particularly artificial lighting, there are far better options; as with all automatic features on any camera, you need to think for yourself and take control when appropriate. For example, if you shoot indoors under normal electric lighting, the color temperature is likely to be lower than 3500K. Alternatively, color temperature is likely to exceed 8000K outdoors in bright overcast conditions, or open shade. In such instances I recommend using the **PRE** preset white balance option.

※ **Incandescent (3000K):** Try using this option in place of the automatic option for indoor shooting under typical incandescent lighting, as its color temperature is more closely matched to such light sources. However, you are likely to find that the result still looks too warm (i.e. the yellow/red content of the pictures is too high), use the fine-tuning control (see page 111) to make further adjustments. Alternatively, use the **PRE** option, which will generally provide the most neutral rendition of color under artificial light sources.

※ **Fluorescent (2,700 – 7,200K):** The light emitted from fluorescent light sources is notorious for causing an unwanted color cast in pictures. This is due to the variability in the color temperature of the light they produce and the manner in which the light is emitted, which follows a discharge/decay cycle at the same frequency as the mains AC power supply. If the white balance is set via the shooting menu there are seven options available for specific types of fluorescent light sources.

※ **Direct sunlight (5200K):** This option is intended for subjects or scenes photographed in direct sunlight from around two hours after sunrise to two hours before sunset. At other times, when the sun is lower in the sky, the light tends to be naturally warmer, which produces pictures with a redder appearance.

Hint: I know that white balance is a subjective issue, but to my eye the color temperature for the ※ option on the D60 is too low (after all, most daylight color film is balanced to 5500K). When shooting in these conditions you may prefer to use the Flash ⚡ or Cloudy ☁ option.

⚡ **Flash (5400K):** As its name implies, this option is intended whenever you use flash as the main light source (Nikon refers to its own flash units as Speedlights).

Hint: As with the ☀ option, I consider the color temperature of the ⚡ option to be too low, since the color temperature of light emitted by Nikon Speedlights is generally in the range of 5500–6000K. Therefore I often select the ☁ option when working with Nikon flash units as the main light source.

☁ **Cloudy (6000K):** This option is for shooting under overcast skies, when daylight has a high color temperature. It ensures the camera renders colors properly without the typical cool (blue) appearance that often results, particularly in pale skin tones, when shooting in such conditions.

🏠 **Shade (8000K):** This option applies a greater degree of correction than the ☁ setting and is intended for those situations when your subject or scene is in open shade beneath a clear blue sky, when the color temperature is likely to be very high. Under these conditions the light will be biased strongly towards blue, as it is comprised principally of light reflected from the sky and has a very low red content.

PRE **White balance preset:** This setting allows the user to measure the color temperature of the light illuminating the subject or scene by making a test exposure (note no picture is recorded). Alternatively, you can use an existing picture stored on the memory card as a reference for the color temperature value. This option is the most effective at achieving a neutral color balance, especially when shooting under artificial, or a mix of different light sources.

Selecting a White Balance Option

The options for white balance settings can be selected in two ways: (1) from the Shooting menu **AUTO** or (2) from the Quick Settings Display; however, the second method does not allow you to select an alternative light source option for the Fluorescent ⚟ white balance item, set a white balance fine-tuning factor, or measure/set a value for the **AUTO** white balance option.

For the first method, press the 🔘 button on the rear of the camera and use the multi selector to open the 📷 shooting menu. Navigate to the white balance item using the multi selector and press it to the right to open the next page, displaying the available options. Scroll down the list to highlight your choice and press the multi selector to right. The menu page that follows will display an option for fine-tuning your selection (see next page for details), except in the case of the Fluorescent 🔆 item, which requires one further step to select the appropriate type of lighting source before the fine-tuning control is displayed.

Note: White balance fine-tuning factors cannot be applied if the **PRE** white balance option is selected, or the camera is set to one of the Digital Vari-Program exposure modes, including 📷. The camera must be set to P, S, A, or M exposure modes in order to fine-tune white balance.

To use the second, and in my opinion much quicker method for selecting a white balance setting, press the ⌨ button to open the Shooting Information Display, then press it again to open the Quick Settings Display. Next use the multi selector to highlight the required white balance item. Press the 🔘 button to display the list of white balance options, and use the multi selector to highlight the desired option. Finally, press the 🔘 button to confirm your selection: the icon for the new white balance setting is displayed in the Quick Settings Display. Press the shutter release button down half way to return the camera to the Shooting Information Display.

Note: If you select a white balance option from the Quick Settings Display, it is not possible to set and apply a fine-tuning factor; do this by selecting the white balance option from the 📷 shooting menu. Also, it is not possible to measure a new value for the **PRE** option if selected from the Quick Settings Display, though you can use the value that was most recently measured and recorded using **PRE**.

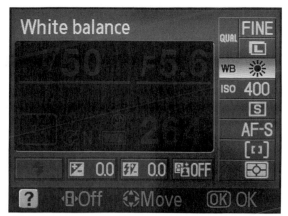

White balance can be set using the Quick Settings Display; here the incandescent option is selected.

Hint: If you expect to alter the white balance option frequently while on a shoot, I recommend using CS-11 to enable selection of the white balance option via the ☉/Fn button. Once set up press and hold the ☉/Fn button, which is located on left side of the camera below the 🗲 button, to open the Quick Settings Display on the LCD monitor: The currently selected white balance option will be highlighted; to change it, rotate the command dial (on back upper right of camera) until the desired option is displayed, then release the ☉/Fn button.

Fine-Tuning White Balance (P, S, A, or M modes only)

This feature enables the white balance to be fine-tuned to compensate for variations in the color temperature of a particular light source, or to create a deliberate colorcast in a picture. The system used in the D60, which effects change in equally spaced MIRED values (see "What is MIRED" panel) offers considerably more precise and consistent control compared with the somewhat arbitrary and counter intuitive method employed by previous Nikon D-SLR cameras, where a value of ±3 is applied with negative values creating a warmer rendition and a positive value a cooler rendition. If you have become familiar with the previous system you will need to invest some time to learn the new one, as the results may not be quite what you expect.

The fine-tuning of white balance can only be applied via the white balance item in the shooting menu. Open the shooting menu and navigate to the white balance item and press ⓞⓚ to display the list of white balance options.

Highlight the required white balance option, then with the exception of the Fluorescent option, press ⓞⓚ to display a color graph; its horizontal axis is used to fine tune for the level of amber (A) and blue (B), while the vertical axis is used to adjust the level of magenta (M) and green (G). If you select the Fluorescent 🌟 white balance option it is necessary to select the light source type first, before the color graph is displayed.

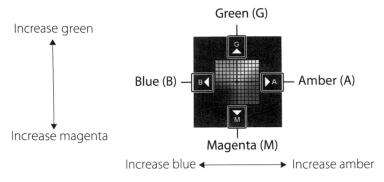

The color graph of the white balance fine-tuning option enables both color temperature and color to be adjusted.

Using the multi selector button a value between 1 and 6 can be selected along each axis of the color graph, working from the central point (see graphic above). Color temperature is fine-tuned by shifting along the amber (A) – blue (B) axis, while color is shifted in a manner similar to using color-compensating (CC) filters by shifting along the green (G) – magenta (M) axis. A combined color temperature and color shift is possible by moving the cursor of the graph display into one of the four quadrants of the graph. Once you have set the fine-tuning adjustment press ⓞⓚ button to save the setting and return to the shooting menu.

Note: If any white balance fine-tuning adjustment is applied ✖ will appear next to the white balance icon shown in the Shooting Information Display.

What is MIRED?

MIRED, or to give it its full title, Micro REiprocity Degree, is a method of defining a shift in color in such a way that each shift in MIRED value is equivalent to the difference in color we perceive. The disadvantage of degrees Kelvin (K) is that a relatively small shift in Kelvin value at low color temperatures (e.g. less than 4000K) create a much larger perceived shift in color compared with a relatively small shift in Kelvin value at high color temperatures (e.g. more than 6000K). The MIRED value is calculated by multiplying the reciprocal of the color temperature by ten to the power six (106). For example, the difference of 1000K between a color temperature of 3000K and 4000K is equal to 83 MIRED, whereas the same difference between 6000K and 7000K is only 24 MIRED.

Hint: Do you want to get creative? It is easy with the white balance control. Try mismatching the selection of the white balance setting on the camera with the color temperature of the prevailing light. For example, rather than shoot a scene lit by daylight using the appropriate daylight white balance value, set the white balance to incandescent. The resulting picture will have a strong blue colorcast. Remember, if the color temperature of the prevailing light is lower than the color temperature of the white balance value set on the camera, the scene will be rendered with a warm (red/yellow) color cast. Conversely, the scene will be rendered with a cool (blue) color cast if the color temperature of the prevailing light is higher than the color temperature of the white balance value set on the camera.

White Balance Preset

The **PRE** option allows you to measure a color temperature value from the light falling on a subject or scene being photographed; in many instances this provides the most accurate way of setting a white balance value. The D60 offers two methods of selecting a WB preset value, either by using the camera to measure light reflected from a white or neutral gray test target, or by using the white balance value from a previous exposure as a reference.

Hint: Nikon suggests using either a white or a neutral gray object as a reference target for the preset white balance option. I strongly recommend that you only use a neutral gray object, such as a Gray Card, for two reasons: (1) many white paper, cards, and plastics often contain pigments, brighteners, or dyes to whiten them, which can cause the camera to render colors inaccurately; and (2) it is more difficult to expose correctly for a pure white object, and errors in exposure can affect the white balance reading you obtain from the test target.

Using the Preset Option

The **PRE** preset white balance option is only available in P, A, S, and M exposure modes. Using this item involves several more steps than the other white balance option that have a fixed color temperature value. Two methods are available to obtain a value for the preset white balance preset option: (1) direct measurement and (2) copying the white balance from an existing picture that was taken on a D60 camera. The camera can store only one value for the preset white balance option, consequently only the most recently measured white balance value will be stored, regardless of the method used.

Direct Measurement

Start by placing a target such as a neutral gray card in the same light that illuminates the scene or subject. The test target does not necessarily have to be at the same location as the subject, just as long as it is in the same light. The exposure mode used is not critical; however, I suggest use of P (Programmed auto), S (Shutter-priority auto), or (A) Aperture-priority auto. If you use either of the two latter options ensure that neither **Hi**, nor **Lo** are displayed in the viewfinder. It does not matter if the camera does not focus on the test target the shutter release remains enabled for the purposes of acquiring the preset white balance measurement.

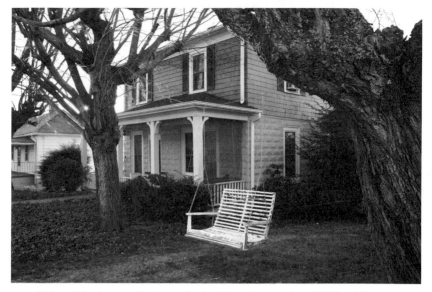

This subject was photographed twice. Once using AUTO white balance and once with the Cloudy option. The results were nearly identical. AUTO white balance often does a great job with standard outdoor subjects. Photo © M. Morgan

Now press the ⊞ button and use the multi selector to open the 📷 shooting menu. Navigate to the white balance item using the multi selector and press it to the right to open the next page to display the available options. Scroll to highlight the **PRE** option and press the multi selector to the right to open the next menu page that displays two further options: Measure and Use photo. Highlight Measure and press the multi selector to the right. The next page displays a message: "Overwrite existing preset data?" Highlight Yes and press the **OK** button. The next page displays a dialog box for a short period with the message: "Take photo of white or gray object filling the viewfinder under lighting for shooting". The Shooting Information Display is then restored and at this point **PRE** will be shown blinking in both the viewfinder and Shooting Information Display.

Note: If you wish to cancel the direct measurement process, highlight No. The white balance preset option will be reset to the last measured value.

Point the camera at your test target (taking care not cast a shadow over it) and make sure it fills the viewfinder frame (there is no need to focus on the test target card). Press the shutter release button all the way down. If the camera is able to obtain a measurement, the message: "Data acquired" will be displayed on the LCD screen and the letters "Gd" will be shown in the viewfinder display. The white balance is now set to the measured color temperature value of the prevailing light being reflected from the test target, automatically replacing any previous value stored on the camera. This value will be retained until you make another measurement, either directly by measurement, or from an existing photograph.

Note: You will need to repeat the process if the message, "Unable to measure preset white balance. Please try again." is displayed on the monitor screen and the viewfinder shows "no Gd." The most common cause for this is the level of ambient illumination being too bright or too dim; so, try setting the lens to a smaller aperture (higher f/# number), or larger aperture (lower f/# number) respectively.

Hint: If you expect to take several preset white balance direct measurements over the course of a shooting period, here are two alternative routes that obviate the need to navigate the menu system thus making them more efficient:

• Press the ◀**⊞**▶ button to open the Shooting Information Display, and then press it again to open the Quick Settings Display. Use the multi selector to highlight the white balance option and press the **⊛** button to show the list of white balance options. Highlight **PRE** and press **⊛** to return to the Quick Settings Display. Now press and hold the **⊛** button for a few seconds until the Shooting Information Display opens and **PRE** begins to blink. Now proceed with the measurement process as described above.

- Alternatively, ensure **PRE** is selected as the white balance option and CS-11 is set to the WB (white balance) option, before pressing the ○/**Fn** button for approximately two seconds. The Shooting Information Display will then appear in the monitor screen, and **PRE** will blink in both the viewfinder and Shooting Information Display. Now proceed with the measurement process as described above.

Once you become adept at handling the D60, either of these methods is considerably quicker than using the 📷 menu to select and measure a white balance preset value.

Copying White Balance From an Existing Photo

It is also possible to set a preset white balance value by copying the white balance value from an existing photograph; however, the photograph used as a reference must have been taken on a D60 camera.

Start by pressing the 🔘 button and use the multi selector to open the 📷 shooting menu. Navigate to the white balance item using the multi selector and press it to the right to open the next page to display the available options. Scroll to highlight the **PRE** option and press the multi selector to the right to open the next menu page that displays two further options: Measure and Use photo. Highlight Use photo and press the multi selector to the right.

The next page displays the title "Use photo" and the last recorded photograph, together with two options: This image and Select image. If you wish to use the displayed photograph as the white balance value reference, select This image and press the multi selector to the right to apply the setting.

To use an alternative photograph, highlight Select image and press the multi selector to the right to display a list of all available folders that contain images. Highlight the required folder and again press the multi selector to the right to display up to six thumbnail images at a time. Scroll through the displayed images using the multi selector ⊚ to highlight a picture; the currently selected photograph will have a narrow yellow border around it. If you wish to view an enlarged display of the selected image, press and hold the ⊕ button. To set the preset white balance value from the highlighted photograph, press the ⊛ button. This will apply the white balance value to the **PRE** option and return the display to the ▣ menu. The White balance preset value will be retained until either you make another direct measurement, or use a value from an existing photograph.

Optimizing Images

In addition to white balance, the D60 has several additional controls that affect the appearance of your pictures. These options can be applied to images shot in P, A, S, and M exposure modes. To select any of them, open the Shooting menu ▣ and navigate to the Optimize image item. Press the multi selector to the right to open the next menu page, which lists the available options. Use the multi selector to scroll to the desired control and press ⊛ to select it. The available options are:

⬚N **Normal**
The default setting, it tends to produce a slightly subdued looking image that benefits from slight enhancement of levels and contrast by processing with imaging software, so it is useful if you intend to deal with images individually using a computer.

⬚SO **Softer**
As the title suggests, this selection produces images with slightly lower contrast and lower edge acuity. It is useful for portraits or for pictures shot with flash as the main light source.

⬚VI **Vivid**
This option increases color saturation and edge acuity (sharpness), adding a little extra bite to images. Use it if you expect to print images directly from the camera without any image processing in the computer.

118

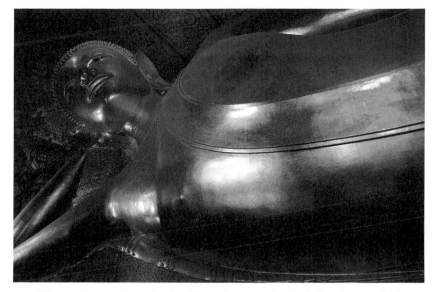

The various options in the Shooting menu's Optimize Image field allow you to choose how sharpening, colors, contrast, etc. are applied to the JPEG file. For unusual subjects such as this, I recommend you experiment till you become familiar with the results.

⊘Vᴵ⁺ More Vivid

An enhanced version of Vivid, this produces results similar to a high saturation color transparency film. It is best used when color intensity is more important than color veracity.

⊘P0 Portrait

This option appears to produce results that are almost identical to the Normal option, particularly in terms of the contrast.

⊘BW Black-and-White

Nikon considers the in-camera technology applied using this option to be commercially sensitive, so the company has not divulged the process used. However, the camera sets sharpening and tone (contrast) to Normal, and appears to average the red, green, and blue values to produce a neutral-toned monochrome image. The algorithm used in this process is not the same as that used in the Monochrome option of the Retouch menu (see page 206).

Note: The D60 always saves a black-and-white picture as an RGB file, using Color Mode Ia, with sharpening, saturation, and tone (contrast) set to Normal, and Hue adjustment set to 0. As with the options available under the Custom item of the Optimize image menu, the effects of the Black-and-white option can be achieved with a far greater degree of control using digital imaging software once the image file has been imported to a computer; however, this option works effectively for images that will be output directly from the camera.

Optimize Image Options

The settings applied in each of the options in the Optimize image menu are fixed, with the exception of the Custom option; the value of each setting is shown in the following table:

Optimize	Color Mode / Space	Tone	Hue	Saturation	Sharpness
Normal	IIIa (sRGB)	Auto	0	Auto	Auto
Softer	Ia / (sRGB)	Low (Less contrast)	0	Auto	Low
Vivid	IIIa / (sRGB)	Normal	0	Enhanced	Medium High
More Vivid	IIIa / (sRGB)	High (More contrast)	0	Enhanced	High
Portrait	Ia / (sRGB)	Auto	0	Auto	Medium Low
Black & white	Ia / (sRGB)	Normal	0	Normal	Normal

Hint: To maximize the level of flexibility and therefore your control over image quality, I strongly recommend that you use the Custom option because no single level of sharpening or tone control is universally applicable.

✐✐ Custom

It is vitally important to understand that the Custom option is the only one that provides full control, allowing you to adjust settings for sharpening, tone compensation (contrast), color mode, saturation (color intensity), and hue adjustment.

120

If you select any of the other Optimize Image options, the camera will automatically apply the settings shown in the table above; the user cannot be altered these. In other words, even if you shoot a series of pictures of a similar scene with those options that apply automatic control to a setting, the values assigned may vary.

To ensure consistent results, use the Custom option but avoid selecting Auto for sharpening, tone compensation (contrast), and saturation, as you relinquish control of these options by doing so.

Another reason for selecting the Custom option is the choice it offers for color space and color mode; a color space describes the range (gamut) of colors that can be recorded by the camera. The color mode defines how accurate the rendition of the recorded colors will be. The settings for color space and color mode have been linked in the D60 (as outlined in the table). The color space is always sRGB in Color modes Ia and IIIa, and it is always Adobe RGB in Color mode II (see pages 125-126). Consequently, if you want Adobe RGB as the working color space, you have to select Color mode II, which is only available in the Custom setting of the Optimize Image options. This is the color space with the widest gamut, and it is linked to Color mode II, which usually ensures the highest level of color accuracy. This is particularly useful if the images will be subject to extensive work using imaging software in the computer, as it provides greater flexibility when modifying color on either a global or localized basis.

Hint: If you expect to use pictures directly from the camera to post to a website, send as an attachment to an email, or produce a print, I recommend using color mode Ia (optimized for portrait pictures) and IIIa (optimized for landscape and nature pictures) accordingly.

Settings Available In Custom-Optimize Image

Select Custom ✐✐ and press the multi selector to the right to open a list of available options. Highlight the desired option using the multi selector and press it to the right; scroll to the setting you want and select it by pressing ⓞⓚ . Once you have finished adjusting the settings, navigate to Done and press the ⓞⓚ button to confirm and save the selected settings; if you fail to carry out this last step the settings will not be saved. The Custom options are:

Image sharpening: This is a process applied to digital data that increases the apparent acuity (sharpness) of a picture. It is used to correct the side effects of converting light into digital data, which often causes distinct edges between colors, tones, and objects to look poorly defined, or fuzzy. The sharpening is a technique that identifies an edge by analyzing the differences between neighboring pixel values. Then the process lightens the pixels immediately adjacent to the brighter side of the edge, and darkens the pixels adjacent to the dark side of the edge. This causes a local increase of contrast around the edge that makes it appear sharper; the higher the level of sharpening applied the greater the contrast at the edge; however, once applied sharpening is virtually impossible to remove so consider carefully how much sharpening is applied during in-camera processing.

Note: Sharpening is not a method for rescuing an out-of-focus picture; once out-of-focus, always out-of-focus!

The D60 offers seven levels of image sharpening:

- **Auto** – The camera applies a level of sharpening that varies according to how the camera analyzes the image data. This is tricky because the level of sharpening can vary from image to image and you have no indication as to how much sharpening the D60 actually applies at this setting.

- **Normal** – Apparently the camera applies a moderate amount of sharpening at a consistent level. I say "apparently" because, again, Nikon does not provide specific values for the level of sharpening the camera applies.

- **Low** – A lesser amount of sharpening is applied than Normal.

- **Medium low** – Sharpening level is slightly higher than Low.

- **Medium High** – Sharpening level is slightly higher than Normal.

- **High** – The D60 applies an aggressive level of sharpening, which may not be appropriate for some subject/scenes.

- **None** – No sharpening is applied to the image data.

Hint: No single level of sharpening is suitable for all picture-taking situations; the level of sharpening should be based on your ultimate intentions for the image (i.e. display on a web page, publication in a book or magazine, or producing a print for framing). Therefore, it is often preferable to apply sharpening as one of the last stages during image processing on a computer, particularly if you want to use an image for a range of different output purposes.

I would make the following suggestions with regard to in-camera sharpening when shooting with the D60:

1. For general photography when using JPEG format files, set sharpening to Low or Medium Low if you intend to process these images later using software in the computer.

2. For general photography when using JPEG format files, set sharpening to Normal if you intend to print pictures directly from the camera without any further image processing.

3. On occasions when you need pictures for publishing on a web page or in newsprint, use the JPEG format and set the sharpening level to Normal or Medium High

4. If you shoot in the NEF (RAW) file format, set sharpening to None

Note: Although the in-camera processing does not apply any sharpening to a NEF (RAW) file, any setting made for sharpening will be stored in the EXIF data (metadata) of the file. Consequently, because some applications automatically read and apply the sharpening level stored in the EXIF file, you may find that sharpening is applied by default when you open a NEF (RAW) file in your chosen RAW converter. Hence, I advise you set in-camera sharpening to none if you shoot NEF (RAW).

Tone compensation: This control allows you to adjust the contrast of an image ("contrast control" would be a better name). It works by applying a tone (contrast) control curve similar to those used in image-processing applications that alter the distribution of tones in an image to fit the selected contrast range, as defined by the contrast curve. Again, there are several levels of Tone compensation:

- **Auto** – The D60 uses its Matrix metering system to assess the differences between the levels of brightness in the scene. If these are significant, the camera assumes the scene has high contrast and applies compensation to lower it. Conversely, if scene contrast is assessed to be low, the camera will increase image contrast.

- **Normal** – The D60 applies a standard tone (contrast) curve that produces images with contrast somewhere between the extremes of Less contrast and More contrast.

- **Less contrast** – This setting produces images with noticeably less overall contrast, which can be a benefit when shooting a subject or scene that contains light tones that are well illuminated. However, it can also affect the density of very dark tones with the result that they lack depth.

- **More contrast** – Image contrast is boosted, which can be a benefit when shooting subjects or scenes that lack contrast. However, this option should be used with care since there is an increased risk that highlight details may appear to be "burned out," and reducing contrast once applied (or over-applied) with this setting can be difficult to achieve without introducing unwanted side effects that affect image quality.

- **Custom** – This option allows you to write your own Tone (contrast) curve and upload it to the camera, but is only applicable if you have access to Nikon Camera Control Pro 2 software. If no custom contrast curve is created and uploaded to the camera, this option performs the same as Normal.

Note: If you expect to perform processing on your JPEG pictures using software in your computer after downloading from your memory card, consider setting Less contrast since it is easier to increase contrast than reduce it at any stage subsequent to the original exposure.

Color Mode: The D60 offers a choice of three color modes, which determine the accuracy of the colors recorded in an image. Your option for Color mode should be chosen based on the use to which the image will be put.

Ia (sRGB only) – Recommended for portraits that will be used or printed without further modification, color mode Ia is biased in favor of those colors that reproduce skin tones with a pleasant appearance (i.e. colors are slightly warm due to increased levels of yellow/red).

II (Adobe RGB only) – This color mode produces the most accurate rendition of colors recorded by the camera. It is used in conjunction with the Adobe RGB color space, which renders a wider range of colors compared with the sRGB color space, thus providing greater flexibility when it comes to subsequent image processing using a computer.

IIIa (sRGB only) – This is the default setting on the D60 and is designed to enhance the rendition of green and blue, although yellow, orange, and red tend to look strong as well. It is a good choice for nature or landscape shots that will be used or printed without further modification.

I recommend using the color mode II unless your pictures will only be displayed on a computer monitor, or will be printed directly with no additional post-processing. Since it is adapted to the Adobe RGB color space, it offers a subtle rendition and well-graduated tonal transitions, increasing the flexibility of an image that will be subject to post-processing in the computer.

Hint: It is essential that any digital imaging application used to handle an image file be set to the same color space (i.e. you work with a color managed system), otherwise the application will more than likely assign its own default color space and you will lose control over the rendition of colors.

Saturation: Adjusting the saturation changes the overall vividness (chroma) of color without affecting the brightness (luminance) of an image. Saturation options are:

- **Auto** – The D60 will adjust the level of saturation automatically according to the assessment of the scene, or subject made by the D60 based on information collected by the 420-segment RGB metering sensor.

- **Normal** – This is the default setting and is probably the option to use for most situations, since the camera offers limited control compared with those that can be applied during post-processing in a digital imaging application at a later stage in a computer.

- **Moderate** – The vividness of colors is reduced, but Nikon provides no information as to the level of adjustment that is applied.

- **Enhanced** – The vividness of colors is increased, but again there is no information about the level of adjustment that is applied.

Hue adjustment: The color modes used by the D60 to produce images is based on combinations of red, green, and blue light. By mixing two of these, a variety of different colors can be produced. If the third color is introduced, the hue of the final color is altered. For example, if the level of red and green data is increased relative to the blue data, the hue shifts (positive adjustment) to a warmer (red/yellow) rendition. If you apply a positive adjustment, the hue shifts causing reds to appear more orange, greens more blue, and blues more purple. A negative adjustment will cause red to shift toward purple, blues to appear greener, and greens more yellow. The default setting for the Hue adjustment control is 0°, and the D60 allows you to set an adjustment of +/- 9° in increments of 3° (the degrees refer to the "color wheel" often used to describe hue).

Hint: I believe it is better to leave control of both color saturation and hue to a later stage when you can apply adjustments with a far greater degree of control during post-processing of an image file in the computer; therefore, I recommend that these controls be set to Normal and 0°, respectively.

ISO Sensitivity

One of the great advantages of digital photography is that digital cameras allow the ISO sensitivity to be adjusted from exposure to exposure; the D60 is no exception. It offers sensitivity settings (in ISO equivalent values) from 100 to 1600, available in steps of 1EV (one-stop), plus the option to select the Hi 1 setting for increased sensitivity (Hi 1 does not equate exactly to an ISO value of 3200 but it is close enough for practical purposes). There is an option for ISO noise reduction set from the Shooting menu for use with the higher ISO settings, plus an item in the Custom Setting menu that enables the D60 to vary the ISO sensitivity value automatically according to the light conditions.

The word "sensitivity" is used advisedly since the sensor in the D60 actually has a fixed sensitivity level equivalent to ISO 100; the higher ISO values are achieved by amplifying the signal from the sensor.

Setting Sensitivity

You can set the sensitivity value on the D60 in two different ways. One method is to open the 📷 shooting menu and scroll to ISO sensitivity. Press the multi selector to the right to display a list of the ISO values, then scroll using ⊚ to highlight the desired value and press the 🆗 button to set it.

Alternatively, press the ◂🔘▸ button to open the Shooting Information Display then press the ◂🔘▸ button again to open the Quick Settings Display; use the multi selector to highlight ISO (sensitivity). Press the 🆗 button to display the list of options: 100, 200, 400, 800, 1600, and Hi 1. Use the multi selector ⊚ to highlight the required option. Finally, press the 🆗 button to confirm your selection: the new ISO value is displayed in the Quick Settings Display. Press the shutter release button down half way to return the camera to the Shooting Information Display.

Hint: If you expect to alter the ISO value frequently during a shoot, I recommend using CS-11 to enable selection of the ISO sensitivity via the ⟳/Fn button. Once set up press and hold the ⟳/Fn button, which is located on left side of the camera below the ❹ button, to open the Quick Settings Display on the LCD monitor: The currently selected ISO value will be highlighted; to change it, rotate the command dial (on back upper right of camera) until the desired value is displayed, then release the ⟳/Fn button.

At high sensitivity settings, an image will show increasing amounts of digital noise that causes a general reduction in image quality, affecting color saturation, contrast, and tonality. A greater degree of graininess will be come increasingly apparent in pictures, as the ISO value is raised.

For optimum image quality, set the D60 to ISO 100. At ISO 200, image quality is maintained at a very high level, with only the slightest degradation apparent at ISO 400. At ISO 800 there is little evidence of noise in the highlights but it does appear in the shadow areas. Subjectively this is random and therefore not as intrusive as the typical noise pattern generated by many digital cameras at high ISO settings, while color saturation remains strong to maintain the visual perception of a fine image quality. The ISO 1600 setting produces images that are remarkably good for such a high value, though the effects of luminance and color noise are clearly perceptible, as is the affect on scenes with high contrast due to the narrower dynamic range that reduces the ability of the camera to record the extremes of deep shadow and bright highlights. In terms of its dynamic range the D60 is good for about nine stops between deepest shadow and brightest high-light when shooting at ISO settings from ISO 100 to around ISO400; this is no doubt due to the benefits of the new Expeed processing and its superior control of ISO noise. Beyond ISO 400 the dynamic range shrinks by around one stop (1EV step) for each full stop (1EV) increase in the ISO value, so by ISO 1600 it is down to about seven stops. However, due to significant noise effects, I suggest the Hi 1 setting should be considered only when no other option (wider aperture or slower shutter-speed) would get the picture.

Hint: If the light level begins to drop as you shoot, you can either raise the ISO setting or use a longer shutter speed. Confronted with this situation, and assuming the subject does not require a fast shutter speed to record it, I recommend putting the camera on a tripod and selecting a longer exposure, so you do not compromise the aperture setting, which would have an immediate effect on depth of field.

ISO Auto

This option should be used carefully because it does not work in quite the way I expect most users imagine. That said, the performance of the D60 at any ISO sensitivity level between 100 and 1600 is likely to satisfy most users, thus leaving the ISO Auto option switched on should not cause any undue concern about overly noisy images. Plus, the D60 does allow you to select a maximum ISO level for this control by using the Max sensitivity option under CS-10.

In Programmed auto (P) and Aperture-priority auto (A) exposure modes, the sensitivity will not change until the exposure reaches the limits of the shutter speed range. The upper limit is always 1/4000 second but the lower limit is set by the user and can be adjusted between 1 second and 1/125 second (default is 1/30 second) using the Min shutter speed option at CS-10.

In Shutter-priority auto (S) exposure mode, the sensitivity is shifted when the exposure reaches the limit of the aperture range available on the lens. Indeed, this is the one exposure mode with which ISO Auto feature might be an advantage, because it will raise the sensitivity setting and thus maintain the pre-selected shutter speed, which in this mode is probably critical to the success of the picture. In M (Manual) exposure mode, the sensitivity is shifted if the selected combination of shutter speed and aperture cannot attain a correct exposure.

Although a blinking warning, ISO-A, appears in the Shooting Information Display, and ISO-AUTO appears in the viewfinder to indicate the sensitivity has been altered from the value set by the user, there is no indication of what ISO value has been set in these displays! You must open page two of the shooting data in the Photo Information Display (available in single-image playback) to see the changed ISO value, which is displayed in red.

Note: ISO Auto control is not available in the AUTO 📷 , and other Digital Vari-program modes, nor does it does not operate at the Hi 1 ISO setting.

TTL Metering

To select one of the three TTL (through-the-lens) metering modes available on the D60, press the ◄**⊞**► button to open the Shooting Information Display then press the ◄**⊞**► button again to open the Quick Settings Display; use the multi selector to highlight the Metering option. Press the ⊙ button to display the list of options: Matrix ▦ , Center-weighted ⊙ , and Spot ⊡ . Use the multi selector to highlight the desired option. Finally, press the ⊙ button to confirm your selection; the metering option is displayed in the Quick Settings Display. Press the shutter release button down half way to return the camera to the Shooting Information Display.

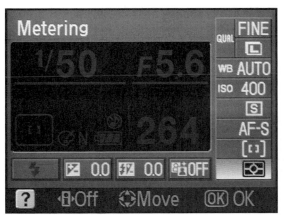

The metering pattern used in the D60 can be set from the Quick Settings Display; here Matrix metering is shown as being selected.

▦ Matrix Metering

The metering pattern for this mode divides most of the image area into a series of segments (a matrix) and assesses the light seen through the lens for a number of attributes. The values for these attributes are then compared to a database of reference images, in the camera's memory, before the camera suggests a final exposure setting. The Matrix metering in the D60 uses a sophisticated 420-segment RGB sensor located in the viewfinder head that divides the frame into 420 segments that cover almost its entire area (the very extreme edges of the frame area are beyond the area cov-

Color Matrix metering II used in the D60 covers virtually the entire frame area, as depicted by the shaded area in the diagram.

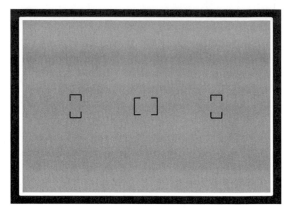

ered by the Matrix-metering pattern), using an alternating pattern of red, green, and blue sensors to measure light values. The D60 uses exactly the same RGB sensor and data-processing algorithms for its Color Matrix metering, as the D80, D40x, and D40 models.

To derive the most from the capabilities of the Matrix metering, use a D-type or G-type Nikkor lens since these provide additional information concerning focus distance, which is combined with information from the Multi-CAM530 AF module, which assists the camera in estimating how far away the subject is from the camera, and where in the frame the it is likely to be (the camera assumes the subject is in the plane of sharp focus and located in the region of the active focus area). Hence, Nikon refers to the system as 3D Color Matrix metering II (it is the second version of this system). When a Nikkor lens that does not communicate focus distance information (i.e. a non D-type or G-type) to the camera is used, the system defaults to standard Color Matrix metering II. If a non-CPU lens (e.g. an Ai-S type manual focus lens) is used the TTL metering system of the D60 does not function.

By assessing color as well as brightness, the Matrix metering system helps reduce the influence of a monochromatic scene or subject, thereby improving its accuracy.

Matrix metering uses four principal factors when calculating an exposure value:

- The overall brightness level of in a scene
- The ratio of brightness (contrast) between the segments
- The active focus area, which suggests the position of the subject in the frame
- The focused distance, provided by the lens (D-type or G-type only)

Active D-Lighting

On the whole I have found the Matrix TTL metering option of the D60 to be remarkably accurate; if it does miss then it is generally when confronted with a situation of high contrast with large areas of very bright highlights and deep shadows, which tends to induce slight underexposure.

Fortunately the D60 benefits from a new feature first introduced in the Nikon D300 camera: Active D-Lighting (not to be confused with the D-Lighting item in the Retouch menu), which can be used to optimize the exposure settings, especially in high contrast situations, when using Matrix metering, to extend the overall dynamic range recorded by the camera.

With the D60 set to use Matrix metering and Active D-Lighting switched on the camera automatically detects situations of high contrast prior to exposure and modifies the exposure level by reducing it to help retain detail in the brightest highlights, and then the highlight, shadow and mid-tone values are preserved by adjusting the subsequent in-camera processing to produce an image with optimum brightness (gamma). The feature is very effective adding around a stop (1EV) of extra highlight range while maintaining shadow and mid-tone values with a relatively normal tone (contrast) curve. The penalty of Active D-Lighting is the slight increase in noise in the darker tones (shadows) but in practical terms this is negligible in the typical situation where the feature is likely to be used (i.e. bright, high contrast lighting, when the ISO is at a low level).

To select Active D-Lighting, press the ◀⚏▶ button to open the Shooting Information Display then press the ◀⚏▶ button again to open the Quick Settings Display; use the multi selector to highlight ⚏ . Press the ⓞⓚ button to display the options: On, or Off. Use the multi selector to highlight the desired option. Finally, press the ⓞⓚ button to confirm your selection; ⚏ is displayed in the Quick Settings Display. Press the shutter release button down half way to return the camera to the Shooting Information Display.

Alternatively, the quick method of enabling or disabling Active D-Lighting is to press the ⚏ button on the top right of the camera and rotating the command dial ⟳ . Check that the Active D-Lighting indicator is displayed in the viewfinder, or Shooting Information Display. The feature can also be set via the ⬛ shooting menu but this is a more long-winded route.

Since the effects of Active D-Lighting are applied proactively during the processing of the original image file before it is saved it is not possible to alter them when recording JPEG files; however, when recording in the NEF RAW format the effects can be altered subsequently using appropriate Nikon software. It is important to note that due to the additional processing that is performed by the Active D-Lighting feature it takes noticeably longer to record each image.

⊙ Center-Weighted Metering

The center-weighted metering pattern dates to the very first TTL metering systems used in early Nikon SLR film cameras. In these models, the frame area was usually divided in a 60:40 ratio with the bias being placed in the central portion of the frame. The D60 uses a ratio of 75:25, with 75% of the exposure reading taken from an 8 mm diameter circle at the center of the frame, and the remaining 25% based on the frame area outside this circle. It is important to note that the focusing screen does not show any markings to define this metering area.

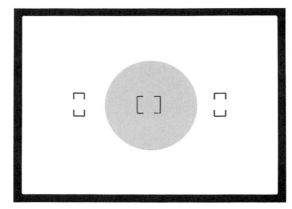

The center-weighted metering system used in the D60 assigns 75% of the metering sensitivity to a central circular area that is 8mm in diameter.

Hint: In my opinion the center-weighted option is the least useful of the three metering patterns available on the D60. Matrix metering will do an excellent job in most situations, and the spot meter is capable of taking readings from a specific area in particularly tricky lighting with greater accuracy than the center-weighted pattern.

[•] Spot Metering

Spot metering is extremely useful for measuring from a highly specific area of a scene. For example, faced with a subject against a very light or dark background, the spot meter allows you to take a reading from the subject without

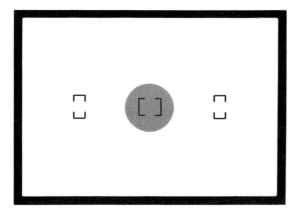

Spot metering assigns sensitivity to a circular area that is approximately 2.5% of the frame ; in single-point AF area mode it can be centered on any one of the three auto focusing points.

it being influenced by the background. In similar circumstances, the Matrix metering system might very well underexpose and overexpose the subject respectively.

The sensing area for the spot metering function is a circle approximately 0.14-inches (3.5 mm) in diameter. The center of the metering area is aligned with the center of the selected (active) autofocus point.

Note: If the AF-area mode is set to closest subject, the camera will perform spot metering using the central autofocus sensing area only. In single-point and dynamic area AF modes spot metering is performed using the area centered on the active AF point. In Dynamic area AF, the D60 attempts to follow a moving subject by shifting focus control between any of the three autofocus points. When this occurs, the spot metering also shifts.

Hint: Every TTL metering system measures reflected light and is calibrated to give a correct exposure for a mid-tone. When using the spot meter, you must make sure that the part of the scene you meter from represents a mid-tone, otherwise you will need to compensate the exposure value.

Exposure Modes

The selected exposure mode is displayed at the top of the Shooting Information Display; here the camera is set to Aperture-priority auto mode.

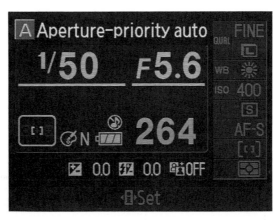

In addition to the ⒶUTO mode and the Digital Vari-Program exposure options, the D60 offers four exposure modes that the user can partially, or fully control: Programmed auto (P), Aperture-priority auto (A), Shutter-priority auto (S), and Manual (M). To select any of these exposure modes, rotate the mode dial on the top right of the camera until the desired mode symbol is aligned with the index mark on the side of the viewfinder head.

Note: The exposure metering system of the D60 is disabled if you attach a non-CPU lens.

P – Programmed Auto

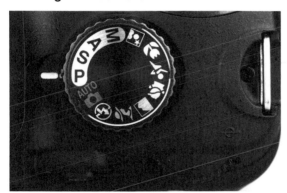

The D60 set to programmed-auto exposure mode.

Program mode, as it is often referred to, automatically adjusts both the shutter speed and lens aperture to produce a correctly exposed image, as defined by the selected metering mode. As in the ⒶUTO Auto and Digital Vari-Program modes, you relinquish control of exposure to the camera. If you want to make informed decisions about shutter speed and aperture for creative photography, it is better to use A, S, or M exposure modes.

However, the photographer does have a bit of influence in this mode. If you decide that a particular combination of the shutter speed and lens aperture chosen by the camera is not suitable, you can override those settings by turning the command dial. An indicator (P *) appears in both the viewfinder and Shooting Information Display to show that you have overridden the settings: This is called the Flexible Program mode. The values for aperture and shutter speed change in tandem, so the overall level of exposure remains the same (i.e. dialing in a shorter shutter-speed decreases the f/#number, and vice versa).

Hint: If you override the Program mode, its new shutter speed and aperture settings will remain locked, even if the meter automatically powers off and is then switched on again by halfway pressing the shutter release button. To cancel the override, you must either rotate the command dial until the P* indicator is no longer visible, change the exposure mode, turn the power switch to OFF, or perform a camera reset.

A – Aperture-Priority Auto

The D60 set to Aperture-priority auto exposure mode.

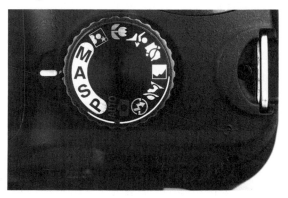

In this mode the photographer selects an aperture value and the D60 will choose a shutter-speed to produce an appropriate exposure. Rotate the mode dial until A is aligned with the index mark; the aperture is controlled by rotating the command dial and is changed in steps of 0.3EV.

S – Shutter-Priority Auto

The photographer selects a shutter-speed and the D60 will choose an aperture value to produce an appropriate expo-

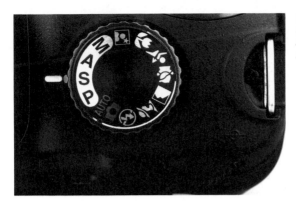

The D60 set to Shutter-priority auto exposure mode.

sure. Rotate the mode dial until S is aligned with the index mark; the shutter-speed is controlled by the command dial and is changed in steps of 0.3EV.

> **Note:** The camera will display **H ᶠ** in the viewfinder as a warning if the subject or scene is too bright for the D60 to achieve a proper exposure in P, A, and S modes. Likewise, if the subject or scene is too dark for the D60 to achieve a proper exposure, it will display **L ▢** in the viewfinder as a warning.

Shutter Speed Considerations

When handholding your camera, a rule of thumb about the minimum shutter speed can be helpful to prevent loss of sharpness due to camera shake. Multiply the focal length by 1.5x, and then take the reciprocal to provide an approximate value for the slowest shutter speed to be used with that lens. For example, with a focal length of 200mm, set a minimum shutter speed of 1/320 second [1/(200 x 1.5)]. Do take care, because shooting with longer focal length lenses, as well as at the higher degree of subject magnification in close-up photography will amplify the effects of camera shake.

Since shutter speed controls the way that motion is depicted in a photograph, it can be used for creative effect. Generally, fast shutter speeds are used to freeze motion, for example in sports or action photography. Slower shutter speeds can introduce a degree of blur that will often evoke a greater sense of movement than a subject that is rendered pin-sharp. Alternatively, you can pan the camera with the subject at a slow shutter speed so that the subject appears relatively sharp against an increased level of blur in the background.

If you want shoot a picture of a static subject but "eliminate" any moving elements from your composition, try using a shutter speed of several minutes or more. While the subject is rendered properly, the moving element(s) do not record sufficient information in any part of the frame to be visible. In many cases, this technique will require a strong neutral density filter in daylight conditions to achieve a sufficiently long exposure time. So the next time you want to take a picture of a famous building and excluded all the other visitors from cluttering up your composition, you know how!

M – Manual

The D60 set to manual exposure mode.

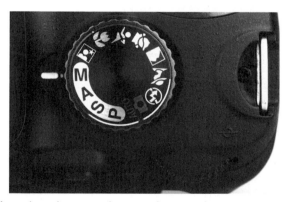

This mode offers the photographer total control over exposure and is probably the most useful if you want to learn more about the relationship between the shutter speed and lens aperture, and how it affects the final appearance of your pictures. You choose and control both the shutter speed by rotating the ⟳ command dial and lens aperture by rotating the command dial, while pressing down on the ⊗ button. An analog scale shown in the viewfinder indicates the level of exposure your settings would produce. If the camera determines the exposure values are set for a proper exposure, a single indent mark appears below the central 0 ⁺··ᵠ··⁻. If the camera determines that the settings would produce an underexposed image, the degree of underexposure is indicated by the number of indent marks that appear to the right (minus) of the 0 point, for example ⁺··ᵠ··⁻ indicates underexposure by 0.3EV. Conversely, if the chosen settings would create an overexposed result, the degree of overexposure is indicated by the number of indent marks to the left (plus) side of the central 0 point, for example ᵗ⃛··⁻ indicates overexposure by more then 2.0EV. The more indent marks that appear, the greater the degree of deviation from a proper exposure. If the deviance is more than +/-2EV, a small arrowhead appears at the appropriate end of the scale.

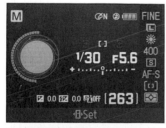

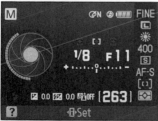

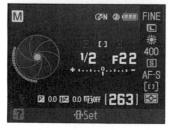

For the less experienced photographer the Graphic Display option in Shooting Information offers a helpful way of visualizing the affect of adjusting the shutter speed and aperture. Note how the representation of the lens aperture is reduced in size as the aperture is set to a higher f/ number and the shutter speed is reduced correspondingly to maintain the same level of exposure, with the analog scale showing no deviation from the central 0 point.

Auto Exposure Lock

If you recompose after taking a meter reading in P, A, or S exposure mode, it is likely the TTL meter sensing area will now fall on an alternative part of the scene that has a different level of reflectivity. The new composition will therefore produce a different exposure value. To deal with this, the D60 allows the auto exposure lock (AE-L) function to lock and retain the initial exposure reading before you recompose and shoot (auto exposure lock has no effect in M exposure mode).

While AE-L can be applied with all three metering modes, it is generally most effective with center-weighted and spot metering. These two modes are most useful in very difficult lighting conditions, when a more accurate exposure reading can be to taken from a specific area of the scene, which may otherwise fool the Matrix metering system.

Select a metering mode and position the part of the scene you want to meter within the sensing area, then press and hold the shutter release button down half way to acquire a reading. Next, press and hold the ⊞ button (this assumes an appropriate option is selected at CS-12 see page 225). You can now recompose and shoot the picture at the metered value ("EL" will appear in the viewfinder display while this function is active). Alternatively you can select On for CS-13, so that once the shutter release button is held half way, the exposure value set in P, A, or S, mode remains locked until the shutter button is released ("EL" is displayed as described).

Note: It is possible to change the settings for shutter speed and aperture while the AE-L function is in effect in P, A, and S exposure modes, although the metered exposure level remains unaltered. Once the exposure is locked, rotating the command dial will cause the shutter speed and aperture values to change, so you can set an alternative value for one and the other will be altered accordingly. In P mode the shutter speed and aperture can be altered as with Flexible Program, in Shutter-priority mode the shutter speed can be altered, and in Aperture-priority the aperture value can be altered.

Exposure Compensation

The TTL metering system on the D60 assumes it is pointed at a scene with a reflectivity that averages to the equivalent of a mid-tone. Note I say tone and not color; tone determines how much light is reflected, light tones reflect more light than dark tones regardless of color. Good examples of mid-tones are green grass, or fire truck red. Nikon appears to calibrate against a reference that has a reflectivity value of approximately 12% to 13%, so using a standard photographic 18% gray reference card to estimate exposure will give results that are approximately 0.3EV to 0.5EV underexposed.

Many scenes you encounter will not reflect 12% to 13% of the light falling on them. For example the light tones of snow, or white sand will reflect far more light than the dark tones of some one dressed in black clothing or an animal with black or very dark brown fur. Unless you compensate your exposure, both of these extremes of tone will "fool" the TTL metering system because it will attempt to rendered them as mid tones; consequently they will look dull and flat, with light tones underexposed and dark tones overexposed. Exposure compensation is available in P, A, and S exposure modes and is most effective with ⊛ and ⊡ metering. Exposure compensation can be set to values between ±5EV in steps of 0.3EV.

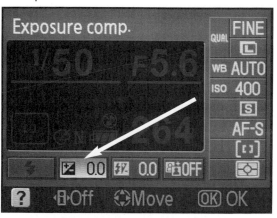

On the D60 exposure-compensation can be set from the Quick Settings Display; here a value of ±0.0 is shown.

To set an exposure compensation factor, press the ◄🅱► button to open the Shooting Information Display, then press the ◄🅱► button again to open the Quick Settings Display; use the multi selector to highlight Exposure comp. Press the 🆗 button to display the current compensation factor (the default is 0.0). Use ◉ on the multi selector to increase or decrease the desired level (the "Assist image" thumbnail will appear, which illustrates the effects of the selected adjustment value accordingly). Finally, press the 🆗 button to confirm and set the exposure compensation value, which is then displayed in the Quick Settings Display, as both a numerical value and on an analog scale (an analog scale is also displayed in the viewfinder where its central 0 blinks as a reminder that exposure compensation is set.) The number of bars shown in these analog scales reflects the amount of compensation set; each bar represents a shift of 0.3EV. Once you have set a compensation factor, it will remain locked until you reset it to 0.0 using the exposure compensation option in the Shooting Information Display (it is not reset if the camera is switched off).

In Manual exposure mode you adjust shutter speed and aperture using the TTL meter's recommended readings as a guide. An analog scale will appear in the viewfinder where a single bar below the central 0 indicates a proper exposure for an average mid-tone scene. When you apply a plus or minus value in M mode using the exposure compensation option, additional bars appear on the analog scale, each representing a shift of 0.3EV. A small "+/-" icon displays to the right of the scale in the viewfinder as a reminder that exposure compensation is applied. However, as you are shooting in Manual mode, the camera will not apply exposure compensation value automatically, as it does in P, S, and A exposure modes; therefore, it is necessary to adjust the shutter speed and/or aperture until the analog scale shows a single bar below the central 0 to put the exposure compensation value into effect. Once set, the compensation factor will remain locked until it is reset to 0.0 via the exposure compensation option in the Shooting Information Display.

144

An alternative (and quicker) way to apply exposure compensation (this method does not apply to M mode) is to hold down the ☒ button, located on the top right of the camera. Rotate the command dial ☟ until the desired plus or minus exposure compensation value is shown in the analog scale that appears in the viewfinder and Shooting Information Display, then release the ☒ button. Once you have set a compensation factor, it will remain locked until you hold down the ☒ button and reset the value to 0.0.

Note: The analog scale that displays in the viewfinder has a range of +/- 2 EV. If you set a greater degree of compensation in P, S, and A modes, you can display the exact compensation value by holding down the ☒ button (it replaces the exposures remaining counter). Also note, the D60 does not have an automated exposure-bracketing feature.

Shutter Release

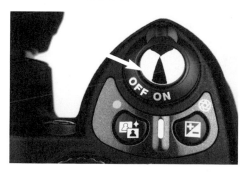

The D60 has a two-touch shutter release. A halfway depression activates the camera's functions such as TTL metering, while full depression releases the shutter mechanism.

The shutter release button is located on the top right shoulder of the camera. If the D60 is powered on, light pressure (pressing no more than half way down) on the shutter release button will activate the metering system and initiate autofocus (assuming an autofocus mode has been selected). Once you let go of the button, the camera remains active for a fixed period, the duration of which depends on the selection of the options available at CS-15 (Auto off timers); the default setting is Normal, which causes the exposure meter to turn off after eight seconds, and the monitor to turn off after twelve seconds if no other activity is performed by the camera.

Pressing the shutter release button all the way down operates the shutter mechanism to make an exposure. There is a short delay between the time the button is pressed all the way and when the shutter opens (referred to as shutter lag). Shutter lag on the D60 is approximately 80 milliseconds (1 millisecond = 1/1000 second); the mirror black out time (the time the viewfinder is obscured from the reflex mirror being in the raised to it returning to its normal position) is approximately double the shutter lag time when shooting at shutter speeds of 1/250-second or faster.

However, release of the shutter can be delayed further, and in some cases prevented, if the certain features and functions are in operation at the time the shutter release button is pressed:

- The capacity of the buffer memory is probably the most common cause of shutter delay. It does not matter whether you shoot in single frame or continuous shooting modes (see below for description), once the buffer memory is full, the camera must write data to the memory card before any more exposures can be made. As soon as sufficient space is available in the buffer memory for another image, the shutter can be released. For this reason, memory cards with fast data write speeds are recommended.

- If single-servo AF mode is selected, the shutter is disabled until the D60 has acquired focus. In low light or low contrast scenes, the autofocus system can often hunt for a while before achieving focus (page 162 for a full explanation), which extends the delay period.

- In low-light situations, the D60 will activate the AF-assist lamp, provided it has been instructed to do so via CS-09, which introduces a short delay while the lamp illuminates and focus is acquired.

Note: The AF-assist lamp only operates in single-servo auto-focus mode (if selected by user in AF-S, or by camera in the AF-A focus modes).

- The Red-eye reduction function, which is one of the flash modes available on the camera, introduces an additional one-second shutter lag. This is the time it takes for the red-eye reduction lamp to emit light causing the subject's pupils to constrict.

- If you select an ISO value above ISO 400 and activate the noise reduction item in the shooting menu the processing time of each exposure is increased, consequently reducing the frame rate. Likewise, even of noise reduction is switched off in the shooting menu the D60 still perform a small level of noise reduction at ISO settings above ISO800, which again can reduce the frame rate.

- Active D-Lighting will increase the processing time when recoding a picture, consequently it also reduces the potential frame rate.

Shooting Modes

The shutter mechanism of the D60 can be operated in a range of shooting modes, including single-frame, continuous shooting, a self-timer option, and via a remote release feature.

To set the Shooting mode, press the ◄🖸► button to open the Shooting Information Display then press the ◄🖸► button again to open the Quick Settings Display; use the multi selector button to highlight the shooting mode option. Press the ⊛ button to display the list of options: Ⓢ single-frame, 🖳 continuous shooting, ⏱10s self-timer, 🖥2s delayed remote, and 🖥 quick response remote. Use the multi selector button to highlight the desired option. Finally, press the ⊛ button to confirm your selection; the new shooting mode option is displayed in the Quick Settings Display. Press the shutter release button down halfway to return to the Shooting Information Display.

ⓢ Single Frame Shooting Mode

A single image is recorded each time the shutter release button is pressed. To make another exposure, the button must be pressed again; you can continue with single presses until the camera's buffer memory is full, in which case you must wait for data to be written to the memory card, or the memory card becomes full.

Hint: You do not have to remove your finger from the shutter release button completely between frames; by raising it slightly after each exposure and maintaining a slight downward pressure on the shutter release button, you keep the camera active, the auto focus locked, and you are ready for the next shot. If you want to take a rapid sequence of pictures in single frame mode, avoid stabbing the shutter button with your finger in quick succession. Instead, keep a light pressure on it and roll your finger over the top of the button in a smooth repeating action to reduce the risk of camera shake.

⊒ᵢ Continuous Shooting Mode

The D60 will continue to record images up to a maximum rate of 3-frames per second (fps) when you press and hold the shutter release button down.

Note: The frame rate is based on the camera set to AF-C mode, Manual (M) or Shutter-priority (S) exposure mode, and a minimum shutter speed of 1/250 second. It is important to remember that a slower shutter speed, the buffer capacity, use of other exposure modes, and the abilities of the autofocus system (particularly in low light) can reduce the frame rate.

⟳10s Self-Timer

When set to the Self-timer option, the camera will not fire the shutter immediately when the shutter release button is pressed. Instead it waits for a predetermined period of time and then makes the exposure. The default delay for the self-timer is 10 seconds, but it can be adjusted to 2, 5, or 20 seconds using the relevant option at CS-16.

Traditionally, the self-timer mode has been used to enable the photographer to be included in the picture, but there is another useful function. By using the self-timer to release the shutter, the photographer does not have to touch the camera after activating the countdown, thus reducing the chance of camera shake. This is particularly useful when shooting with a shutter speed in the range of 1/2 to 1/30 second, and precise timing of the shutter release is less critical.

You should normally place your camera on a support such as a tripod when you want to use self-timer mode. Compose the picture and make sure focus is confirmed before depressing the shutter release button (the shutter release will be disabled unless focus is acquired).

Hint: If you expect to use the self-timer feature frequently while on a shoot, I recommend using CS-11 to enable its selection via the ↻/**Fn** button. Once set up press the ◄**⊞**► to open the Shooting Information Display, and then press the ↻/**Fn** button, which is located on left side of the camera below the **⊕** button, to switch between the currently selected shooting mode and the self-timer mode. The self-timer delay set via CS-16 will be applied; the duration of the delay is shown in the Shooting Information Display. To activate the self-timer function press the shutter release button all the way down. Once the exposure has been made, the D60 is returned to the selected shooting mode. If, after selecting the self-timer option by pressing the ↻/**Fn** button, you decide you do not wish to use it, press the ↻/**Fn** button again to return to the selected shooting mode.

Hint: When using autofocus, you must make sure nothing passes in front of the lens when the shutter release is pressed down all the way to activate the self-timer function, as this may cause the AF system to shift the point of focus and result in an out of focus subject. I recommend setting the camera on Manual focus mode when using Self-timer.

Note: In all exposure modes except manual, it is essential to cover the viewfinder with the supplied DK-5 eyepiece cap when the camera is operated remotely using the self-timer. This is because shutter speed and aperture settings are not altered by the camera in M mode, but in all other exposure modes the camera sets at least one of these values based on assessment of the light by the TTL metering system. In normal shooting when the photographer has their eye to the viewfinder light is blocked from entering the viewfinder eyepiece; however, as the metering sensor is located in the viewfinder head, light entering the viewfinder eyepiece (as opposed to the lens) when it is not covered will influence the metering sensor, causing incorrect exposure.

Hint: Fitting the DK-5 requires removal of the DK-20 rubber eyecup; this is a nuisance and increases the risk that the eyecup might be lost. I find it far quicker and more convenient to keep a small square of thick felt material in camera bag to drape over the viewfinder eyepiece when using the self-timer mode.

After the shutter release button is pressed, the AF-assist lamp will begin to blink (it will also beep if the audible warning has been activated in CS-01) until approximately two seconds before the exposure is made, at which point the light stops blinking and remains on continuously (the frequency of the beep will increase) until the shutter operates. The release mode is reset to either single-frame or continuous after the exposure is made. To cancel self-timer operation after the countdown has begun, turn the camera off.

Using a Remote Release
The D60 uses the Nikon ML-L3 wireless infrared (IR) remote release that is common to several other Nikon D-SLR cameras. Pressing the transmit button on the ML-L3 sends an IR signal to the receiver on the camera, which is located behind a small widow on the front of the camera just below the camera's shutter release button. The system has a maximum effective range of approximately 16 feet (5 m).

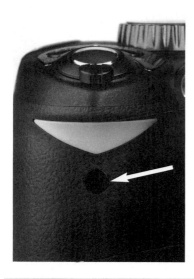

The sensor for the IR remote release is located behind the small window on the handgrip of the D60.

Hint: Though it is most effective to have an unobstructed line of sight between the ML-L3 and the receiver on the camera, it is not essential. It is possible to bounce the IR signal from the ML-L3 off a reflective surface such as a wall or window, which increases the potential of this feature.

The ML-L3 can be used to release the shutter in two different ways:

🔲 2s **Delayed remote** – The shutter is released with a delay of approximately two seconds after you press the transmit button on the ML-L3 remote control. The self-timer lamp will illuminate for approximately two-seconds, before the shutter is released.

🔲 **Quick-response remote** – The shutter is released as soon as you press the transmit button on the ML-L3 remote control. The self-timer lamp will flash immediately after the shutter is released.

Regardless of which remote release modes you choose (Delayed or Quick-response), the D60 will cancel it automatically after a fixed period of camera inactivity. At the default setting this period is one minute, but you can also set it to 5, 10, or 15 minutes via CS-17).

Note: If you require a flash unit to be used with either of the remote release options in P, A, S, and M exposure modes, ensure that it is switched on and that the flash ready light is illuminated before you press the release button of the ML-L3.

Hint: If you want to make extremely long exposures, select manual exposure mode and set the shutter speed to **buℓb**. Then select either Delayed remote or Quick-response; a pair of dashes (blinks) replaces **buℓb** in the Shooting Information Display. To start the exposure, press the transmit button on the ML-L3 once; then press a second time to end the exposure (the maximum duration of a single exposure is 30 minutes). A single flash of the AF-assist lamp confirms completion of the exposure. Before attempting any long time exposure, make sure the battery is fully charged and activate the noise reduction feature available in the shooting menu.

The Autofocus System

The autofocus system of the D40 marked a significant departure from the design of all previous Nikon AF D-SLR cameras because it was the first model that did not incorporate a built-in motor to drive the focusing mechanism of Nikon lenses. The same design has been adopted for the D60; consequently, it only supports autofocus with either AF-S or AF-I type Nikon lenses that have a built-in focusing motor. If you have a Nikon AF or AF-D type lens, it will be necessary to perform manual focus when used with the D60, although all other camera and lens functions will be supported.

Autofocus Sensor
The D60 uses the Multi-Cam 530 autofocus module, first seen in the D40, which has 530-photosites, as part of a phase detection auto focus system. The system uses a beam splitter comprising two optical prisms in a small semi-trans-

parent area of the main reflex mirror that capture the light rays coming from the opposite sides of the lens, they are coupled with a small secondary mirror located behind the main mirror that directs the light from these prisms to the Multi-Cam 530 module, which is located in the base of the mirror box at the bottom of the camera an AF sensor at the bottom of the camera. The double image projected on to the AF module is then analyzed for the patterns of light intensity and the phase difference between them is then calculated to determine whether the subject is in front of, or behind the current plane of focus. This not only informs the AF system which way the focus must be adjusted but also by how much. The focus point is adjusted immediately and the phase difference checked; provided it is within the tolerances of the AF system focus will not be altered again, as the camera has determined that focus has been acquired.

The 530 sampling points on the Multi-CAM 530 are divided in to three defined areas; each one approximately aligned to the three small square bracket pairs marked on the focusing screen, which are arranged parallel to the long edge of the frame. Only the central sensing area is a cross-type; this area is sensitive to detail in both a horizontal and vertical orientation, therefore, it is the most reliable and offers the best performance in low light conditions. The other two outer sensing areas are line-types, sensitive only to detail in a direction that is perpendicular to their vertical orientation, detecting detail aligned with the long edge of the viewfinder frame.

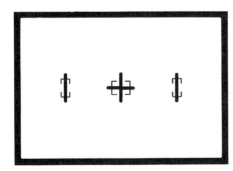

The actual area of coverage of the auto focus points extends beyond the area defined by the bracket pairs displayed on the focusing screen; the diagram shows the approximate coverage of the AF points in the D60. Note the central point is a cross-type, while the outer two are line-types.

153

Hint: Sometimes when using one of the outer line-type sensing areas, the autofocus system of the D60 will hunt, driving the focus of the lens back and forth, without attaining focus. This usually occurs when the AF point covers an area of continuous tone, a very fine pattern, or a very bright highlight and any detail is aligned in the same orientation as the AF sensing area. If this occurs, try twisting the camera slightly, 10 to 15-degrees is usually sufficient, to allow the camera to acquire focus, by disrupting the alignment of the AF point and subject detail. Once focus is confirmed, lock it (see page 160) and recompose the picture before releasing the shutter.

Focusing Modes

The D60 has two principal methods of focusing, AF (autofocus) and M (manual focus). The autofocus system offers three options known as the autofocus modes: AF-A (auto-servo), AF-S (single-servo), and AF-C (continuous-servo).

To select the AF mode, press the ◄**⊟**► button to open the Shooting Information Display then press the ◄**⊟**► button again to open the Quick Settings Display; use the multi selector to highlight the focus mode option. Press the **⊙** button to display the list of options: AF-A, AF-S, AF-C, and MF. Use the multi selector to highlight the desired option. Finally, press the **⊙** button to confirm your selection; the new focus mode is displayed in the Quick Settings Display. Alternatively the focus mode can be selected from the 🖉 menu via CS-02.

- **AF-A (Auto-servo)** – In an attempt to remove the burden of choosing which of the two principle autofocus modes (AF-S and AF-C) you should use, Nikon developed this option, (inherited from the D50), which is the default AF mode. In AF-A mode, the D60 assesses the focus information and selects either AF-S, or AF-C mode, depending on whether the camera determines that the subject is stationary, or moving. More often than not, the AF-A option will select the appropriate AF mode, but if it makes the wrong choice the result can spell disaster for your photos!

154

Hint: In my opinion, the fully automated nature of the AF-A option simply does not provide sufficient reliability for correct autofocus mode selection. I recommend you select the specific AF mode you require.

- **AF-S (single-servo)** – The D60 focuses the lens as soon as the shutter release button is pressed (either half or all the way). The shutter can only be released once focus has been locked, displaying the in-focus indicator, a green dot, in the viewfinder.

- **AF-C (continuous-servo)** – The D60 focuses the lens while the shutter release button is pressed halfway, continuously shifting focus to follow the subject if the camera-to-subject distance changes, regardless of whether the subject moves constantly or stops and starts periodically. This occurs until either the shutter is released or you remove your finger from the shutter release button. In this mode the shutter may in certain circumstances, be released before the in-focus indicator has been displayed in the viewfinder; however, the D60 does not perform any predictive focus tracking (see page 157).

- **MF (manual focus)** – The user must rotate the focusing ring of the lens to achieve focus. There is no restriction on when the shutter can be operated. The in-focus indicator, a green dot, is displayed in the viewfinder as a confirmation that focus has been achieved, which is particularly useful in low light, or low contrast conditions.

Note: Normally the focus mode is set via the Quick Settings Display; however, if you have selected one of the AF modes and wish to switch to manual focus, then provided the lens you are using has a switch to select either M/A or M, and it is set to the M/A position, you need only turn the focusing ring manually to disengage the AF system. As soon as you release the focusing ring and press down halfway on the shutter release, the camera will resume autofocus operation. If the switch on the lens allows selection of either A or M, then set it to M to disengage the AF system; it can now be focused manually.

AF-S vs. AF-C

It is important to appreciate the fundamental difference between the AF-S and AF-C autofocus modes. In AF-S, the autofocus system acquires focus and locks it at that distance for as long as the shutter release button is pressed halfway; the shutter cannot be released until focus has been locked. AF-S mode is most useful when photographing static subjects. Even if the shutter release is pressed all the way down immediately, operation of the shutter is delayed until the camera has locked focus. In most shooting conditions, particularly in good light, this delay is so brief that it is not perceptible, and it is has no practical consequence. However, under certain conditions, such as low-light or photographing subjects with low contrast, there can be a discernable lag between pressing the shutter release button and the shutter opening, particularly if one of the two line-type sensing areas is used.

Conversely in AF-C, the autofocus system monitors focus continuously, even after focus has been acquired, provided the shutter release button is pressed halfway. Hence, AF-C mode is most useful when photographing moving subjects, because the focusing system will follow the subject, even if it moves after focus is first acquire. However, unlike the AF-S mode, the shutter can be released in AF-C mode before focus has been locked.

Hint: When using AF-C mode to photograph a subject that is moving, or likely to move, it is imperative that the camera is given as much time as possible to assimilate focusing data. Rather than use the shutter release button to initiate the AF system, use Custom Setting CS-12 to select the AF-ON option for the function for the 🔘 button, and press and hold it down to keep the focusing system active; this removes the risk of the AF system switching off if you inadvertently remove you finger from the shutter button, allowing you to concentrate on timing the shutter release.

Hint: There is a short delay between the time when the reflex mirror lifts out of the light path to the camera's sensor and when the shutter actually opens. If a subject is moving toward or away from the camera, the camera-to-subject distance will change during this delay. In these circumstances some Nikon D-SLR cameras use a predictive tracking system, which estimates the likely position of the subject at the point when the shutter opens, and shifts the point of focus to compensate for the change in camera-to-subject distance, regardless of whether the subject is moving at a constant speed, accelerating, or decelerating. The camera achieves this by comparing multiple samples of phase detection as the camera monitors subject movement. Unfortunately the AF system of the D60 lacks such a feature; therefore, if you know that your subject is going to follow a particular path you may obtain better results by pre-focusing on a specific point the subject will pass, anticipate the movement it will reach it, and release the shutter slightly in advance of the moment to allow for the delay of the reflex mirror movement.

Trap Focus

It is possible to use the AF system to perform the trap focus technique, which allows the camera to be pre-focused at a specific point and have the shutter released automatically as soon as a subject passes through the pre-selected point. This technique can be very effective provided you can predict the path of the subject.

To use this technique, open CS-12 (AE-L/AF-L) and choose the option for AF-ON. Focusing will now be performed only when the 🔲 button is pressed, not when the shutter release button is pressed. Select AF-S mode, single-area AF mode, and if the lens has a focus mode switch on it, set it to either A or M/A to ensure that autofocus operates. Pre-focus the lens to a point the same distance from the camera as the point through which the subject will pass by aligning the selected AF point with it (you can use any of the three sensing areas). Then push the 🔲 button to acquire focus, and then release it. Recom-

157

pose the picture and make sure the active AF point covers the point through which the subject will pass. Keep the camera active by maintaining a light pressure on the shutter release button. When the subject arrives at the predicted position and covers the selected AF point, the camera will detect focus and the shutter will be released.

AF-Area Modes

The D60 has three area modes for autofocus (not to be confused with the three autofocus modes described on pages 154-155) that determine how each of the three AF points is selected. To set the AF-area mode, press the ◄⚏► button to open the Shooting Information Display, then press the ◄⚏► button again to open the Quick Settings Menu; use the multi selector to highlight Focus mode. Press the ⓞⓚ button to display the list of options: Closest subject AF (default), dynamic-area AF, and single-point AF. Use the multi selector to highlight the required option. Finally, press the ⓞⓚ button to confirm your selection; the new AF-area mode is displayed in the Quick Settings Display. Press the shutter release button down halfway to return to the Shooting Information Display. Alternatively the AF-area mode can be selected from the ✐ menu using CS-03.

[■] **Closest subject AF** – The focusing system selects the AF point that detects a subject closest to the camera. Note I say a subject; not necessarily the subject: This is a fully automated process and the D60 provides no choice about which AF point is used; hence, the camera can end up focusing on something other than the intended subject! After determining which AF point to use, the camera will lock focus. If you lift your finger from the shutter release button momentarily and then press is down halfway again the selected AF point is highlighted in red on the focusing screen; always double check to see if the camera has selected an appropriate point of focus before you release the shutter.

Hint: Closest subject AF selects the correct AF point a majority of the time, but it is far from foolproof. For predictable and precise control of the AF system, I strongly recommend either single point AF (for a static subject) or dynamic area AF (for a moving subject).

[⚬] **Dynamic area AF** – The D60 focuses using the AF point selected initially by the user. However, if the subject moves outside of the coverage of this AF point, even just briefly, the AF system will assess information from all three AF points and shift focusing to one of the other AF points if necessary to maintain focus. The AF point selected originally is highlighted on the focusing screen and also shown in the viewfinder information display and Shooting Information Display even if the subject moves outside its coverage. This option is selected automatically in the 🏃 mode.

[⬜] **Single point AF** – The focusing system uses only the single AF point currently selected for focusing; the camera takes no part in choosing which AF point to use. The selected AF point is highlighted on the focusing screen and also shown in the viewfinder information display and Shooting Information Display. This option is selected automatically in the 🌷 mode.

Hint: Manual selection of the AF point is only possible in either [⚬] dynamic-area AF, or [⬜] single-point AF. To select the required AF point, press the multi selector to the left or right ◉ . I recommend avoiding use of [▦] closest subject AF, since you have no control over which AF point is used by the camera.

AF Mode and AF-Area Mode Overview

If you are new to Nikon's AF system, it will probably take a while to get used to the functionality of the focus modes and focus-area modes available on the D60. In conjunction with the descriptions above, refer to the following table that summarizes the various autofocus operations.

AF Mode	AF-Area Mode	Selection of Focus Area
AF-S - single-servo	Single-point	User
AF-S - single-servo	Dynamic-area	User [1]
AF-S - single-servo	Closest subject	Camera [2]
AF-C - continuous-servo	Single-point	User
AF-C - continuous-servo	Dynamic-area	User [1]
AF-C - continuous-servo	Closest subject	Camera [2]

1. *In dynamic-area mode, the user selects the focus point to be used initially, but if the camera determines subsequently that this AF point no longer covers the subject, it will assess focus based on information from all three AF points to maintain focus (the focus point used initially remains highlighted in the viewfinder).*

2. *If closest subject AF is chosen, the camera selects the focus point that it determines to be most appropriate, automatically; the user has no control over the active AF point.*

Focus Lock

Once the D60 has attained focus, it is possible to lock the autofocus system so the shot can be re-composed with out the focus distance being altered, even if an AF point no longer covers the intended subject.

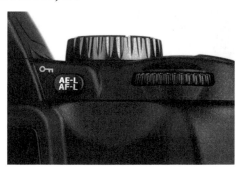

The AE-L/AF-L button can be used to lock focus and/or exposure; various options are available via CS-12.

When using AF-S, press the shutter release button halfway to activate autofocus. As soon as focus is attained, the in-focus indicator, a green dot, is displayed in the viewfinder and focus is locked. It will remain locked as long as the shutter release button remains depressed half way and the composition can be changed at will. Alternatively, assuming one of the appropriate AF options has been selected at CS-12 (AE-L/AF-L), press and hold the 🔘 button to lock focus; once focus is locked using the button, it is not necessary to keep the shutter release button depressed halfway.

When AF-C is selected, the autofocus system constantly adjusts the focus point while the shutter release button is held down halfway, so the picture must be composed with an AF point covering the subject. To lock focus and enable you to recompose the picture without keeping an AF area on the subject, press and hold the 🔘 button. Again, this is assuming one of the appropriate AF options has been selected at CS-12 (AE-L/AF-L).

Hint: Use CS-12 to assign the function of the 🔘 button, which can be used for several purposes: To lock both exposure and focus, to lock exposure only, or to lock focus only. Once focus has been locked in either AF-S or AF-C focus modes, ensure the camera-to-subject distance does not change. If it does, re-activate AF and re-focus at the new distance before using the AF lock options.

AF-Assist Illuminator

The D60 has a built-in AF-assist lamp on the front of the camera that is designed to facilitate autofocus in low light condition, though I consider this feature is largely superfluous. Here are a few reasons why I suggest using CS-09 (AF Assist) to cancel operation of this lamp.

• The lamp only works if you have a compatible autofocus lens (AF-I or AF-S type) attached to the camera, if the focus mode is set to AF-S, or if AF-S is selected in the AF-A mode. It is only usable with focal lengths between 24mm–200mm (ensure any lens hood is removed).

- The operating range is restricted to distances between 1 foot 8 inches and 9 feet 8 inches (0.5–3.0m).

- The lamp overheats quite quickly (6–8 exposures in rapid succession is usually sufficient) and will automatically shut down to cool. Plus, at this level of use, it also drains the battery faster.

Hint: Provided the conditions described above are met, it is possible to use the built-in AF-assist Illuminator lamp of either the SB-600 or SB-800 Speedlights. If you want to use either the SB-600 or SB-800 off camera, the SC-29 TTL flash lead has a built-in AF-assist lamp that attaches to the camera's accessory shoe.

Limitations of AF System

Although the autofocus system of the D60 is quite effective, there are some circumstances or conditions that limit its performance:

- Low light (use the central AF point for optimum auto focus performance).
- Low contrast (use the central AF point for optimum auto focus performance).
- Highly reflective surface.
- Subject too small within the area covered by the AF point.
- The AF point covers a subject comprised of fine detail.
- The AF point covers a regular geometric pattern.
- The AF point covers a region of high contrast.
- The AF point covers objects at different distances from the camera.

If any of these conditions prevent the camera from attaining focus, either switch to manual focus mode, or focus on another object at the same distance from the camera as the subject and use the focus lock feature before re-composing the picture.

Using Non CPU-Type Lenses

With electronic communication between the lens and camera for the purposes of exposure metering and autofocus, a number of changes have been introduced to the Nikon F lens mount. Consequently, older non-CPU type lenses (i.e. those that lack electrical contacts around their mounting bayonet) offer a restricted level of compatibility with the D60. If a non-CPU type lens is attached to the camera, only Manual exposure mode is available (the shutter release is automatically disabled if you select another exposure mode). The lens aperture must be set using the aperture ring on the lens, and the autofocus system, TTL metering system, electronic analog exposure display, and TTL flash control do not function. However, the electronic rangefinder does operate, provided the maximum effective aperture is f/5.6 or larger (for full details and lists of lens compatibility, see pages 274-279).

Depth of Field

When a lens brings light to focus on a camera's sensor, there is only a single plane-of-focus that is critically sharp. However, in the two-dimensional picture produced by the camera, there is a zone in front of and behind the plane of focus that is perceived to be sharp. This area of apparent sharpness is often referred to as the depth of field, and its extent is influenced by the camera-to-subject distance, together with the focal length and aperture of the lens in use.

If the focal length and camera-to-subject distance is constant, depth of field will be shallower with large apertures (low f/ numbers) and deeper with small apertures (high f/ numbers). If the aperture and camera-to-subject distance are constant, depth of field will be shallower with long focal lengths (telephoto lens) and deeper with shorter focal lengths (wide-angle lens). If the focal length and aperture are constant, depth of field will be greater at longer camera-to-subject distances and shallower with closer camera-to-subject distances. Depth of field is an important consideration when deciding on a particular composition; it has a direct and fundamental effect on the final appearance of the picture.

It is important to understand that images shot on a D60 exhibit slightly less depth of field than those shot on a 35mm film camera. This is due to the smaller size of the sensor compared with a 35mm film frame. The digital picture must be magnified by a greater amount compared with 35mm film to achieve any given print size. Therefore, at normal viewing distances, detail that appears to be sharp in a print (i.e. within the depth of field) made from a film-based image may no longer look sharp in a print of the same dimensions made from a digital file.

You will maximize depth of field in landscape photos by setting a small aperture (high f/ number). It is also worth observing that at mid to long focus distances; the zone of apparent sharpness will extend about one-third in front of the point of focus and two-thirds behind it. Therefore, by placing the point of focus about a third of the way into the scene, the coverage of the depth of field for the shooting aperture will be maximized.

In portrait photography, is often preferable to render the background out-of-focus so it does not distract from the subject(s). The simplest way to achieve this effect is to use a longer focal length lens (70 to 105mm is ideal) in combination with a large aperture (low f/ number).

In close-up photography, depth of field is limited, so convention suggests you set the lens to its minimum aperture (highest f/ number) value. However, I strongly recommend that you avoid doing this because the effects of diffraction at or near the minimum aperture of a lens cause a significant loss of image sharpness. Generally, you will achieve superior results at an aperture about two-stops more (lower f/ number) than the minimum value of the lens. Although it does vary slightly from lens to lens, I have found the effects of diffraction become apparent around f/11 to f/13. Also, do

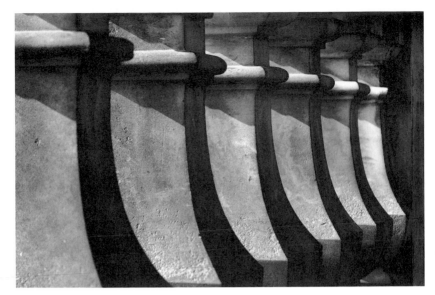

Using a small aperture and controlling the point of focus, so that it was about 1/3 of the way into the picture, created the large depth of field in this image.

consider using a tripod because the shutter speed is likely to be rather slow, even in good light, when shooting with a small lens aperture.

Unlike the distribution of the depth-of-field zone for mid to long focused distances, at very short distances the depth of field extends by an equal amount in front of and behind the plane of focus. By placing the plane of focus with care, you can use this fact to further maximize depth of field.

Two-Button Reset

If you want to restore settings that can be altered from the Quick Settings Display of the D60, or the Flexible Program option, to their default values hold down the 🔼 and 🔍

buttons for approximately 2 seconds (the monitor will turn off briefly during the reset). The green dots beside each button are a reminder of their function for this feature.

Two-button Reset Default Values

Option	Default
Release mode	Single frame
Focus mode	AF-A (Auto-area)
AF-area mode [1]	Closest subject
Focus area	Center
Metering	Matrix
Active D-Lighting	Off
Exposure Compensation	+/- 0
Flash Sync mode	Fill flash [2]
Flash compensation	+/- 0
Image Quality	JPEG Normal
Image Size	Large
White Balance	Auto [3]
ISO	100 [4]
Flexible Program	Off

1   *In* 🏃 *mode – Dynamic-area, and in* 🌷 *– Single-area are set*
2   *In* 🅰 🏃 🌻 🌷 *modes – Auto is set, and in* 🌃 *mode Auto slow-sync is set.*
3   *Fine tuning set to 0*
4   *ISO Auto is set in* 🅰 *and the Digital Vari-program modes*

Image Playback Options

One of the most useful features of a digital camera is the ability to get nearly instant feedback on photographs as you shoot. Using the playback functions on the D60 will allow you to see not only the images you have taken, but also a range of helpful and interesting information. Keep in mind that the small image displayed on the screen is not represented with sufficient precision to make critical analyses of such attributes as color or exposure. I believe that the image displayed is helpful to confirm that an exposure has been recorded, the success (or otherwise) of its composition, its potential accuracy in terms of exposure based on the histogram display, and its degree of sharpness using the zoom function.

Image Review

Immediately after taking an exposure, the image can be reviewed on the LCD monitor as long as On is selected at CS-07 (Image review); the duration of the display is determined by the option selected at CS-15 (Auto off timers). In single frame and self-timer shooting modes, the image is displayed almost immediately after the exposure is made. In the continuous shooting mode, the camera must write the image data from the buffer memory to the memory card for all of the images recorded, so a short delay may occur; the camera displays each image chronologically as soon as it has been saved.

Hint: Select Off for the Image review option at CS-07 if you do not want the camera to display the image automatically after shooting; this can be an effective way of reducing power drain fro the camera battery.

Basic Single Image Playback

Press the ⬛ button on back of the camera to the left of the LCD monitor to display the most recent image taken by the camera. If you wish to view other images saved on the memory card, simply press the multi selector to the left or right ◉ to scroll through them. Pressing the shutter release button halfway returns the camera to its shooting mode.

Note: If you want images shot in an upright (vertical) composition to be displayed in the correct orientation, select On for the Auto image rotation option in the setup menu, and select On for the Rotate tall option in the Playback menu.

Photo Information Pages: A useful feature of the playback function is the host of information that can be accessed while viewing the image on the monitor. This data can help confirm your composition as well as give detailed information about how, when, and where the exposure was made. Up to six different pages of information can be displayed for each image file displayed on the LCD monitor.

To access these, first display an image for playback by pressing the 🔘 button, and then press the multi selector up and down ⊚ to scroll back and forth through the following pages:

- **File Information** – this Photo Information page displays an unobstructed view of the image while providing the following additional information about the photo: Retouch indicator; Protect status; Frame number/Total number of frames; Folder name; File name; Image quality; Date of recording; Time of recording; and Image size.

- **Shooting Data Page 1** – A block of information is superimposed over the center portion of the screen, obstructing the view of the image, while providing the following additional information: Retouch indicator; Protect status; Camera name; Metering method; Shutter speed; Aperture; Exposure mode; Exposure compensation; Focal length; Flash sync mode; Frame number/Total number of images.

Note: This screen can be particularly useful if you are trying to achieve consistent results in similar shooting conditions, learning about your shooting style, and attempting to understand which settings produce particular results.

- **Shooting Data Page 2** – A block of information is superimposed over the center portion of the screen, obstructing the view of the image, while providing the following additional information: Retouch indicator; Protect status; Image optimization; ISO sensitivity *; White balance; White balance fine tuning; Image size/Image quality; Tone compensation; Sharpening; Color mode/Hue adjustment; Saturation; Image comment; Frame number/Total number of images.

* If the ISO Auto feature (CS-10) is active and adjusts the ISO value automatically, the new value is displayed in red.

168

Note: This screen can help you understand the effects of image settings and adjustments on the appearance of your picture.

- **Active D-Lighting and Retouch History** – A block of information is superimposed over the center portion of the screen, obstructing the view of the image. It displays: Retouch indicator; Protect status; Active D-Lighting *; Retouch history, which lists changes made to image using Retouch menu options, with most recent change shown first; Frame number/Total number of images.

* AUTO is displayed if the picture was recoded with Active D-Light switched on.

- **Highlights** – Displays an unobstructed view of the image: Retouch indicator; Protect status; Highlights; Frame number/Total number of images.

Note: This screen is very useful for checking if information may have been lost as a result of overexposure; any relevant areas that may be affected will flash alternately black and white. Use the histogram display to check exposure and adjust as necessary.

- **Histogram** – Provides a composite histogram of the red, green, and blue channels, superimposed over the center portion of the screen. It displays: Retouch indicator; Protect status; Histogram; Frame number/Total number of images.

Assessing The Histogram Display

The histogram is a graphical display of the tonal values recorded by the camera. The shape and position of the histogram curve indicates the range of tones that have been captured in the picture. The horizontal axis represents 256 different tonal values from pure black at the extreme left end to pure white at the extreme right end with brightness, with darker tones distributed to the left of the histogram graph and lighter tones to the right. The vertical axis represents the number of pixels that have that specific tonal value.

In a well exposed picture of a scene containing an average distribution of tones that includes a few very dark shadows, a sizable number of mid-tones, and a few bright highlights, where no clipping of shadow or highlights has occurred, the curve will extend across much of the horizontal axis; in this case all tones in the scene will have been recorded.

Obviously not all scenes contain an even spread of tones; many have a natural predominance of light or dark areas. In these cases the histogram curve will be biased to the right with scenes containing mainly light tones, or the left when the scene contains mainly dark tones; this is not an indication of over or underexposure respectively, but an indication of the limited range of tones in the scene. Hence there is no single, perfect or ideal histogram curve for all scenes and subjects; the shape of the histogram curve will vary widely depending on the nature of the scene recorded. However, provided the histogram curve stops on the bottom axis before it reaches either end of the graph, the image will contain the fullest range of tones from the darkest to the lightest in the scene being photographed.

However, if the curve begins at a point part way up the left or right vertical axis of the histogram display (i.e. it does not end on the horizontal axis but the histogram curve looks as though it has been cut off abruptly), the camera will not have recorded some tones. This is often referred to as "clipping". If the curve is stacked up against the left axis the darker tones (i.e. shadows areas in the image) will likely be compromised due to underexposure, whereas if the curve is stacked up against the right axis the lighter tones (i.e. highlight areas in the image) will likely be compromised due to overexposure. The exception would be in a scene were there were very bright specular highlights, such as the sub reflecting off water, or streetlights in a night time cityscape – these small areas will almost invariably be much brighter than most of the other light tones in the scene and therefore it is of little consequence if they are overexposed. Significant under or overexposure is to be avoided if possible but especially the latter as it is unlikely that highlight areas that have been overexposed will be able to render any detail and nothing can be done to rectify this in post-processing. It is often possible to recover shadow detail lost due to underexposure; however, there is likely to be a penalty of reduced image quality in these areas due to the effects of noise.

Many photographers adopt a technique known as "expose to the right", in which they adjust the exposure to the point that the histogram curve is as far to the right as it can be without clipping occurring to ensure they capture as wide a tonal range as possible and with as many levels to describe those tones.

As mentioned the "clipping" of the histogram curve is usually an indication of under, or over-exposure but do remember that the preview image, including those for NEF RAW files, is always derived from a JPEG file to which the camera settings (white balance, contrast and saturation, etc) have been applied, and it is the tonal distribution of this JPEG file that the histogram describes. A NEF RAW file will contain more data and have a wider range of tonal values; therefore an overexposed highlight in the JPEG preview may well not be an overexposed highlight when the NEF RAW file is examined in a RAW file converter such as Nikon Capture NX. Even if a NEF (RAW) file has been incorrectly exposed it is possible to apply retrospective exposure compensation using software such as Nikon View NX, or Nikon Capture NX, between about -1.0EV to +1.5EV; no such flexibility is possible with a JPEG file.

Scenes that are low in contrast will have a rather narrow curve that ends before reaching either the left or right-hand extremities of the bottom axis. You have two choices about how to deal with this situation: (1) In the Shooting menu, select Tone compensation, which is within the Custom

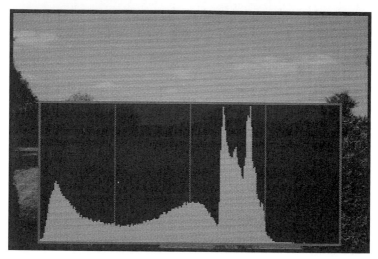

A typical histogram for a scene with a wide range of tones that has been well exposed; the full range of tones has been recorded, with no indication of any clipping.

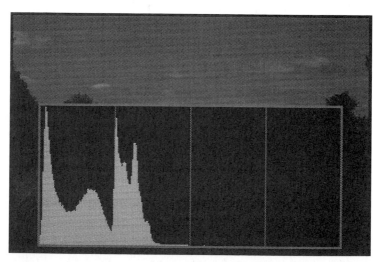

A typical histogram for a scene with a wide range of tones that has been underexposed; the range of tones has been compromised and shadow tones have been clipped, resulting in a loss of shadow detail.

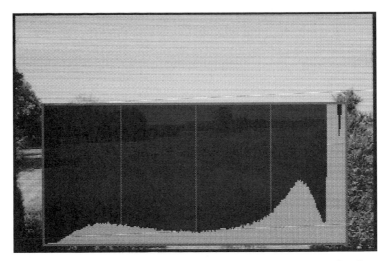

A typical histogram for a scene with a wide range of tones that has been overexposed; the range of tones has been compromised and highlight tones have been clipped, resulting in a loss of highlight detail.

option of the control for Optimize image (see page 118) to have the contrast control performed by the camera; or (2) adjust the contrast level at a later stage using an image-processing software application. I would recommend the latter approach, as it offers a far greater degree of control.

Hint: It is always preferable to err on the side of lower image contrast because it is easier to boost contrast than it is to try and reduce it at any stage subsequent to the original exposure.

Thumbnail Playback

If you wish to view multiple images on the monitor, press the ◉ button; press once to view four and press again to view nine images simultaneously. To view fewer images press the ◉ button. A yellow border surrounds the highlighted image: To scroll through the images, press the multi selector left, right, up, or down. Once an image is highlighted, use the ◉ button to show the image full frame, and press the ◉ button to return to multiple image display. Protect an image by pressing the ◉ button, located on back of camera to right of viewfinder. Delete an image by pressing the 🔘 button, located on back lower right of camera. To return the camera to the shooting mode, press the shutter release button.

Playback Zoom

The image displayed on the LCD monitor is usually too small to check with any certainty for sharpness; the playback zoom will allow you to enlarge the image by up to 25x. To do so, press the ⊕ button. The image will appear slightly enlarged, and a thumbnail with a yellow border indicating the sectional view of the image is displayed briefly before turning off automatically. To increase the degree of magnification, press the ⊕ button repeatedly until the required zoom is achieved. You can navigate around the enlarged image by pressing the multi selector in the direction you want to shift the view. It is possible to examine other images at the same location of the frame and the same degree of magnification by rotating the Command dial. To zoom out, press the ⊖ button repeatedly.

Protecting Images

To protect an image against inadvertent deletion, display it on the LCD in either the full-frame single image playback or multiple image display (ensure the image is highlighted with a yellow border), and press the 🔳 (⊶) button. A key icon will appear in the upper left corner, superimposed over the image. To remove the protection, open the image and press 🔳 (⊶) again, checking that the key icon is no longer displayed.

Note: Protected images will retain that status even when the image file is transferred to a computer or other storage device. However, all protected images on a memory card will be erased during card formatting.

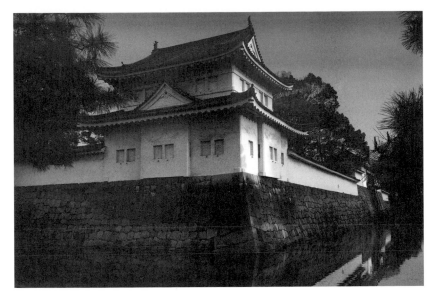

If you capture an image that is a "keeper" you can protect it against accidental erasure using the ⊡ (⊶) button. Be aware, however, that this does not protect the image from being erased during card formatting.

Deleting Images

Images can be deleted using one of two methods. The quickest and easiest is to press 🗑 button while the image is displayed on the LCD monitor. The first press opens a warning dialog box that asks for confirmation of the delete command. To complete the process, press the 🗑 button again. To cancel the delete process, press the ▶ button to return to viewing the image. Images can also be deleted by selecting the Delete option in the ▶ Playback menu. There are two options: delete Selected images, or delete All images stored on the memory card.

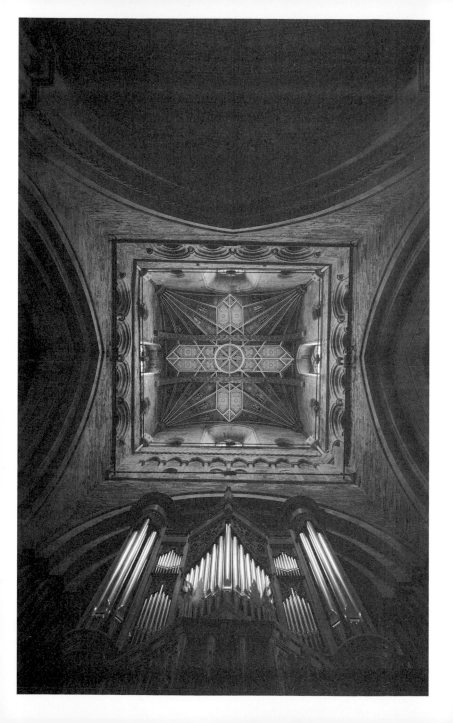

Camera Menus

The D60 makes extensive use of a sophisticated and comprehensive menu system that is displayed via the LCD monitor on the rear of the camera. The menus are divided into five main sections:

▶ **Playback Menu** – used for reviewing, editing, and managing the pictures stored on the memory card.

◯ **Shooting Menu** – used to select more sophisticated camera controls that have a direct influence on the quality and appearance of the pictures recorded by the camera.

✐ **Custom Setting Menu** – the items available allow the user to select and set a wide range of controls to fine-tune camera operation to meet specific requirements.

♈ **Setup Menu** – used to establish the basic configuration of the camera.

☑ **Retouch menu** – offers useful features for performing a range of enhancements and modifications to images recorded by the D60 and stored on the installed memory card.

○⃔ *The D60's menu system offers an impressive range of features that give you a remarkable degree of control over your photography. If the multitude of options seems intimidating at first, it is well worth programming your own Custom Setting Menu to allow quick access to the specific settings you use most frequently.*

Note: While Nikon should be commended for including the items available in the Retouch menu, I believe it is important to put them in perspective, as they cannot be considered as comprehensive or sophisticated as those available in the many good digital imaging software applications available today. They are intended to provide a convenient and largely automated method of producing a modified version of the original image, without the need to use a computer, to enable the user to produce a finished picture direct from the camera.

Access to Menus

To open the menu display press the 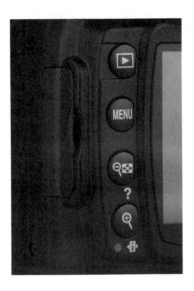 *button on the rear of the camera.*

To gain access to any menu, push the ⓜ button, and then press multi selector to the left to highlight one of the five tabs used to identify each main menu (top to bottom): Playback menu ▶ , Shooting menu ⏺ , Custom Setting menu ∅ , Setup menu ⚏ , and the Retouch menu ☑ . Highlight the desired menu tab by scrolling up or down with the multi selector and the first level of menu options will open. Press the multi selector to the right to highlight an option in the selected menu. To navigate to a specific menu item within the selected menu press the multi selector up or down. To display the second level of the menu, the sub-options available for each menu item, press the multi selector to the right. Again, to select a specific sub-option press the multi selector up or down. To select an enable the highlighted sub-option in any menu, press the ⊙ button (although pressing the multi selector to the right, which is quicker and more convenient, has the same effect in most instances). To return to the previous menu level without making a selection, press the multi selector to the left once. To exit the menu system and return to the D60 to its shooting mode, press the shutter release button down halfway; the monitor will turn off.

Note: The menus have multiple options and sub-options that frequently cannot be displayed on a single page. Keep scrolling up or down to access those options or sub-options not originally displayed on the screen. If a menu item, option, or sub-option is gray, it is not available at the current camera settings.

Many of the options within the menu system can be set using buttons and the command dial in conjunction with the Quick Settings Display. Where such an alternative route is available it will generally improve the efficiency of camera handling. If you need a reminder about the function or effect of a particular menu option, or camera setting, press and hold the ? button to display a descriptive dialog box. You may need to press the multi selector up or down to scroll through this display.

⚘ Setup Menu (Simple Option)

The Setup menu is used to establish the basic configuration of the camera. Once configured, the items in this menu are generally not changed very frequently. This menu can be displayed in either an abbreviated format, Simple (the default setting) that shows a partial list of the available items, or alternatively in an unabridged format,

(Full), that shows the complete listing of all available items. Furthermore, the setup menu is home to the My menu item, which enables the user to select only those options from all five menus that they wish to display. This effectively allows the entire menu system to be customized to the user's specific requirements.

The following ten items will be displayed in the Setup menu if the Simple option (default) is selected, which is one of three choices under the CSM/Setup menu item (see below).

CSM/Setup Menu

This option is used to determine whether the camera displays an abbreviated list of all the options available in both the setup menu and the custom setting menu (this does not affect the display of options in the other three camera menus).

To select which options are displayed in the menu system:

1. Select CSM/Setup from the Setup menu.
2. Highlight Simple to display only the abbreviated form of the Setup and Custom Setting menu, Full to display all the options in all menus, or My Menu to display only those menu items you will choose, or have already chosen to be selected and displayed from all five of the camera's menus.
3. Press the ⊛ button to confirm your selection of either Simple, or Full.

To use the My menu option it is necessary to select which menu items you want to be included in its display. Highlight My menu and press the multi selector to the right to display a list of the five camera menus. Select one by highlighting it and press the multi selector to the right. A list of all items in the menu will be shown with a check box next to each one. Use the multi selector to scroll through the menu items and press it to the right to select, or deselect it (a check mark is shown in the box for each item that is selected). Once you have finished making your selection for the menu, highlight Done and press the ⊛ button to confirm the selection of the menu item and return to the set up menu display. Repeat this process for each main menu item. Finally, highlight Done in the list of main menus and press the ⊛ button to confirm the settings and return to the Setup menu. It is essential that Done be confirmed in both instances, otherwise your changes will not be saved.

Format Memory Card

A new memory card should always be formatted when it is first placed into the D60. It is also good practice to format any memory card whenever you insert it in to the camera. This is particularly important if you use your memory cards between different camera bodies, or you have added / deleted any files from the card using a computer.

To format a memory card:

1. Select Format memory card from the Setup menu.
2. Select Yes or No.
3. Press the ⊛ button to confirm your selection.

To help prevent accidental deletion of image files, the No option is the default when the sub-menu of options is displayed. If you select Yes, the camera will display the following message on the monitor screen: "All pictures on memory card will be deleted. OK?" During the formatting process, "Formatting memory card," followed by, "Formatting complete" will be displayed on the LCD monitor.

Make certain that power to the camera is not interrupted during formatting. A loss of power could damage the card, so ensure the battery is adequately charged, or use the optional EH-5 / EH-5a AC adapter and EP-5 DC power connector.

Note: The D60 supports the SDHC version 2.00 standard, which allows it to use a memory card with a capacity in excess of 2GB.

The formatting process does not permanently delete image files and data from the memory card, as stated in Nikon instruction manual to the D60, but actually overwrites the file directory, so that it is no longer possible to access any image files stored on the card. If you should format a card inadvertently, it may be possible to recover the image files using appropriate data recovery software.

Info Display Format
The D60 offers three different styles for the Shooting Information Display: Classic, Graphic, and Wallpaper. It is possible to have one style displayed when using the 🅐ᵁᵀᴼ and Digital Vari-Program modes, and another style when shooting in the P, S, A, and M exposure modes.

To select a style for the Shooting Information Display:

1. Select Info display format from the Setup menu.
2. Highlight Digital Vari-Program or P, S, A, M and press the multi selector to the right.
3. Highlight the desired option from Classic, Graphic, or Wallpaper, and press the multi selector to the right.
4. The Classic and Graphic options offer a further choice as to the background color, while the Wallpaper option offers a choice of font color. Highlight the choice for the background color or font color, and then press the **OK** button to confirm the settings selection.

If you wish to use an existing photograph as the background in the Wallpaper display:

1. Select Info display format from the Setup menu.
2. Highlight Select wallpaper and press the multi selector to the right.

3. Up to six thumbnail pictures will be shown on the monitor. Use the multi selector to highlight the picture you want to display (a yellow frame is shown around the currently selected picture). Press the ⊕ button to display an enlarged view of the picture). To confirm the selection, press the ⓞⓚ button.

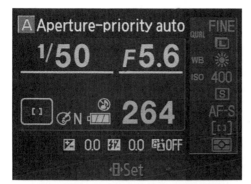

I recommend using the Classic display, because it offers the greatest clarity; in my opinion the Wallpaper display is entertaining but depending on the background picture it can be difficult to discern.

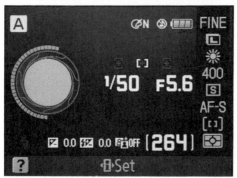

The Graphic display may be more helpful to less experienced photographers, because it provides a visual representation of the lens aperture and shutter speed.

Auto Shooting Info

This option enables the camera to display shooting information automatically as soon as a picture has been recorded and displayed on the monitor screen. When On is selected at CS-07 (Image review) the picture recorded by the camera will be displayed on the monitor screen immediately after the shutter has been released. If On is selected for Auto Shooting Info, press the multi selector up or down to display the required Photo Information page; thereafter, each subsequent exposure will cause the same page to be displayed, superimposed over the recorded picture. If Off is selected at CS-07 (Image review) while this function is enabled, the normal Shooting Information Display will be shown automatically on the monitor after a picture has been recorded. This feature is useful if you need to check camera settings frequently as you shoot.

To set Auto Shooting Info:

1. Select Auto shooting info from the Setup menu, and press the multi selector to the right.
2. Highlight Digital Vari-Program or P, S, A, M and press the multi selector to the right.
3. Highlight On or Off as desired, and press the ⓞⓚ button to confirm your selection.

Shooting Info Auto Off

This item determines whether the eye-sensor feature of the D60 is enable or disabled. If On is selected (default) for this item the sensor located beneath the viewfinder eyepiece will detect when the user's face is in close proximity to the viewfinder, while the exposure meter is active, causing the Shooting Information Display to be turned off and the viewfinder display to be turned on, automatically. Moving the camera away from the user's face reverses the process. This not only reduces the drain on the battery by having only one display active at a time but also prevents the bright glow from the monitor screen from distracting the user while their eye is to the viewfinder.

If Off is selected at Shooting info auto off, the eye-sensor function is disabled and both the viewfinder display and the Shooting Information Display will remain on while the exposure meter is active.

To set Shooting Info Auto Off:

1. Select Shooting info auto off from the Setup menu, and press the multi selector to the right.
2. Highlight On or Off as desired, and press the ⓞⓚ button to confirm your selection.

World Time
World time enables you to set and change the date and time recorded by the camera's internal clock, and also how this information is displayed. Once you have selected World time from the Setup menu, four options are displayed: Time zone, Date, Date format, and Daylight savings time. Each one requires the user to input information.

To set Time Zone:

1. Select Time zone from the options list.
2. Scroll right or left through the world map using the multi selector until the relevant time zone is highlighted.
3. Press the ⓞⓚ button to select it.

To set Date:

1. Select Date from the options list.
2. Scroll through the settings by pressing the multi selector left or right, and press it up or down to set each value in the date and time fields.
3. Press the ⓞⓚ button to confirm the date/time.

To set Date Format:

1. Select Date format from the options list and press the multi selector to the right.
2. Highlight the desired configuration for the date display.
3. Press the ⓞⓚ button to confirm the selection.

To set Daylight Savings Time:

1. Select Daylight savings time from the options list and press the multi selector to the right.
2. Highlight either On or Off depending on whether or not daylight saving is in effect in the current location.
3. Press the ⊕ button to confirm the selection.

LCD Brightness

The brightness of the LCD monitor can be adjusted to help improve the visibility of any displayed image or page of information. A negative adjustment will darken the screen while a positive adjustment will brighten it; the screen displays a gray scale to help you judge the brightness effect on the full tonal range present in your images. This feature is particularly helpful, as I consider the default level to be too bright, which can be misleading when trying to assess images. Try setting a monitor brightness level of -1 to give a more accurate representation of the recorded image. Even with such an adjustment the image displayed on the monitor screen should only be used a guide as to the success or otherwise of the picture; due to the limitations of the monitor screen it is not possible to assess color, contrast, or exposure level with any degree of accuracy.

To adjust LCD Brightness:

1. Select LCD brightness from the Setup menu, and press the multi selector to the right
2. Adjust the brightness value by pressing the multi selector up or down
3. Press the ⊕ button to set the brightness value you have chosen

Video Mode

This option allows you to select the type of signal used by video equipment to which you may connect your camera, such as a DVR/VCR or television. This should be set before connecting your camera to the device with the optional EG-D2 video cord.

To set Video Mode:

1. Select Video mode from the Setup menu and press the multi selector to the right.
2. Use the multi selector to highlight either NTSC (used in USA, Canada, and Japan) or PAL (most other countries).
3. Press the ⓞⓚ button to confirm your selection.

Language

The Language option on the D60 allows you to select one of 15 languages for the camera to use when displaying menus and messages.

To set the Language:

1. Select Language from the Setup menu and press the multi selector to the right.
2. Highlight the desired language from the list displayed by pressing the multi selector up or down.
3. Press the ⓞⓚ button to confirm the selection.

Image Comment

You can attach a short comment (note) up to 36 characters in length to an image file. It may contain letters and/or numbers. Since the process requires each character to be input individually, this is not a feature you will use for each separate picture. However, it is useful to assign a general comment (e.g. the name of a location, or event). Alternatively it can be used to note authorship, or a copyright of the recorded picture.

Note: The "keyboard" used for inputting a comment is the same one used for file and folder naming.

To attach an Image Comment:

1. Select Image comment from the Setup menu and press the multi selector to the right.
2. Select Input comment from the options list.
3. To enter your comment, highlight the character you wish to input by using the multi selector and press the ⊙Ⓚ button to select it. If you accidentally enter the wrong character press the 🗑 button to erase it.
4. Press the 🔍 button to save the comment and return to the Image comment options list.
5. To attach the comment to your photographs, scroll to the Attach comment option and select Set. A small check mark will appear in the box to the left of the option. If you fail to select Set and place a check mark in the box, the image comment will not be attached to the image file.
6. Finally, once you have completed this process highlight Done and press the ⊙Ⓚ button to confirm the selection.

If you wish to exit this process at any time without attaching a comment or changing an existing one prior to step 5, simply press the 🔍 button.

When the check mark is present in Attach comment, the saved comment will be attached to all subsequent images shot on the camera. To prevent the comment from being attached to an image, simply return to the Image comment menu and uncheck the Attach comment box. The comment (note) will remain stored in the camera's memory and can be attached to future images by rechecking the Attach comment box.

Note: The first fifteen characters of the comment will be displayed on the second of the Photo Information Pages, available via the Image review option, which is selected from CS-07. The full comment can be viewed when using the supplied Nikon View NX software, or optional Nikon Capture NX 2.

Folders

The D60 uses a folder system to organize images stored on the installed memory card. The Folders option in the Shooting menu allows you to select which folder your images will be saved in, and it also enables you to create new folders.

If you do not use any of the options pertaining to folders, the camera creates a folder named "NCD60" automatically in which the first 999 pictures recorded by the camera will be stored on the memory card. The folder will automatically be assigned a three-digit prefix, so the title of the default folder will be "100NCD60." If you exceed 999 pictures, the camera creates a new folder named "101NCD60", and so on for each set of 999 pictures. You can create your own folder(s); the user can set the folder title, which can have a maximum of five characters, but it will always be preceded by a three-digit number between 100 and 999.

If you use multiple folders, you must select one as the active folder to which all images will be stored until an alternative folder is chosen, or the maximum capacity of 999 pictures in the active folder is exceeded. In the latter case, the D60 will create a new NCD60 folder and assign a three-digit prefix with an incremental increase of one (e.g. if folder "100NCD60" becomes full, the D60 creates folder "101NCD60" into which subsequent pictures will be stored).

Note: If the folder that has reached full capacity is folder number "999ND60," the camera will disable the shutter release button, preventing you from making an exposure. You will have to create a new folder with a lower number, or choose another folder on the card that still has space to hold new images. To create a new folder:

1. Select Folders from the Shooting menu and press the multi selector to the right.
2. Select New from the list of options.
3. Designate the new folder by highlighting the required letter or number from the displayed keyboard and pressing ⊙ to select it. Use the command dial to shift the cur-

sor position. Repeat this process up to four more times to create the new five-character folder name.

4. To delete a character, press the 🗑 button.
5. Press the 🔍 button to confirm the new folder title and return to the Setup menu.

To select an existing folder:

1. Select Folders from the Shooting menu and press the multi selector to the right.
2. Choose Select folder from the options list and press the multi selector to the right.
3. Highlight the folder you wish to use by pressing the multi selector up or down.
4. Press the 🆗 button to confirm the folder in which pictures will be stored, and return to the Shooting menu.

Note: It is possible to rename a folder. Select Folders from the Shooting menu and press the multi selector to the right, and then choose Rename from the options list and press the multi selector to the right. Select the required folder from the list displayed under the Rename option. Use the method described above to rename the existing folder.

Note: To delete a folder, first ensure that it contains no images. Select Folders from the Shooting menu and press the multi selector to the right, and then choose Delete from the options list and press the multi selector to the right. Select the required folder from the list displayed under the Delete option.

Folders may be useful if you expect to take pictures of a variety of subjects. For example, on a touring vacation you can create a folder for each location visited, and file your images on the memory card(s) location-by-location. However, I find that using multiple folders is time consuming and potentially confusing. If you have more than one different Nikon digital camera model and move memory cards between them, the individual cameras will not be able to display images in folders created by another camera. Even multiple folders created by the D60 can present problems, as images will be saved to the currently selected folder with the highest prefix number. I would rather use a browser application such as Nikon View NX, or Nikon Capture NX 2 to view and organize my images after they have been imported to a computer.

File Number Sequence

D60 file names contain three letters (DSC), a four-digit number, and the three-letter file extension (.JPG or .NEF). There will be an underscore next to DSC, either as a prefix to denote Adobe RGB, or as a suffix to denote the sRGB color space (e.g. _DSC0001.JPG denotes a JPEG file, number 0001, saved in the Adobe RGB color space; DSC_0001.JPG is saved in the sRGB color space). The file number sequence option in the Shooting menu allows you to select whether file numbering is reset to 0001 whenever a new folder is created, the memory card is formatted in camera, or a new memory card is inserted. Alternatively, the file number can be set to increase incrementally as each new folder is created by the D60, or can be reset to 0001 at any point that the user wishes.

To use File No Sequence:

1. Select File no sequence from the Setup menu and press the multi selector to the right.
2. Highlight Off (default) to reset the file number to 0001 whenever a new folder is created, the memory card is formatted in camera, or a new memory card is inserted. Select On to continue numbering from the last number used after a new folder is created, the memory card is formatted in camera, or a new memory card is inserted. Select, Reset to number the next image file 0001 and continue numbering as if the On option had been selected.
3. Press the ⊛ button to confirm the selection and return to the Shooting menu.

Clean Image Sensor

In an effort to help reduce the effects of such deposits on the OLPF and reduce the frequency with which external cleaning measures need be applied, Nikon has incorporated a self-cleaning mechanism into the D60 that vibrates the OLPF at four different frequencies using a piezo-electric oscillator. The cleaning process can be set to activate automatically when the camera is turned on, turned off, or both. Alternatively, it can be activated at anytime the user deems it necessary.

This feature is effective at reducing the effect of loose, dry material that settles on the surface of the OLPF, but it will not deal with smear marks, or more tenacious material, such as precipitates that form when moisture evaporates from its surface.

To set the Clean Image Sensor:

1. Select File no sequence from the Setup menu and press the multi selector to the right.
2. Highlight Clean now option and press ⓄⓀ to activate the cleaning process immediately (graphic will be displayed on the monitor screen with the message "Image sensor cleaning," while the function is in operation.
3. Alternatively, highlight the Clean at option and press the multi selector to the right.
4. Highlight one of the four options: Startup and shutdown (default), Startup, Shutdown, or Cleaning off and press the ⓄⓀ button to select it.

Hint: For best results when using the Clean Image Sensor feature place the camera on a flat horizontal surface while the cleaning process takes place, as this will ensure that any material that is dislodged will fall to the bottom of the mirror box on to a strip of highly adhesive material that is located beneath the OLPF, where it will be retained.

Mirror Lock-Up

This feature is exclusively for cleaning or inspecting the low-pass filter (it cannot be used to lock the reflex mirror in its raised position to reduce camera vibration while shooting). It is essential not to interrupt the camera's power supply when Mirror lock-up is active, particularly if you have cleaning utensils in the camera at the time, as the reflex mirror will drop to its normal position with potentially dire consequences. Make sure the camera battery is fully charged or use the optional EH-5 / EH-5a AC adapter with EP-5 DC power adapter.

Note: This option will not function if the battery charge indicator displayed in the Shooting Information Display shows ▭ or is ▭ shown blinking.

To use Mirror Lock-up:

1. Select Mirror lock-up from the Shooting menu and press the multi selector to the right.
2. Highlight On and press the ⊛ button. A message with instructions on how to proceed will be displayed on the monitor screen and a series of dashes will appear in the control panel.
3. Press the shutter release button fully; the mirror will lift and the shutter will open. Proceed with any necessary inspection/cleaning.
4. To return the reflex mirror to its normal position, turn the camera off.
5. If you wish to cancel the function, select Off at step 2, and press the ⊛ button.

Note: Exceptional care should be taken whenever the Mirror lock-up function is in use because the optical low-pass filter (OPLF) is exposed; therefore there is an increased risk that dust or moisture might settle on its surface. Always keep the camera facing down: gravity is your best friend in this situation! Full details of how to clean the OPLF can be found on pages 50-55.

Firmware Version

Select Firmware version to see the current version (A & B) of the firmware installed on the camera. It is worthwhile to check periodically on the various Nikon technical support web sites (details of these are listed on page 325) to see if any firmware updates have been released for the D60. The first firmware version issued for the D60 was A=1.00/B=1.00.

Dust Off Ref Photo

The Dust off ref photo option on the D60 is specifically designed for use with the Image Dust Off function in Nikon Capture NX 2. The image file created by this function creates a mask that is "overlaid" electronically on a NEF file to enable the software to reduce or remove the effects of shadows that are cast by dust particles on the surface of the low-pass filter.

Note: This function can only be used with NEF files. To obtain a reference image for this function, you must use a CPU-type lens, and Nikon recommends use of a lens with a focal length of 50mm, or more.

To use Dust Off Ref Photo:

1. Select Dust off ref photo from the Setup menu and press the multi selector to the right.
2. Highlight Start and press the **OK** button. A message will instruct you to "Take photo of bright featureless white object 10 cm from the lens. Focus will be set to infinity."
3. Point your camera at an evenly lit, white featureless surface, such as a card, positioned approximately 4 inches (10 cm) from the front of the lens, ensuring the white surface fills the viewfinder frame.
4. Press the shutter release button halfway and focus will be set to infinity automatically. Alternatively, in Manual focus mode set the lens to infinity focus.
5. Fully depress the shutter release button to acquire the reference frame for the Image Dust Off function in Nikon Capture NX 2.

6. Alternatively, select Clean sensor, then start at step (2); the message "Take photo of bright featureless white object 10 cm from the lens. Focus will be set to infinity," will be displayed once the cleaning process is completed. Then proceed as in steps (3) to (5) above.

If the Dust off reference frame is displayed on the camera it appears as:

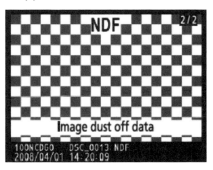

If the lighting conditions for your subject are too bright or too dark, the camera will display the error message: "Exposure settings are not appropriate. Change exposure settings and try again." In these conditions it is not possible to complete the process, so either increase or decrease the level of exposure by adjusting the exposure settings (i.e. in P, S, and A modes use the exposure compensation feature, while in M mode you can adjust the shutter speed / aperture accordingly). Alternatively choose another reference target.

Note: The Dust off reference photo only records the position of extraneous material on the optical low-pass filter at the time of its exposure. If any of the material moves position while shooting, this function will not be effective at masking the effects. Therefore, it is worthwhile to record several Dust off reference photos as you proceed if you are engaged in a protracted period of shooting.

Auto Image Rotation

The D60 automatically recognizes the orientation of the camera as it records an image, whether formatted horizontally or vertically depending on how you hold the camera. At its default setting, the D60 stores this information so the image can be rotated automatically during image playback, or when viewing images on the computer with compatible software, such as Nikon View NX, or Nikon Capture NX 2.

How to set Auto Image Rotation:

1. Select Auto image rotation from the Setup menu and press the multi selector to the right.
2. Highlight On (default) or Off.
3. Press the ⓞⓚ button to confirm the selection.

If you do not wish the camera to record its orientation, or if you shoot with the camera pointed up or down, which will usually render this feature unreliable, select Off.

Note: I have encountered some digital imaging software that is incapable of recognizing the image orientation information written to the image file, which can prevent the software from opening the file. I recommend testing pictures shot on the D60 with whatever software you use and turning this feature off if you encounter problems with image orientation when opening files.

◘ Shooting Menu

The options in this menu help determine the attributes of the recorded image file. The Shooting menu also contains specialty features, such as noise reduction for high ISO/long time exposures. You can use the My menu option, which is chosen from the CSM/Setup menu item in the Setup menu, to select any item in Shooting menu and have it displayed in My menu to facilitate access. The full Shooting menu contains the following options:

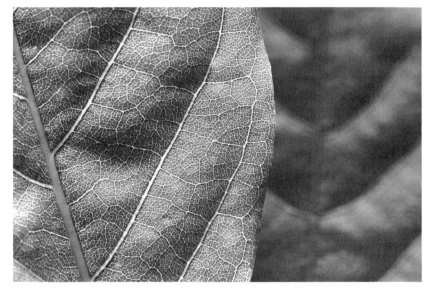

The D60 allows you to shoot pictures in black-and-white recording mode. This will allow you to view the image in grayscale on the camera's LCD.

Optimize Image

The Optimize image option allows you to make changes to sharpening, contrast, color mode, saturation, and hue based on the current shooting situation and/or the user's preferences. It also allows you to select a variety of options for shooting pictures in the black-and-white recording mode. See pages 118-121 for full details.

Image Quality

The Image quality option allows you to select the file format(s) to be used for images recorded by the camera. See pages 103-106 for full details.

Image Size

The selection for Image size determines the file size, or resolution, of an image in terms of pixel quantity. See pages 103-106 for full details.

Note: Image size adjustments will only apply to images saved using the JPEG format. NEF files are always saved at the camera's highest resolution of 3,872 x 2,592 pixels.

White Balance

The White balance option allows you to select the color temperature applied to the images you are shooting. There are eight options available when shooting in the P, A, S, and M exposure modes. See pages 106-117 for full details.

ISO Sensitivity

This item for ISO sensitivity is the digital equivalent to film speed. It emulates the light sensitivity of film bearing the same ISO number. The ISO sensitivity in the D60 is a measure of the degree of amplification applied to the signal from the sensor, since the sensitivity of the sensor is fixed at its base level, which is approximately equivalent to ISO 100. See pages 127-130 for full details.

Noise Reduction

Images taken at high ISO settings and/or using a long exposure will often exhibit the effects of electronic noise, which is the result of amplification processes that are applied to the data captured by the sensor. Noise generated by using a high ISO setting can result in a slight loss of color saturation (colors can look flat) and reduction in contrast. Noise produced during a long exposure is manifest as irregularly placed bright, colored pixels that disrupt the appearance of an image, particularly in areas of even tonality. The noise reduction feature of the D60 will help reduce the appearance of both these types of noise.

If On is selected for Noise reduction, it will be applied to pictures shot at an ISO above 400 and/or at a shutter speed of approximately 8 seconds or longer. If this option is applied to counter the effect of noise produced during a long exposure, the processing time for each recorded image will increase and be approximately equal to the duration of the shutter speed used for the exposure. **Job nr** will appear, blinking, in place of the shutter speed and aperture value displays in the viewfinder until the process is complete, and the green access lamp will glow. No other picture can be taken while ꓤоᑕ ⲛⲅ is displayed.

If Off is selected for Noise Reduction, it will not operate at an ISO of 800 or less; however, a low-level of noise reduction is always performed at ISO sensitivities above 800.

Nikon D60 – Noise issue

Long time exposures made at high ISO settings will generate a noticeable noise pattern in images recorded by the D60; notice the bright patches in the top corners of the frame. The solution is to always use the Noise Reduction feature in the Shooting menu when making long exposures, particularly at high ISO settings.

During testing of my own D60 camera I have noticed that when used for long exposures (i.e. a minute, or more) and at high ISO settings (1600, or H1) there was a significant level of noise produced by sensor signal amplification. The noise is particularly prevalent and clearly visible in the top corners of the long edge of the frame when the image is reviewed on the monitor screen. A smaller, less troublesome area occurs about a third the way along the top edge of the frame from the left side (see the dark frame exposure example). Remember, in the camera these areas are at the bottom of the sensor, as the image formed by the lens on the sensor is upside down, which suggests that a localized increase in temperature due to heat generated by a component close to sensor are at the root of this issue.

I have tested several other D60 cameras with similar results (this issue also occurs in the D40x and D80 models); therefore, if you use your D60 at high ISO settings (i.e. 1600, or H1) with an exposure duration of 30 seconds, or longer, with the Noise Reduction feature in the Shooting menu set to Off you will more than likely see noticeable levels of noise in the top corners of the frame, especially if you perform any subsequent adjustment in computer post-processing, which significantly raises the level of these photosites (pixels) , in these areas.

Thankfully the Noise Reduction feature of the camera is very effective at reducing the level of noise present in the image, so if you want to shoot long exposures my advice is to always set Noise Reduction to On, and keep the ISO setting as low as possible, preferably ISO 400, or lower.

Note: The process used by the D60 to perform noise reduction for long exposures involves making a second exposure known as a "dark frame exposure," during which the shutter remains closed but the camera maps the sensor and records the values of each photosite (pixel). It's possible for a photosite to retain a value that is erroneous. This can occur if the sensor becomes too warm due to prolonged use, although other influences such as the ambient atmospheric temperature also contribute to noise. After mapping the sensor for hot (overly bright) photosites, the camera subtracts the "dark frame" photosite values from the photosite values of the main exposure in an effort to reduce the effect of noise in the final image.

☑ Retouch Menu

This menu contains a range of items that create copies of image files stored on the camera's memory card. These options enable you to create retouched (modified), trimmed (cropped), or resized versions of the original image file, plus create JPEG-format copies of NEF (RAW) format images. The Before and After item allows the retouched copy to be displayed side-by-side with the original image. The original image is always preserved.

You can use the My menu option, which is chosen from the CSM/Setup menu item in the Setup menu, to select any item in Retouch menu and have it displayed in My menu to facilitate access.

While the items in this menu can be useful, they are not nearly as sophisticated as their equivalents in many of the more powerful digital imaging computer software applications. The selections in the Retouch menu are intended to provide a quick, convenient, automated method to modify the original image without the need to use a computer.

Retouch Copies – General Restrictions

• The same option cannot be applied to the same copy more than once.

• The Quick Retouch, D-lighting, Red-eye correction, Monochrome, and Filter effects items, except Cross screen, are not available if the original image was recorded with the Black-and-white option under Optimize image in the shooting menu.

• With the exception of the Small picture options (see page 208), all other effects in the Retouch menu can also be applied to a copy image on the memory card (previously created with the Retouch menu). However, each option can only be applied once and this may result in a loss of image quality, depending on the option.

Selecting Images

Images can be selected for processing using the items in the Retouch menu from either single image, full-frame playback display with the exception of the Image overlay item, or from the Retouch menu itself.

Create Retouch Copy in Full-frame Playback

To select and produce a copy of an image from the single image playback view, display the image on the monitor screen and open the Retouch menu by pressing the 🆗 button. Scroll with the multi selector to highlight the desired menu item (Image overlay is not available using this route), and then press the multi selector to the right to display the available options. Again, press the multi selector up or down to highlight the required option, and press 🆗 to apply it. You can return to single image playback at anytime without creating a copy image by pressing the ▶ button.

Create Retouch Copy from Retouch Menu

To select and produce a copy of an image directly from the Retouch menu, open the menu and highlight the desired item using the multi selector, and then press the multi selector to the right to display up to six thumbnail images on the monitor screen. Note that pressing the multi selector to the right after highlighting Monochrome, Filter effects, or Small picture items opens a further page of sub-options; select the required sub-option and press the multi selector button to the right again.

A yellow border frames the selected thumbnail picture; then either scroll individual pictures with the multi selector or rotate the command dial to move through the pictures six at a time. To view an enlarged version of the selected picture, press and hold the 🔍 button. Once you have selected the picture to be modified and copied, press the 🆗 button. You can return to single image playback at anytime without creating a copy image by pressing the ▶ button.

Note: With the exception of the Small picture and Stop-motion movie items, copy files created using other items in the Retouch menu have file names beginning with "CSC_" (e.g. CSC_0001.JPG).

Quick Retouch

As its tile implies, this item enables the automated modification of an image saved on the memory card. The D-Lighting function (see below) is applied to the selected image, and the contrast and saturation are enhanced, automatically. The amount of adjustment is selected by pressing the multi selector up or down to highlight one of three options: High, Normal, and Low. The effect can be previewed in the edit display that shows the original source image (left) beside the modified image. Press the ⊕ button to create the retouched copy and return to the full frame playback.

Note: Copies created with Quick retouch cannot be modified further using D-Lighting.

This item has nowhere near the finesse or flexibility of adjusting gamma, contrast, and saturation in digital imaging software using a computer, plus the limitations of the monitor screen make assessment of any adjustment a largely cursory process. However, for the user who wishes to produce a finished picture direct from the camera with a minimum of effort, the Quick retouch menu provides an easy solution.

Note: The retouched copy is recorded at the same image quality and size settings as those of the source image, unless the source image was recorded at an image quality of RAW, or RAW+B, in which case the copy is recorded at a quality of JPEG Fine, and image size of 3.872 x 2,592.

D-Lighting

The D-lighting feature brightens shadow areas to reveal more detail. It is not a simple global brightness control, rather its application is selective and only affects the shadow areas of the recorded image. It should not be confused with the Active D-Lighting option available in the shooting menu, which modifies exposure settings prior to an image being recorded and influences highlights, mid-tones, and shadows during in-camera processing ahead of the image file being saved to the installed memory card.

Highlight D-lighting in the Retouch menu and press the OK button to display two thumbnail images; one unmodified and the other modified (the latter allows you to preview the effect). You can select three levels using this feature that increase brightness respectively from Low to Normal to High. Press the OK button to apply the desired level and create the copy.

Note: Copies created with D-Lighting cannot be modified further using Quick retouch

Red-Eye Reduction
This option is only available with pictures taken using either the built-in or external Speedlight (if an image was not shot using a Nikon Speedlight flash unit, a yellow box that is crossed through appears in the center of the thumbnail indicating the effect cannot be applied). First, examine the picture in single image playback and use the Q button to zoom in and the button to zoom out of the image. You can navigate around the image using the multi selector (a navigation window is displayed while these buttons are pressed).

If you see red-eye in the image, return to single image playback by pressing the OK button. Then press the OK button again; the D60 will then analyze the original image data and assess it for red-eye. If the camera determines that red-eye is present, it creates a copy image with reduced red-eye. However, since this is a completely automated process, it is possible for the camera to apply the red-eye correction to areas of an image that are not affected by red-eye, which is why it is prudent to check the preview image before selecting this item. If no red-eye is detected, a message is displayed accordingly and the full image playback/Retouch menu display is restored.

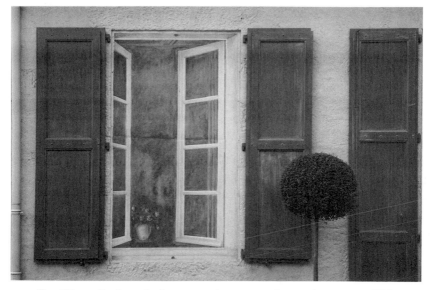

The Trim adjustment allows you to crop an image in camera. This is helpful in situations where you want to print an image directly to a printer.

Trim

This item enables you to crop the original image to exclude unwanted areas. The selected image is displayed along with a navigation window to show the location of the border that marks the crop area (you can navigate the crop border around the image using the multi selector). As you use the 🔍 and 🔍 buttons to zoom in and out of the single, full-frame image, the crop size is displayed in the top left corner of the image and shows the pixel dimensions (width x height) of the crop area (the ratio of the long and sort edges of the crop area is always 3:2). Once you have decided on the size and location of the crop area, press the ⓞⓚ button to create a cropped copy of the original picture and return to the single image playback.

Note: Copies created by Trim cannot be modified further.

Monochrome

This item allows you to save the copy image in one of three monochrome effects: Black-and-white (grayscale), Sepia (brown tones), and Cyanotype (blue tones). In all three cases the image data is converted to black and white using an algorithm dedicated to this feature (apparently it is different than the algorithm used for the black-and-white options in the Optimize image item in the Shooting menu). Once converted to black and white, the image data is still saved as an RGB file (i.e. it retains its color information).

If you select either Sepia or Cyanotype, the appropriate color shift is applied after the copy is converted to black and white; a preview image is displayed and the saturation of the color can be increased or decreased by pressing the multi selector up or down respectively. Once you are satisfied with the effect shown in the preview image, press the ⓞⓚ button to save the processed copy.

Note: Quick retouch, D-Lighting, Red-eye correction, and Filter effects other than Cross screen cannot be applied to monochrome copies.

Filter Effects

There are seven options in this menu. One emulates a skylight filter and another the type of color correction (warm) filter used for color photography, while a third produces the effect of a cross screen (star burst) filter. There are individual options for intensifying (increasing saturation of) red, green, and blue colors. The final option is a color balance that allows you to adjust the amount or red, green, blue, and magenta in the image.

Skylight and Warm filter

If you select either the Skylight, or Warm filter, a full-frame preview image is displayed. To apply the effect and save a copy of the image, press the ⓞⓚ button.

- **Skylight** – the effect is a subtle reduction in the level of blue in the picture.

- **Warm filter** – the effect increases the amount of red in the image to produce a result similar to the use of a Wratten 81-series color correction filter. Again, the effect is subtle and proper control of the white balance should obviate the need to use this option.

Color Intensifier

If you select either the Red, Green, or Blue intensifier, a full frame preview image is displayed. Use the ⊚ button to increase (make lighter) or decrease (make darker) the intensity of the selected color. To apply the effect and save a copy of the image, press the ⊛ button.

Cross screen

If you select Cross screen a preview image is displayed with the currently selected options for: Number of points, Filter amount, Filer angle, and Length of points applied. Each of these options can be adjusted; use the multi selector button to highlight the required option and press the multi selector to the right to display the three sub-options available in each case. Select the required sub-option and press the ⊛ button to apply it. Repeat the process for each option, as required.

Once the settings have been made, highlight Confirm and press the ⊛ button to apply the settings (an egg-timer icon is displayed during processing). Highlight Save and press the ⊛ button to create a copy image and return to full-frame playback.

Color Balance

Selecting Color balance causes a thumbnail image to appear alongside histograms for the red, green, and blue channels. Below the thumbnail image is a color-space map; vertical and horizontal axes bisect it, and at the center there is a small black square cursor. Press the multi selector up to increase the level of green, and down to increase the level of magenta. Pressing to the left increases the level of blue, and right increases the level of red. The cursor will shift accordingly, and the thumbnail image can be used to preview the effect. Once you are satisfied with the adjustment, press the ⓞⓚ button to apply the color shift and save a copy of the image.

Note: Copies created with Filter effects set to any option other than Cross screen can only be modified further by using the Cross Screen option in the Filter effects item.

Small Picture
The Small picture item offers options to reduce the resolution of the original image to create a copy that has a far smaller file size:

1. 640 x 480 pixels – suitable for playback on a television set.
2. 320 x 240 pixels – suitable for display on Web pages.
3. 160 x 120 pixels – suitable for sending as an attachment in an e-mail.

Note: The selection of a picture for processing in this menu from single image playback is described on page 202. However, using this route the method of selecting a photo after choosing Small picture differs from the method described previously. It is necessary to select the image size as the first step, and then select the picture(s) to which the process will be applied.

Note: Copies created by Small picture cannot be modified further.

Note: Small copy file created with the small picture option have file names that begin with "SSC_" and end with the file extension ".JPG" (e.g. SSC_0001.JPG)

Using the Retouch menu route proceed as follows:

1. Open the Retouch menu, highlight Small picture and press the multi selector to the right to display two options: Select picture and Choose size.
2. Use the multi selector to highlight Choose size, and then press the multi selector to the right to display the three size options (listed above), and highlight the required size.

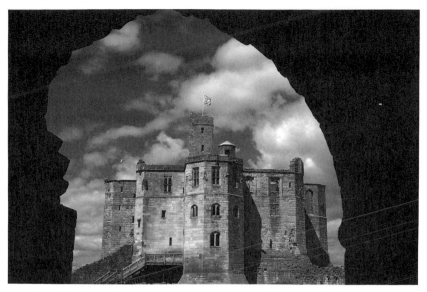

Small Picture allows you to reduce the resolution of a file in camera. However, once this is done, the image cannot be further modified.

3. Press the button to confirm your choice and return to the previous page. Highlight Select picture and press the multi selector right to display up to six thumbnail images. The currently selected image is shown framed by a yellow border.

4. Use the multi selector to highlight a desired image (the yellow border will shift accordingly), then press the multi selector up or down to select it (a small icon appears in the top right corner of the thumbnail to indicate it has been selected). Press to view an enlarged picture.

5. Repeat as required; once you have selected all the images you want to reduce in size, press the button. A confirmation page will be displayed indicating how many images will be processed.

6. Select Yes to proceed with the process, or No to return to the previous page. If you select Yes, press the button to apply the effect and save the copy picture(s).

Note: To identify images saved using the Small picture item, they are displayed with a gray border during full-frame playback, thumbnail playback, and when a picture selection dialog page is displayed; it is not possible to use the ⊕ zoom function with these images.

Image Overlay

Image overlay enables the user to combine a pair of NEF (RAW) files to form a single, new image (the original image files are not affected by this process and are preserved). The images do not have to be taken in consecutive order but must have been recorded by a D60 camera and be stored on the same memory card.

Since any overlay image created using this option can be saved at the image quality and size settings applied via the Quick Settings Display or the Shooting menu, the first step is to select these settings before selecting the Image overlay item to ensure the image overlay copy is saved at the required quality and size. If the overlay image is saved as a NEF (RAW) file it can be combined with another NEF (RAW) file to create a new overlay image.

To use Image Overlay:

1. Select Image overlay from the Retouch menu, and press the multi selector to the right.
2. The Image overlay page will open with Image 1 highlighted.
3. To select the first picture, press ⊛ and a thumbnail view of all NEF (RAW) files stored on the memory card will be displayed. Scroll through the images by pressing the multi selector left or right to highlight the image you wish to select. Pressing ⊕ displays the highlighted image full frame.
4. Press ⊛ and the selected image will appear in the Image 1 box and the Preview box.
5. Highlight the Image 2 box and press ⊛ to select the second picture to be combined with the first. Use the same process as step 3.

210

6. Press ⓞⓚ to select the second image, which will appear in the Image 2 box and in the Preview box, overlaying the first image.

7. Adjust the gain value, in either Image 1 or Image 2, by highlighting it (the gain value is shown beneath the selected picture), and then scrolling up and down using the multi selector to adjust the value. To highlight either image, press the multi selector to the left or right. The effect of the gain control can be observed in the Preview box (the default value is 1.0).

8. Once you have adjusted the gain of both images to achieve the desired effect, highlight the Preview box by pressing the multi selector to the left or right.

- To view a larger version of the preview image, press the 🔍 button. Press the ⊞ button to return to the thumbnail view.

- To generate an enlarged preview of the new image, highlight Overlay using the multi selector, and press ⓞⓚ . To save the new image press ⓞⓚ . To return to the Image overlay editing screen press the ⊞ button.

- To save the image without creating an enlarged preview image, highlight Save and press the ⓞⓚ button.

Note: Image attributes such as white balance, sharpening, color mode, saturation, and hue will be copied from the image selected as Image 1. Similarly, the shooting data is copied from the same image.

Note: Although limited to combining only two separate images, the Image Overlay feature can be used to emulate the effect of a double-exposure. For example, try shooting two exposures of the same subject, one in focus and the other slight out of focus, and then combining them to create a soft focus effect. If the new image overlay copy is saved as a NEF (RAW) file it can be combined with another NEF (RAW) file to create a new overlay image.

NEF (RAW) Processing

This item can be used to create JPEG format copies of pictures saved and stored on the installed memory card at an image quality of NEF (RAW), or NEF (RAW) + B.

To use NEF (RAW) processing:

1. Highlight NEF (RAW) processing in the retouch menu and press the multi selector button to the right.
2. Select the required NEF (RAW) picture from the displayed thumbnail pictures by pressing the multi selector to the left or right. Note only NEF (RAW) pictures will be displayed. Press the ⓞⓚ button to select the highlighted picture.
3. A preview image is now displayed next to a menu of options:

   • **Image quality:** Choose image quality from, JPEG Fine, JPEG Normal, or JPEG Basic.

   • **Image size:** Choose image size from, Large, Medium, or Small.

   • **White balance:** Choose white balance settings, specify fluorescent lighting type, apply white balance fine-tuning, including photographs taken at a white balance of preset manual, but these can only be subjected to fine-tuning from the preset manual white balance option. The preset manual option is only available for pictures taken at this white balance setting.

   • **Exposure compensation:** Adjust the exposure level ±3EV.

   • **Optimize image:** Choose an Optimize image option, including Custom.

4. Highlight the required option and press the multi selector to the right. Select the required setting and press the ⓞⓚ button to return to the preview image and menu display. Repeat the selection process for any other options to be used.

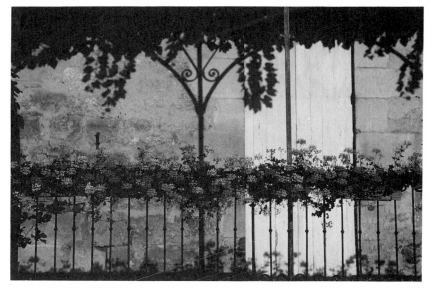

You can process NEF (RAW) files in-camera with the Nikon D60. This may come in handy if you need to share images immediately.

5. Once all settings have been adjusted, highlight EXE.
6. Press **OK** to create and save a JPEG format copy and return to the full-frame playback.
7. Press the **MENU** , or **▶** buttons to return to the full-frame playback without creating a copy image.

Note: The exposure compensation option should be treated with caution, as the ±3EV range is overly optimistic. The extended dynamic range of NEF (RAW) files recorded by the D60 does permit some adjustment to the exposure level, but only across a far more limited range if image quality is to be preserved. I would suggest that ±2EV is the practical limit of adjustment using this option, and preferably lower if possible. To maximize image quality the original exposure should be as accurate as possible.

Note: The exposure compensation option cannot be selected if the original picture was taken when the Active D-Lighting feature was set to On.

Note: The White balance option cannot be selected for a copy image created using the Image overlay feature.

Note: Copies created with NEF (RAW) processing > Optimize image > Black-and-white cannot be modified further using Quick retouch, D-Lighting, Red-eye correction, or Monochrome. The only further modification possible is with Cross screen in Filter effects.

Stop-motion Movie

This item enables creation of a stop-motion movie from images stored on the installed memory card. These movies are saved in the AVI file format, and can be played back directly in the D60, or on a computer using suitable software such as Nikon View NX (1.1.0, or later) and Apple's QuickTime.

To create a stop-motion movie:

1. Open the Retouch menu and highlight the Stop-motion movie item. Press the multi-selector button to the right to display three options:

    • **Create movie:** choose the pictures that will comprise the stop-motion movie and create the movie file.

    • **Frame size:** choose from 640 x 480, 320 x 240, or 160 x 120

    • **Frame rate:** choose from 15 frames-per-second (fps), 10 fps, 6 fps, or 3 fps

2. Highlight Frame size and press the multi selector to the right to display the frame size options. Select the required option and press the ⊙ button to apply the setting and return to the stop-motion menu page.

3. Highlight Frame rate and press the multi selector to the right to display the frame rate options. Select the required

option and press the ⓞⓚ button to apply the setting and return to the stop-motion menu page.

4. Highlight Create movie and press the ⓞⓚ button. The highlighted image will be shown with a yellow border and the word "Start" within it. Press the multi selector left or right to select the start image for the stop-motion movie. Hold the multi selector button down to scroll rapidly through the thumbnail pictures. Press the ⓞⓚ button to select the start image.

5. The yellow border will now contain the word "End". Press the multi selector left or right to select the ending (final) image for the stop-motion movie. Hold the multi selector button down to scroll rapidly through the thumbnail pictures. Up to a maximum of 100 images can be selected for a stop-motion movie.

6. Press the ⓞⓚ button to select the ending (final) image. The start, ending, and all images between will be indicated with a check mark.

7. To remove unwanted pictures, or edit either the start or ending image, select Edit and press the ⓞⓚ button. The next page displays four options:

- **Starting image:** to alter the start image, highlight Start image and press the ⓞⓚ button. Press the multi selector to the left or right to highlight the new start image, and then press the ⓞⓚ button to select it. The monitor display will revert to the create movie display, with options to Edit and Save.

- **End image:** to alter the end image, highlight End image and press the ⓞⓚ button. Press the multi selector to the left or right to highlight the new end image, and then press the ⓞⓚ button to select it. The monitor display will revert to the create movie display, with options to Edit and Save.

- **Middle image:** to remove unwanted images from the stop-motion movie, highlight Middle image and press the ⓞⓚ button. Scroll through the thumbnail images, select the unwanted image, and then press the multi selector up or down to remove the check mark. Repeat the process for each unwanted image. Press the ⊙ button to apply the new selection of images to be retained in the movie file.

- **Cancel:** to create the stop-motion movie without editing, highlight Cancel and press the ⊙ button.

8. Highlight Save and press the ⊙ button. The next page displays four options:

- **Save:** choose this option to save the movie file. Highlight Save and press the ⊙ button. Once the movie file is saved the display will revert to showing the start image in full-frame playback.

- **Preview:** choose this option to playback the movie file before it is saved. Highlight Preview and press the ⊙ button. During preview of the movie file the same operations available with stop-motion movie playback, including pause, rewind and advance, can be applied.

- **Frame rate:** choose this option to alter the frame rate. High light frame rate and press the ⊙ button, highlight the required frame rate and press the ⊙ button, again to revert to the create movie display.

- **Edit:** choose this option to return to step (7) above. Highlight Edit and press the ⊙ button.

Note: Movie files created with the stop-motion movie option have file names that begin with "ASC_" and end with the file extension ".AVI" (e.g. ASC_0001.AVI).

Note: Stop-motion movies can be played by pressing the ⊙ button in full-frame playback, or by using the Stop-motion movie item in the playback menu.

Before and After Comparison

Use this item to perform a side-by-side comparison of a retouched copy image with an original source image. This option is only available when a retouched copy image or an original source image for a retouch copy image is displayed in full frame playback, and the ⊙ button is pressed. This action opens the Retouch menu in full-frame playback; use the multi selector to highlight Before and after, and then press the ⊙ button.

The source image is displayed on the left and the retouched copy on the right of the monitor screen. The option(s) used to create the copy image are listed above the images. Press the multi selector in the direction of the arrowhead adjacent to the yellow border to switch between images, and use the ⊙ button to view an enlarged version of the highlighted picture. To return to the full-frame playback mode with the highlighted image displayed, press ⊙ .

⊘ Custom Setting Menu

Many of the default settings for the various functions and features of the D60 can be altered to suit your shooting style. This is achieved using the ⊘ Custom Setting (CS) menu that has nineteen items, with multiple options and sub-options.

At the camera's default setting for menu displays, it is necessary to scroll through the list of available options in the Custom Setting menu each time you want to make an adjustment to a particular one. In an effort to simplify and speed-up this process, the D60 offers two different levels of Custom Setting menu, Simple (default) and Full. The Simple option will display only the first six of the nineteen items available in the Custom Setting menu. The Full option enables access to all items in the CS menu. Each of the two Custom Setting levels and the selection for My menu is set from the CSM/Setup option in the ⚈ Setup menu. Likewise, you can use the My menu option to select any item in the Customs Settings menu and have it displayed in My menu to facilitate access (see page 180 for a description of how to set different options in CSM/Setup).

To view the Custom Setting menu, press the ⊕ button and use the multi selector to highlight the ⌀ Custom Settings tab. Press the multi selector to the right, and then press it up or down to scroll through the menu. To save time, the menu will wrap-around in a continuous loop in both directions as you scroll by just keeping the multi selector pressed, either up or down. Once your chosen menu item is highlighted, press the multi selector to the right to display its options. Highlight the desired option by pressing the multi selector button up or down, and select/set it by pressing the ⊛ button.

⏻ Help Button

Rather than try to remember what each option does, or refer to printed instructions, a built-in help function provides a brief description on the LCD monitor screen of each Custom Setting item. Highlight the item and press and hold the ⏻ / ⊛ button to display a descriptive text on the screen (if necessary press the multi selector button down to scroll through the text).

(R) Custom Setting Reset

All nineteen items in the Custom Setting menu have a default value (indicated in the follow descriptions). If you wish to cancel all your user-set options and restore the camera to its default Custom Settings, select Reset (CS-R) and highlight Yes, then press the ⊛ button. This action only resets the Custom Setting menu; it does not restore default settings in any other camera menus.

CS-01 Beep

An audible signal can sound when the camera has performed certain functions, such as the countdown during self-timer operation and delayed remote release mode, confirmation that focus has been acquired in AF-S, and that shutter operation has been activated with the ML-L3 remote control in Quick-response release mode.

- **On (default)** – The camera will beep. A musical note icon is shown in the Shooting Information Display. However, the sound can be a distraction in many shooting situations, so it is advisable to set this item to Off.

- **Off (camera is silent)** – The camera is silent. A musical note icon with a strike through is shown in the Shooting Information Display.

CS-02 Focus Mode

These options determine how the camera's auto focusing system operates.

- **AF-A (Auto-servo AF)** – The default, in this mode the AF system will decide to select either AF-S, or AF-C based on whether it determines the subject is static or moving.

- **AF-S (Single-servo AF)** – The AF system will acquire focus when the shutter release is pressed halfway, or is activated by using the AF-ON option of CS-12, and will lock the focus distance. It is ideal for stationary subjects.

- **AF-C (Continuous-servo AF)** – The AF system will acquire focus when it is activated by pressing the shutter release halfway, or using the AF-ON option of CS-12. It will continue to monitor the focus distance, adjusting focus if subject-to-camera distance changes. It is ideal for moving subjects.

- **MF (Manual Focus)** – The user must rotate the focus ring of the lens to alter the point of focus.

CS-03 AF-Area Mode

The D60 has three different autofocus area modes that determine which focus sensing areas are used. (Also see pages 158-159 for a full description of the autofocus area modes.)

[■] **Closest subject** – This is the default for all exposure modes except ⚡ Sport and ✿ Close-up Digital Vari-Programs. The camera selects the AF point used for focusing based on what it determines to be the closest subject; the user has no choice.

[⊡] **Dynamic-area** – A single user-selected AF point is used to acquire focus unless the AF system detects the subject moving out of this area, in which case it uses information from all three AF points in an effort to maintain focus on the subject. (Default for [■] Sport Digital Vari-Program.)

[⊡] **Single-point** – Only the single user-selected AF point is used to acquire focus. (Default for ✿ Close-up Digital Vari-Program.)

CS-04 Release Mode

The D60 offers five release modes that determine how and when the shutter is released. (Also see pages 147-151 for a full description of the shooting modes.)

[S] **Single frame (default)** – One exposure is made each time the shutter release button is pressed down all the way.

[⊒] **Continuous** – Exposures are recorded at a maximum rate of 3 per second while the shutter release button is pressed down fully.

⟳10s **Self-timer** – The exposure can be delayed for a fixed duration (default 10-seconds)

📷2s **Delayed remote** – Use the ML-L3 remote to release the shutter after a short delay

Quick-response remote – Use the ML-L3 remote to release the shutter immediately

CS-05 Metering

The D60 has three methods of measuring light using its TTL (through the lens) metering system. This applies to P, S, A, and M exposure modes only. (Also see pages 131-135 for a full description of the metering modes.)

Matrix (default) – The camera uses its 420-segment RGB sensor to evaluate brightness, contrast, and color. Using compatible lenses, the focus distance and likely position of the subject within the frame area are provided by the AF system.

Center-weighted - 75% of the metering is based on an 8 mm diameter circle at the center of the frame area, while the remainder is taken from the rest of the frame area outside this circle.

Spot – The TTL metering system reads from an area approximately 3.5 mm in diameter, centered on the active AF point.

CS-06 No Memory Card?

To prevent you from thinking the camera is recording pictures when in fact there is no memory card installed, the shutter release of the camera is disabled (although this can be overridden to allow the camera to save pictures directly to a computer using appropriate Nikon software).

- **Release locked (default)** – The shutter will not operate if a memory card is not installed.

- **Enable release** – The shutter release will operate normally even with no memory card installed in the camera. The photograph is displayed on the LCD monitor with the word "Demo" but the image data is NOT saved, and the picture cannot be printed

Hint: Leave this option set to Release lock (default). Otherwise it might appear that the camera is operating normally but no pictures will be recorded and saved!

CS-07 Image Review

The D60 can display a picture on its LCD monitor almost as soon as an exposure is made.

- **On (default)** – Pictures are shown almost immediately on the LCD monitor after an exposure is made. The duration of the display is set via CS-15 (Auto timers off).

- **Off** – Pictures are not displayed on the LCD monitor after an exposure is made. They can be displayed by pressing the ▶ button.

Hint: I suggest in most instances to set this option to On unless you need to conserve battery power. Displaying the picture acts as confirmation that an exposure has been made. You can also show the histogram automatically at the same time by using the Auto shooting info item in the Setup menu, and selecting the appropriate Photo Information page. As soon as you have finished looking at the picture/histogram, you can switch the monitor off and return the D60 to its shooting mode by pressing lightly on the shutter release button. One exception might be when shooting in low-light conditions when the brightness of the monitor screen display may be a distraction.

Note: The eye-control system has no affect on Image review if the default setting of On is selected; the recorded image will be displayed on the monitor screen, even when the user's eye is to the viewfinder.

CS-08 Flash Compensation (P, S, A, and M modes only)

The amount of light output by the built-in Speedlight (flash), or a compatible external Speedlight (SB-800, SB-600, and SB-400) can be adjusted (compensated) in a range from -3EV to +1EV in steps of 1/3EV.

Hint: If you set a flash output compensation level, it will remain locked until you restore the value to ±0.0 (default), even if the camera is powered off and then switched on again.

CS-09 AF-Assist

The AF-assist lamp will light automatically when the camera determines that light levels are low and there is a risk that the AF system will not be able to acquire focus. However, there are limitations depending on the type of lens in use; AF-assist is only effective with focal lengths between 24 and 200mm, and any lens hood should be removed. Plus it has a maximum effective range of only 9 feet 10 inches (3 m).

- **On (default)** – AF-assist lamp will light automatically in AF-S, or when AF-S is selected in AF-A.

- **Off** – The lamp will not operate regardless of the ambient light conditions.

Hint: I prefer to keep this set to Off. Not only does using the lamp drain the battery, it is often a distraction to the subject. In addition, its limited range means it is of no value with many of the subjects I shoot!

Note: AF-assist is not available in ■ or ♣ exposure modes.

CS-10 ISO Auto

This function is available in P, S, A, and M modes only. The camera will automatically shift the ISO sensitivity if an optimal exposure cannot be made at the selected value. Although the camera displays "ISO-AUTO" in the control panel and the viewfinder when this option is selected, and this icon flashes as a warning when the camera has changed the ISO value, there is no indication as to what ISO setting is in use without opening page two of the shooting data shown by the Photo Information pages in image playback mode. The ISO value is displayed in red if the camera has altered it. The operation of this function is also dependent on the exposure mode you select.

- **Off (default)** – The camera retains the ISO (sensitivity) setting selected by the user and will not change it.

- **On** – Assuming certain exposure conditions prevail, the camera will alter the ISO setting to compensate if an optimal exposure cannot be made (the flash output is adjusted appropriately). In P and A, exposure modes the maximum ISO setting can be set by selecting Max sensitivity; the sensitivity is only adjusted if underexposure would occur at the lowest shutter speed selected by the user at the Min. shutter speed option.

Hint: I suggest turning this function Off if you want to be sure of the exact sensitivity level used in order to keep ISO noise at a minimum.

CS-11 Fn Button
The Fn button can be set to offer a quick and convenient way to activate several different camera functions.

- **Self-timer (default)** – Press the ☉/Fn button to set self-timer operation (the duration of the delay is determined by the setting selected at CS-16) in the Shooting Information Display, and press the shutter release to start the function.

- **Release mode** – Press the ☉/Fn button to highlight the shooting mode setting in the Shooting Information Display (the rest of the display is dimmed), and rotate the command dial to adjust it.

- **Image Quality/Size** – Press the ☉/Fn button to highlight the image quality and image size settings in the Shooting Information Display (the rest of the display is dimmed), and rotate the command dial to adjust them.

- **ISO sensitivity** – Press the ☉/Fn button to highlight the ISO setting in the Shooting Information Display, and rotate the command dial to adjust it.

- **White balance** – Press the ☉/Fn button to highlight the white balance setting in the Shooting Information Display (the rest of the display is dimmed), and rotate the command dial to adjust it (P, A, S, and M exposure modes only).

Hint: Selection of the Fn button operation will depend on the shooting situation and specific user requirements. For what it is worth, I generally select either ISO sensitivity or White balance when shooting in available light.

CS-12 AE-L/AF-L

This item assigns a variety of functions to the AE-L/AF-L button.

🔒 **AE/AF lock (default)** – The exposure value and autofocus are locked when the 🔒 button is pressed and held down.

🔒 **AE lock only** – The exposure value is locked but autofocus continues to operate when the 🔒 button is pressed and held down. This may be the most useful option because you can take a reading from a specific area, lock it, and then re-compose before releasing the shutter.

🔒 **AF lock only** – Autofocus is locked but exposure value can continue to be altered when the 🔒 button is pressed and held down. This can be useful when you know where the subject is going to be but want auto exposure to operate right up to the moment you make the exposure.

AE **AE Lock hold** – Exposure value is locked when the button is pressed and released and remains locked until it is pressed again.

AF **AF-ON** – Camera will only autofocus when the button is pressed; pressing the shutter release button will not activate autofocus. AF-ON has two distinct ways of being used. First, it can be considered an alternative to the AF lock feature; press the button in AF-S mode to focus on a subject, and then release it. The focus distance will remain locked. Now, provided the active AF point covers the subject (any one of the three can be selected) the picture can be recomposed at will and the shutter released as many times as you wish, as long as the camera to subject distance is not altered. Alternatively, this option can be used to perform the trap focus technique (see page 157 for details).

CS-13 AE Lock

This item determines if the D60 locks an auto exposure value when the shutter button is pressed halfway down.

- **Off (default)** – The exposure is not locked when you press the shutter release button half way.

- **On** – The exposure value is locked when the shutter release button is pressed down halfway (P, S, A, and Digital Vari-Program modes)

Hint: I set this option to On since I find it far simpler and quicker to lock exposure using the shutter release button.

CS-14 Built-in Flash / Optional Flash

This item sets the flash mode for the built-in Speedlight when using P, S, A, and M exposure modes. It does not affect external Speedlight units, other than the SB-400.

TTL **TTL (default)** – The built-in flash operates in the i-TTL mode for fully automatic control of flash output and always emits monitor pre-flashes.

M ⚡ Manual – The flash output is fixed at a predetermined level selected from options in this item. The [⚡] icon flashes in the Shooting Information Display and viewfinder when this option is selected.

Hint: You will probably want to select TTL when using either the built-in Speedlight or optional external Speedlights (currently only the SB-800, SB600, SB-400, and SB-R200 units are compatible; the SB-R200 requires either an SB-800 or SU-800 as a commander unit). This option offers the most sophisticated level of TTL flash exposure control.

CS-15 Auto Off Timers

This item sets the duration of display on the LCD monitor and of the TTL metering display in the viewfinder, assuming no other function/action is activated that would otherwise turn it off.

- **Short** – The monitor will turn off after 8-seconds if no camera operation is performed while in playback mode or menu display. If Image review (CS-07) is On, the picture is displayed for 4 seconds after the exposure is made. The exposure meter remains on for 4 seconds

- **Normal (default)** – The monitor will turn off after 12-seconds if no camera operation is performed while in playback mode or menu display. If Image review (CS-07) is On, the picture is displayed for 4 seconds after the exposure is made. The exposure meter remains on for 8 seconds.

- **Long** – The monitor will turn off after 20-seconds if no camera operation is performed while in playback mode, or menu display. If Image review (CS-07) is On, the picture is displayed for 20 seconds after the exposure is made. The exposure meter remains on for 1 minute.

- ⏱🖊 **Custom** – The display duration for monitor, image review, and exposure meter display can be chosen as follows:

  Playback /menus: 8s, 12s, 20s, 1 minute, and 10 minutes.

  Image review: 4s, 8s, 20s, 1 minute, and 10 minutes.

  Auto meter off: 4s, 8s, 20s, 1 minute, and 30 minutes.

Hint: I recommend selecting shorter durations because the monitor consumes a relatively high level of power. Remember, you can always switch off the monitor display by pressing the shutter release button down halfway.

Note: If you connect the D60 to the Nikon EH-5 / EH-5a AC adapter via the EP-5 DC power adapter, the displays do not turn off automatically. This cannot be altered.

CS-16 Self-Timer (Delay of Self-Timer Operation)
When using self-timer, this setting lets you select several different durations for the delay between the time the shutter release is pressed and when the exposure is made. The options are: two seconds (2s), five seconds (5s), ten seconds (10s default), and twenty seconds (20s)

Hint: A delay of 2 seconds is ideal for releasing the shutter when you want to minimize camera vibration caused by touching it. The ML-L3 remote release is probably a more practical option since you do not need to press the camera's shutter release button to initiate the shutter action and the timing of its release can be controlled with precision. This also allows you to release the shutter some distance from the camera.

CS-17 Remote on Duration
This item allows you to determine the duration in which the D60 can receive the infrared (IR) control signal from the ML-L3 remote control before it automatically cancels the remote

release function. The setting options are: 1 min (default), 5 min, 10 min, and 15 min.

Hint: The camera draws more power than usual when it remains active awaiting the IR signal. Therefore I recommend you set the shortest duration possible, based on the shooting conditions.

CS-18 Date Imprint

This item enables the date and time of picture recording to be imprinted within the image area. The date and time are shown using the format selected at the Date option under the World time item of the setup menu. The feature is only available for pictures recorded in the JPEG format; photographs recorded using the RAW and RAW+B quality settings cannot have the date / time imprinted using this feature.

Hint: It is important to understand that the imprinted information form part of the original image file data; therefore it cannot be simply deleted but would require the picture to be retouched using digital imaging software on a computer. I recommend you consider, very carefully, whether you want to use this feature, as the date and time of recording are stored automatically in the EXIF information of the image file, which can either be displayed using the appropriate Photo Information page, via the playback menu, or accessed subsequently using compatible software, such as Nikon View NX and Nikon Capture NX 2.

- Off (default setting) – no information is imprinted within the picture

- **DATE** **Date** – the date currently set on the camera's internal clock is imprinted in the lower right corner of the picture.

- **DATE⊕** **Date and time** – the date and time currently set on the camera's internal clock is imprinted in the lower right corner of the picture.

- **⊞⊞⊞** **Date counter** – if this option is selected the D60 calculates the number of days remaining until, or the number of days elapsed since a specified date, and prints this number as a prefix to the imprinted date. Up to three key dates can be saved by the camera. The period between the current date set on the camera's internal clock and the selected key date can be displayed in one of three ways: number of days, years and days, or years, months and days.

To set up this feature, open the Date imprint item, highlight the Date counter item, and then press the multi selector to the right. On the next menu page, highlight Choose date and press the multi selector to the right. If the date counter is being applied for the first time, or the multi selector button is pressed to the right after selecting one of the three key date options, the Set date screen will be displayed. Enter a date using the multi selector button, pressing it up or down to adjust settings, and left or right to shift between fields. Once the key date has been entered press **OK** to return to the Date counter page. Up to three key dates can be stored, to select another stored key date highlight it using the multi selector button and press **OK** .

Highlight Display options and press the multi selector to the right. Highlight one of the three options: number of days, years and days, or years, months and days, and then press **OK** to return to the Date counter page.

Finally, highlight Done and press **OK** to apply the settings.

CS-19 Rangefinder

Selecting On for this item converts the analogue exposure display in the viewfinder to be converted to a rangefinder display to facilitate manual focus in all shooting modes except manual exposure, provided manual focus mode has been selected either via the Quick Settings Display, or CS-02. The rangefinder display provides an indication of not only the degree of focus or defocus but also the direction in which the focus ring of the lens should be turned to achieve focus.

Note: This feature requires a maximum lens aperture of f/5.6 or greater, and may not function properly in situations where the auto focus system has difficulty in acquiring focus (see page 152 for further details).

The range finder display options are as follows:

Rangefinder Display	Explanation
0	In focus – the area within the selected AF point is in focus
0	Focus point is slightly in front of the subject
0	Focus point is a significant distance in front of the subject
0	Focus point is slightly beyond the subject
0	Focus point is a significant distance beyond the subject
	Unable to determine focus point

Playback Menu

The following items are displayed in the Playback menu. If the installed memory card contains no pictures, all items except Playback folder and Rotate tall will be shown in gray. You can use the My menu option, which is chosen from the CSM/Setup menu item in the Setup menu, to select any item in the Playback menu and have it displayed in My menu to facilitate access.

Delete

You can choose to erase individual images, a group of images, or all of the images on the card by using this function. To delete images one by one, it is quicker and easier to use the 🗑 button on the rear of the camera. However, to erase a group of images, the Delete function in the Playback menu will probably save you a lot of time (and button pushing!).

To delete a group of images:

1. Select Delete from the Playback menu and press the multi selector to the right.
2. Highlight Selected and press the multi selector to the right.
3. Thumbnails of all of the images stored in the active folder will be displayed on the LCD monitor. Scroll through the images by pressing the multi selector to the left or right; a yellow border is shown around the selected image. To see an enlarged view of the selected image, press the 🔍 button.
4. To select the highlighted image for deletion, press the multi selector up or down. A small icon of a trashcan will appear in the upper right corner of the thumbnail image.
5. Once all the files to be deleted have been selected, press the 🆗 button.
6. The total number of images to be deleted will be displayed, along with two options: No or Yes. Select the require option and press the 🆗 button to either complete (Yes), or cancel (No) the delete process.

Note: If All is selected from the Playback folder item (see below), you can view all images stored in all folders on the memory card, not just those in the active folder.

To delete all images:

1. Select Delete from the Playback menu and press the multi selector to the right.
2. Select All and press the multi selector to the right: A warning appears, "All pictures will be deleted. OK?"

3. Highlight either Yes or No.
4. Once you have selected the desired option, press the
   ⊙ button to either complete (Yes), or cancel (No) the
   delete process.

Note: This process cannot delete pictures that have been
protected. Images that have been hidden will not be displayed, and therefore cannot be selected for deletion.

Hint: It can take a long time to delete a high volume of pictures. To save draining the camera battery and placing additional wear and tear on your D60, when erasing a large
quantity of files it is probably better to connect your memory card to a computer (using a card reader) and use the
computer to carry out the deletion process.

Playback Folder
This option allows you to determine which images on the
installed memory card will be displayed during playback.
There are two options available:

- **Current (default)** – Only the images in the folder
  currently set for image storage, via the Folders option
  in the Setup menu, will be displayed during playback.

- **All** – All of the images stored on the card are displayed, regardless of which folder they are stored in.

To apply the Playback folder:

1. Select Playback folder from the Playback menu and press
   the multi selector to the right.
2. Highlight the desired option: Current or All.
3. Press ⊙ button to confirm your selection.

As soon as a new picture is recorded, Current is selected
automatically even if All was previously selected at this
menu item. Select All again to view images from all folders.

Rotate Tall

Use this option to automatically turn pictures taken in the vertical (portrait) format and display them on the LCD in their proper orientation. The Auto image rotation option in the Setup menu must be turned on for the Rotate tall function to operate, otherwise all images will be displayed in a horizontal (landscape) orientation regardless of the camera orientation at the time of exposure.

To set Rotate tall:

1. Select Rotate tall from the Playback menu and press the multi selector to the right.
2. Highlight On or Off.
3. Press ⊛ button to confirm your selection.

Hint: You will probably prefer to leave this feature switched Off, since rotating an image to a vertical orientation for display on the monitor screen will decrease the overall size of the image by about 1/3.

Slide Show

The Slide show option lets you view all images in the current folder in sequential order. This can be a useful and enjoyable feature, especially if the camera is connected to a television for viewing.

To use Slide show:

1. Select Slide show from the Playback menu and press the multi selector to the right.
2. Start will be highlighted; to begin the slide show immediately, press the ⊛ button (images will be displayed for approximately two seconds). To alter the display duration highlight Frame interval and press the multi selector to the right; choose either 2, 3, 5, or 10 seconds, and then press ⊛ .
3. To pause the slideshow, press the ⊛ button again. This displays a sub-menu of Restart, Frame interval (you can choose a display duration of either 2, 3, 5, or 10 seconds), and Exit to stop the slide show.

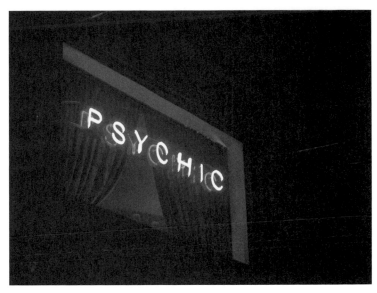

You can connect the D60 to a television set and present your pictures to others using the Slide Show feature in the Playback menu.

To skip back and forth, press the multi selector to the left and right respectively; to view the shooting information for an image press the multi selector up, or down. To end the slide show and return to the playback menu, press the 〔MENU〕 button. To end the slide show and return to the full-frame, or thumbnail playback, press the 〔▶〕 button. To return the D60 to its shooting mode press the shutter release button down halfway.

Print Set (DPOF)

The Print Set option enables the user to create and save a set of images to be printed automatically by a compatible printing device. This "print order" will communicate which images should be printed, how many prints of each image, and the information that is to be included on each print. This information is saved on the installed memory card, in the Digital Print Order Format (DPOF), to be read subsequently by DPOF compatible printing device. See pages 303-309 for more details.

Stop-motion Movie (Viewing)

This item is used to view the movie files created with the stop-motion movie item of the Retouch menu.

To view a stop-motion movie:

1. Select Stop-motion movie from the Playback menu and press the multi selector to the right.
2. A thumbnail of the first frame of each saved stop-motion movie file will be displayed. The total number of frames in the movie is shown in the lower right corner of the thumbnail, and a yellow border surrounds the currently selected movie file. Use the multi selector button to choose an alternative movie file. To enlarge the thumbnail of the first press and hold the ⊕ button.
3. Press the ⊙ button to play the selected movie file. At the end of the playback the screen reverts to the movie file thumbnail display.

During movie file playback it is possible to activate a number of controls: pause, rewind, advance, and end. The icons for these four controls are displayed in the lower left corner of the monitor screen. During movie file play back press the multi selector button left or right to highlight the required control and then press the ⊙ button to activate it.

The following table sets out the control options and their effects:

Control option	Use	Explanation	
Rewind	◀◀	Rewind movie. Playback will resume when ⊙ is pressed	
Advance	▶▶	Advance movie. Playback will resume when ⊙ is pressed	
Pause	❚❚	Pause playback; while paused the following operations can be performed	
		◀❙	Rewind movie by one frame. Press ⊙ to progress frame rewind
		❙▶	Advance movie by one frame. Press ⊙ to progress frame advance
		▶	Resume playback
End	■	End playback and return to the thumbnail view of movie files. Return to the full-frame playback when movie file was played from full-frame playback mode	

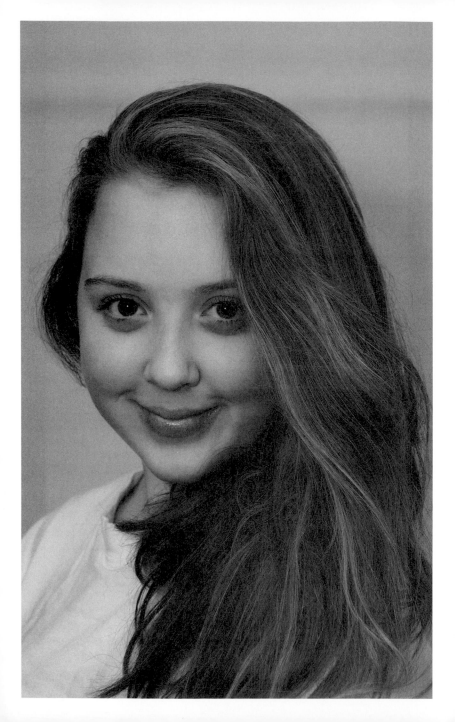

Nikon Flash Photography

Before we take a look at the flash capabilities for the D60 it is important to understand a few basic principles of flash photography. Light from a flash unit decreases in intensity as it travels away from its source, as described by the Inverse Square Law. Put simply, if you double the distance from a light source the intensity of light drops by a factor of four. This is because light spreads out as it travels away from its source; so if the distance is doubled, the area covered is four times larger. Since a flash unit emits a precise amount of light, it will only light a subject correctly at a specific distance depending on the amount of light emitted by the flash unit. Consequently, if the flash exposes the subject correctly at a given distance, then anything closer to the flash will be over-exposed, and anything further away will be increasingly underexposed. Also, to produce a balanced exposure between the subject and its surroundings you will often want to balance the light from the flash with the prevailing ambient light.

When the built-in Speedlight of the D60, or alternatively an external Speedlight such as the SB-400, SB-600, or SB-800 is used with a D-type or G-type Nikkor lens, and the camera is set to Matrix metering, 3D Multi-sensor Balanced Fill-flash is active. In this mode, the camera attempts to balance ambient light with the flash output. The i-TTL (intelligent TTL) flash exposure control system used in the D60 is the third generation of TTL flash exposure control developed by Nikon and is their most sophisticated flash exposure control system to date. It is part of a wider set of flash features and functions that Nikon refers as the Creative Lighting System (CLS).

For this photo an SB-600 was mounted in the camera's hot shoe and the flash head was tilted upward to "bounce" the flash off the white ceiling. Bounce flash is often a good technique for portrait photography because the light from the flash is softened and diffused when it is reflected off the ceiling. Since it falls on the subject from above, it has lends a pleasing, natural appearance to the image.

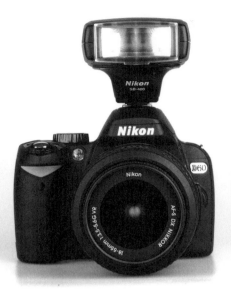

The Nikon D60 with SB-400 Speedlight.

Note: Currently the SB-800, SB-600, SB-400, and SB-R200 Speedlights are the only external Nikon flash units to support CLS. If any other external Nikon Speedlight is attached to the D60, TTL flash exposure control is not be supported.

The Creative Lighting System

During 2003 Nikon raised the bar a considerable distance for photography with portable, camera mounted, flash units by introducing the SB-800 Speedlight and D2H digital SLR camera, the first two components of their Creative Lighting System (CLS). The CLS encompasses a range of features and functions that are as much a part of the cameras that support it, as the Speedlight units themselves. These features include: i-TTL, Advanced Wireless Lighting for wireless TTL control of multiple compatible Speedlights, Flash Value (FV) Lock,

Flash Color Information Communication, Auto FP High-Speed Sync, and Wide-Area AF-Assist Illuminator. However, the D60 does not support the Auto FP High-Speed Sync, nor the FV Lock feature; furthermore, its built-in Speedlight does not support the Advanced Wireless Lighting control.

i-TTL (Intelligent TTL) Flash Exposure Control

Nikon's most recent TTL flash exposure control system, i-TTL uses only one or two pre-flash pulses that have a shorter duration and slightly higher intensity than those used for the TTL and D-TTL system used in previous Nikon cameras and Speedlights. Currently, the D60 supports i-TTL with the following compatible Speedlights: the built-in Speedlight of the camera, SB-800, SB-600, SB-400, plus the SB-R200 via the SU-800 commander unit) at sensitivity settings between ISO 100 and ISO 1600. The SB-400 is not compatible with wireless TTL control; it is a small, compact, basic unit capable of TTL, or manual flash exposure control when used with the D60.

Note: Due to its design, the SB-R200 cannot be mounted on the accessory shoe of the D60; it can be used only as a remote flash, controlled wirelessly by either the SU-800 Commander unit or an SB-800 Speedlight. The built-in Speedlight of the D60 does not support direct wireless control of remote CLS compatible Speedlights.

There are several key differences between the i-TTL system and the earlier TTL and D-TTL systems. When shooting with the flash units listed above and the D60 these include:

- i-TTL uses fewer monitor pre-flashes but they have a slightly higher intensity. The greater intensity of the pre-flash pulses improves the efficiency of obtaining a measurement from the TTL flash sensor, and by using fewer pulses the amount of time taken to perform the assessment is reduced.

- The D60 uses its 420-segment RGB sensor to measure and control the output of flash, regardless of whether you use a single Speedlight attached to the camera (directly, or via a dedicated TTL flash cord such as the SC-28), or multiple CLS compatible Speedlights in a wireless TTL configuration.

- Monitor pre-flashes are always emitted before the reflex mirror is raised, regardless of whether the camera is used with one or more compatible Speedlights; if you look carefully you can often observe the pre-flash emission a fraction of a second before the viewfinder blacks out as a result of the reflex mirror being raised.

The following is a summary of the sequence of events used to calculate flash exposure in the D60, when used with a single or multiple compatible Speedlights (the built-in unit, SB-800, SB-600, SB-400, or SB-R200) and a D-type or G-type Nikkor lens:

1. Once the shutter release is pressed the camera reads the focus distance from the D-type or G-type lens.

2. The camera sends a signal to the Speedlight to initiate pre-flash; the system emits one or two very brief pulses of light from the Speedlight(s).

3. The light from these pre flashes is bounced back from the scene, through the lens on to the 420-segment RGB sensor housed in the camera's viewfinder head, via the reflex mirror.

4. The information attained from the pre-flash analysis is combined with assessment of the ambient light by the 420-segment sensor and focus information from the lens and auto focus sensor module. The camera's microprocessors determine the amount of light needed from the Speedlight(s) and set the duration of the flash discharge accordingly.

5. The reflex mirror lifts up out of the light path and the shutter opens.

6. The camera sends a signal to the Speedlight(s) to initiate the main flash discharge, which is quenched the instant the amount of light pre-determined in Step 4 has been emitted.

7. The shutter closes at the end of the predetermined time duration, and the reflex mirror is lowered to its normal position.

Note: The emission of pre-flashes occurs before the reflex mirror is raised. In some shooting situations, because of the slight delay between the mirror being raised and the shutter opening, photographers may fail to realize that this can cause a blink reflex in the eyes of their subject(s).

Note: The SB-400 does not support the Advanced Wireless Lighting system that provides wireless control of control multiple Speedlights using i-TTL flash exposure control.

Flash Output Assessment

The crucial phase in the sequence is step 4 (above), when the output from the flash is calculated. I understand from Nikon technicians and engineers that, in Matrix metering mode, three distinct elements are considered during this process:

- **Brightness** – In Matrix metering mode the camera will assess the overall level of brightness, using its 420-segment RGB sensor.

- **Contrast** – The camera compares the relative brightness of each sampling point in its 420-segment RGB sensor. The camera is preprogrammed to recognize specific lighting patterns across the metering segment array. For example, outer segments that detect a high level of brightness and a central segment with a lower level of brightness indicate a strongly backlit subject in the center of the frame. The camera then compares the detected pattern with patterns pre-stored in its database of approximately 30,000 example exposures. If the first comparison generates conflicting assessments the segment pattern maybe re-configured and further analysis is performed. Finally, if any segment detects an abnormally high level of brightness in comparison to the others (as might occur if a highly reflective surface such as glass or a mirror caused a specular reflection in part of the scene), the camera will usually ignore this information in its flash exposure calculations.

- **Focus Information** – This is provided in two forms: camera-to-subject distance, and the level of focus/defocus at each of the three focus sensing areas. The D60 uses this focus information to assess how far away the subject is likely to be and its approximate location within the frame area, which is based on the assumption that the subject will be located under the focus sensing area that reports focus.

Generally, the focus-distance information will influence which segment(s) of the Matrix metering sensor contribute to overall exposure calculations. For example, assuming the subject is positioned in the center of the frame and the lens is focused at a short range, the camera will place more emphasis on the outer metering segments and less on the central ones. An exception to this occurs if the camera detects a very high level of contrast between the central and outer sensors it may, and often does, reverse the emphasis, weighting the exposure according to the information received from the central sensors. Conversely, if the subject is positioned in the center of the frame and the lens is focused at a mid to long range, the camera will place more emphasis on the central metering segments and less on the outer ones. Essentially what the camera is trying to do in both cases is prevent over exposure of the subject, which it assumes is in the center of the frame.

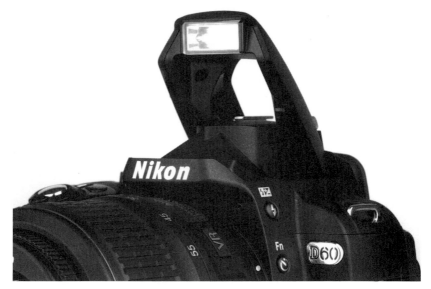

Used with Matrix metering the D60 performs a range of complex cal-culations to control flash output from both its built-in Speedlight (shown here) and compatible external Speedlights.

Note: To provide focus-distance information, a D-type or G-type Nikkor lens must be mounted on the camera; the appropriate designation is marked on the lens barrel of each lens

Individual focus sensor information is integrated with focus-distance information, as each focus sensing area is checked for its degree of focus. This provides the camera with information about the probable location of the subject within the frame area. Using the examples given in the previous paragraph the camera notes that the central focus sensing area is reposting focus while the two outer focus sensing areas report a level of defocus. Therefore exposure is calculated on the assumption that the subject is in the center of the frame and the camera biases its computations according to the focus-distance information it receives from the lens.

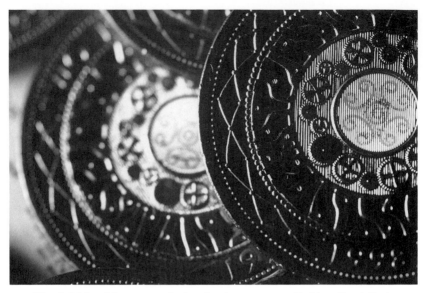

The light for this macro study of coins was supplied by direct flash from two SB-800 Speedlights—one served as the main light and a second was set up as a fill light.

However it is important to understand that other twists occur in the interaction between exposure calculation and focus information. For example, if you acquire and lock focus on a subject using the center focus sensing area and then recompose the shot so that the subject is located elsewhere in the frame (so the central focus sensing no longer detects focus), the camera will, generally, use the exposure value it calculated when it first acquired focus. However, if it detects that the level of brightness measured by the central metering segment has consequently changed significantly from the point when focus was acquired with the subject in the center of the frame the camera can, and often does adjust its exposure calculations but not necessarily for the better!

The Built-In Speedlight

The built-in Speedlight of the D60 (Speedlight is Nikon's proprietary name for its flash units) has a Guide Number (GN) 39 in feet (12 in meters) at ISO100 (in manual flash mode the GN is 42 feet /13 meters). It can synchronize with the shutter at speeds up to 1/200 second. It has a minimum range of 2 ft (.6 m); at shorter ranges the flash/camera will not necessarily calculate a correct flash exposure.

If the D60 determines that the ambient light level is low, or the subject is backlit strongly, the built-in Speedlight is raised automatically in the 🔆 , 🏃 , 👥 , 🌷 , and 🏃 Digital Vari-program modes; however, it is not available in 🚫 , 🏔 , or 🏃 DVP modes. In P, S, A, and M exposure modes it must be activated manually by pressing the 🔆 button, which causes the flash head to pop up.

The built-in Speedlight draws its power from the main battery of the camera; therefore, extended use of the flash will drain battery power significantly. As soon as the flash unit pops up it begins to charge. The flash ready symbol 🔆 appears in the viewfinder to indicate charging is complete and the flash is ready to fire. If the flash fires at its maximum output, the same flash ready symbol will blink for approximately three seconds after the exposure has been made, as a warning of potential under-exposure. This flash ready symbol operates in the same way when an external Speedlight is attached and switched on.

External Speedlights

In addition to the built-in Speedlight, the D60 offers full i-TTL flash exposure control with three external Speedlights that are compatible with the CLS:

* **SB-400** – Guide number 69/21 (ISO100, ft/m, 18mm)
* **SB-600** – Guide number 98/30 (ISO100, ft/m, 35mm)
* **SB-800** – Guide number 125/38 (ISO100, ft/m, 35mm)

All three models can be mounted to the camera's flash shoe, or connected via a dedicated TTL remote flash cord, such as the SC-28 or SC-29.

Note: The D60 does not support TTL flash exposure control with any other Nikon flash shoe-mounted Speedlight. The SB-R200 can only be controlled as part of a wireless flash system using either the SB-800 or SU-800 as a Commander Unit.

SB-400

Weighing 4.5 oz. (127 g), this lightweight Speedlight is fully compatible with the i-TTL flash exposure control system of the D60. It offers a fixed angle of coverage equivalent to that of a focal length of 18mm (when used on the D60 with its DX-format sensor), and the flash head can be tilted in four positions: horizontal, 60, 75, and 90 degrees for bounce flash. However, the flash head does not swivel.

Used with the D60 the SB-400 supports the following flash sync modes: Front-curtain sync, Slow Sync, Red-eye reduction, Red-eye reduction with Slow-sync, Rear-curtain sync. When attached and switched on the flash control mode for the SB-400 is selected via CS-14 (Optional flash unit).

SB-600 and SB-800

Aside from being more powerful, the SB-600 and SB-800 Speedlights are considerably more versatile than the built-in flash on the D60, or the SB-400, since their flash heads can be tilted and swiveled for bounce flash. They also have an adjustable auto zoom-head (SB-800, 24-105mm) (SB-600, 24-85mm) that controls the angle-of-coverage of the beam of light emitted from the flash, and a wide-angle diffuser for creating a broader beam to cover the angle of view of a focal length of 14mm.

Note: Unlike earlier Nikon Speedlights, which cancelled monitor pre-flashes if the flash head was tilted or swiveled for bounce flash photography, the SB-800 and SB-600 emit pre-flashes regardless of the flash head position.

Hint: The focal lengths used by the SB-600 and SB-800 Speedlights in their zoom heads assume the units are used with 35mm film format (24 x 36 mm) cameras, and not digital SLR cameras, such as the D60 with its reduced angle-of-view due to the smaller size of its DX-format (15.8 x 23.6 mm) sensor. Therefore, the flash will illuminate a greater area than is necessary when used on the D60, which means you will be squandering light and consequently restricting your shooting range. Use the following table to maximize the performance and shooting range of an external Speedlight on the D60:

Focal length of lens (mm)	Zoom head position (mm)
14	20
18	24
20	28
24	35
28	50
35	50
50	70
70	85
85	105 [1]

1 - Available on SB-800 only.

TTL Flash Modes
(Built-In and External Speedlights)

The D60 supports two methods for TTL control flash exposure with either its built-in Speedlight, or a compatible external Speedlight.

- **i-TTL Balanced Fill-flash** – the most sophisticated version of Nikon's TTL flash exposure control system the Speedlight(s) emit an short series of nearly imperceptible pre-flashes (sometimes referred to in Nikon literature as monitor pre-flashes) a faction of a second before the reflex mirror lifts to record the exposure. The light from these pre-flashes is reflected from all areas of the scene within the camera's frame area is detected by the 420-segment RGB-metering sensor of the D60 and assessed as described above to adjust the flash output so it produces a balanced exposure of the main subject and the background lit by any ambient light. The most precise calculations are obtained when either a D, or G-type lens is attached to the D60, since focus information including distance in included in the computations for flash output.

• **Standard i-TTL Flash** - this differs from i-TTL balanced fill-flash control method just described as the 420-segment RGB-metering sensor and metering system of the D60 determine the output of the flash, exclusively, so measurement of the ambient light in the background remains wholly independent, and is not integrated in any way with the flash exposure calculations. For reasons I explain below standard i-TTL flash control can often be the best option when flash exposure of the main subject is the priority, or when flash output compensation is used.

Note: Standard i-TTL Flash has very important implications when mixing ambient light with light from a Speedlight for the fill-flash technique, as any exposure compensation level selected for either the ambient light exposure, or the flash exposure, or both will be applied at the level pre-determined by the photographer and is not influenced by the any automated adjustment the camera may apply.

Note: Standard i-TTL Flash can be set from an external compatible Speedlight (it is not available with the SB-400).

Note: Selecting spot metering on the D60 will cause the flash exposure control to default to standard i-TTL Flash when used with either the built-in, or an external Speedlight.

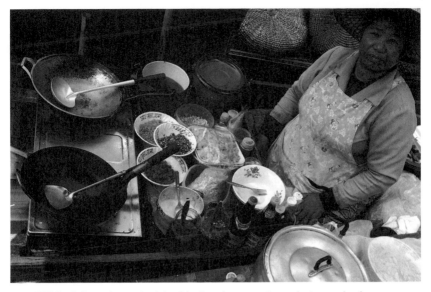

Fill flash is an important tool in the documentary photographer's arsenal. It can be used to reduce exposure latitude and make colors pop, accent detail in surroundings, or highlight the subject in the scene.

Understanding Nikon Flash Terminology

Many photographers fail to understand how their choice of exposure mode can affect the appearance of a photograph made with a mix of flash and ambient light. All too often they assume that because the camera is performing automated i-TTL balanced fill-flash that both the subject and background will be rendered properly. Their frustration deepens when they realize that any exposure compensation factor that they apply on the camera, Speedlight, or both, is often either overridden, or ignored completely!

The i-TTL balanced fill-flash is a fully automated process, so the photographer is not the one in control here! The camera is responsible for all exposure decisions in i-TTL balanced fill-flash when the camera is set to any of the automatic exposure modes (P, A, S, ͣᵁᵀᴼ , or other Digital Vari-program modes that support flash use), and all flash output decisions in i-TTL balanced fill-flash, when the camera is set to manual exposure mode.

Furthermore, if you select either the P or A exposure modes, or one of the DVP modes that support use of flash, the available range of shutter speeds is restricted (see the table, below). If the level of ambient light requires a shutter speed outside of this range, as is usually the case when shooting in low-light conditions such as a dimly lit interior, the areas of the scene lit predominantly by ambient light will be underexposed.

Exposure Mode	Flash Sync Shutter Speed range
P, A, 🅰️ 📷 🎭 🏞️	1/200 – 1/60 second
🌷	1/200 – 1/125 second
🌃	1/200 – 1s
S, M	1/200 – 30s

Hint: If you use any exposure modes, other than S and M, with flash consider setting Slow sync flash mode (do not confuse this with Rear-curtain sync mode) as it overrides this restriction on shutter speed range, and allows the full range of speeds available on the camera, between the maximum flash sync speed and the slowest shutter speed to be used, so areas lit by ambient light appear more balanced with those lit by flash.

Another clue as to what occurs in i-TTL balanced fill-flash is the word "balanced"; this means that the camera assess the flash output level and the ambient light to create a balanced exposure using both light sources. The camera achieves this more often than not by compensating the flash output, the exposure for the ambient light, or sometimes both. As mentioned above any exposure compensation factor to adjust either the ambient light, or flash output compensation applied by the photographer is frequently overridden, or even ignored, because i-TTL balanced fill-flash is a wholly automated process, which can make achieving consistent repeatable results difficult to accomplish.

The reference to fill-flash in the name of this flash control method just serves to confuse users even further! Fill-flash is a recognized lighting technique in which the flash is used to provide a supplementary light to the main ambient light source, and as such its output is always set at a level below that of the ambient light. Generally, the purpose of this fill light from the flash is to provide additional illumination in the shadows and other less well-lit areas of a scene to help reduce the overall contrast range, although many photographers also use the technique to put a small catch light in their subject's eyes.

The use of the term fill-flash by Nikon is misleading on two counts in the context of i-TTL balanced fill-flash: first, depending on the prevailing light conditions, generally when the level of ambient light is very low, the Speedlight becomes the principal light source for illuminating the scene, and second, as discussed above "balanced" implies that the exposure for the ambient light and flash comprise equal proportions, which is neither the desired, nor achieved result in this case.

So, whenever you see the term i-TTL balanced fill-flash remember that existing ambient light and flash will be mixed in a fully automated process to produce the final exposure; how the two light sources are mixed and in what proportion will depend on a wide variety of factors, including ISO sensitivity, lens aperture, exposure mode, exposure compensation value, brightness of both the ambient and flash illumination, and nature of the scene being photographed.

If you want to achieve consistent repeatable results when using a true fill-flash technique, where the flash is the supplementary light I recommend you use standard i-TTL flash, as any flash output compensation, or exposure compensation you set will be applied without influence from the camera. Likewise in any situation where you wish to use flash as the main source of illumination and have control over the flash output level and any exposure of ambient light, I suggest you select standard i-TTL flash.

Non-TTL Flash Modes (SB-800 Speedlight)

When using the SB-800 external Speedlight with the D60 there are two additional non-TTL flash modes available.

(AA) Auto Aperture – in this mode the SB-800 reads the ISO sensitivity setting and lens aperture from the camera automatically, and also receives the "fire flash" signal from it as well. It can be used in aperture-priority auto, or manual exposure modes. Thereafter the flash output level is determined using a sensor on the front panel of the Speedlight to monitor the flash exposure and as soon as this sensor detects that the flash output has been sufficient, the flash pulse is quenched. If, between exposures, you decide to alter the focal length, or change the lens aperture the Speedlight will adjust its output accordingly to maintain a correct flash exposure. The problem with this option is that the sensor does not necessarily "see" the same scene as the lens, which can lead to inaccuracies in flash exposure.

(A) Automatic (non-TTL) – this is the only automatic (non-TTL) flash mode available with the earlier DX-type Speedlights, such as the SB-80DX, as well as the SB-800. It can be used in aperture-priority auto, or manual exposure modes. Similar to the AA mode a sensor of the front of the SB-800, or DX-type Speedlight, monitors flash levels and shuts off the flash when the Speedlight calculates sufficient light has been emitted. However, the lens aperture and ISO sensitivity values must be set manually on the Speedlight to ensure the subject is within the flash shooting range. As with the AA mode the sensor does not necessarily "see" the same scene as the lens, which can lead to inaccuracies in flash exposure.

Manual Flash Mode (Built-in Speedlight)

In Manual flash mode the user sets the output of the Speedlight (built-in or external) to a fixed level. It is necessary to calculate the correct lens aperture based on the flash to subject distance and the Guide Number (GN) of the Speedlight.

At its base sensitivity of ISO 100 (equivalent) the built-in Speedlight of the D60 has a Guide Number (GN) of 42 ft (13 m). The output level of the built-in Speedlight and SB-400 is set via CS-14, where a value between 1/1 (full output) and 1/32 can be selected (available in P, S, A, and M exposure modes only).

Since there is only one specific exposure value for any given level of sensitivity at a particular flash-to-subject distance, it is necessary to calculate the lens aperture required to record a proper exposure. Use the following equation:

Aperture = GN/Distance

So for example using the built-in Speedlight of the D60 set to 1/1 (its full output), and at a shooting distance of exactly 7.5 ft, the lens aperture for a correct exposure of the subject will be f/5.6. (5.6 = 42/7.5).

Note: Similar calculations will have to be performed when using an external Speedlight in manual flash mode. Check the Guide Number for the Speedlight model and ensure that you conduct the calculations using the same measuring system (feet or meters) throughout.

Flash Sync Modes

Not to be confused with the flash control modes available with the D60, described above, the Flash Sync (synchronization) Modes determine when the flash is fired and how it combines with the shutter speed. These apply to the built-in Speedlight, and the compatible external Speedlights.

To set a flash sync mode on the D60 press the ◀🔲▶ button to open the Shooting Information Display then press the ◀🔲▶ button again to open the Quick Settings Display; use the multi selector button to highlight the flash mode ⚡ option. Press the 🆗 button to display the list of options indicated by the relevant icons and

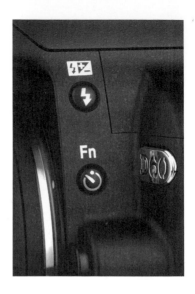

The built-in Speedlight is activated in P, A, S, and M exposure modes by pressing the flash button on the side of the viewfinder head.

thumbnail "assist images." Use the multi selector to highlight the required option. Finally, press the **OK** button to confirm your selection; the new flash mode is displayed in the Shooting Information Display and Quick Settings Display.

An alternative and quicker route to select and set the flash mode is to press and hold the **⚡** button, to show the flash mode highlighted in either the Shooting Information Display, or Quick Settings; rotate the command dial to scroll through the various options until the icon for the desired flash sync mode appears. Release the **⚡** button to confirm the selection.

Flash Sync in P, S, A, and M Modes
⚡ - **Fill flash (Front-curtain) sync** – the flash fires as soon as the shutter has fully opened. In P and A exposure modes the flash will sync with a shutter speed between 1/60 and 1/200 second. In S and M exposure modes the Speedlight synchronizes at shutter speeds between 1/200 second and 30 seconds.

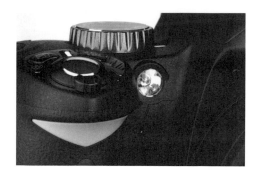

The AF-assist lamp located next to the finger grip is used for the red-eye reduction feature.

⚡ 👁 - **Red-eye reduction (Front-curtain) sync** – the D60 uses the AF-assist lamp on the front right side of the camera body to light for approximately one second before the main exposure in an effort to reduce the size of a subject's pupils. Shutter speed synchronization is the same as for fill flash (front –curtain) sync.

Hint: This mode does cause an inordinate delay in the shutter's operation by which time the critical moment has generally passed and you have missed the shot! Personally, I never bother with this feature.

⚡ **+ SLOW** - Slow sync is only available in P and A exposure mode; the flash fires as soon as the shutter has fully opened and at all shutter speeds between 30 seconds and 1/200 second. It is useful for recording low-level ambient light as well as those areas of the scene or subject illuminated by flash.

⚡ 👁 **+ SLOW** - Slow sync with red eye reduction; is the same as Slow sync (above) except the red-eye reduction lamp is switched on for approximately one second before the shutter opens for the reason stated above under Red-eye reduction.

Hint: The same advice applies – avoid this mode!

⚡ **+ REAR** - Rear-curtain sync; in S and M exposure modes, the flash fires just before the shutter closes at all shutter speeds between 30 seconds and 1/200 second. Any image of a moving subject recorded by the ambient light exposure will appear to be behind (i.e. following naturally) the parts of the subject illuminated by the flash output.

⚡ + SLOW + REAR - Slow Rear-curtain sync; available with P and A camera exposure modes only, the flash fires just before the shutter closes at all shutter speeds between 30 seconds and 1/200 second. Any image of a moving subject recorded by the ambient light exposure will appear to be behind the parts of the subject illuminated by the flash output. This effect can be useful for accentuating a sense of movement by the subject.

Flash Sync with Digital Vari-Program Modes

Using the built-in flash with the 📷ᴬᵁᵀᴼ , 🏃 , 🌇 , 🌷 , and ◼ Digital Vari-program modes provides the following flash sync modes:

⚡ + AUTO - Auto flash in 📷ᴬᵁᵀᴼ , 🏃 , 🌇 🌷 modes only, the flash fires as soon as the shutter has fully opened; the camera selects a shutter speed between 1/60 and 1/200 second (1/125 – 1/200 second in 🌷 mode), automatically.

⚡ + 👁 + AUTO - Auto Flash with red-eye reduction; in 📷ᴬᵁᵀᴼ , 🏃 , 🌇 , 🌷 , modes only, the AF-assist lamp on the front right side of the camera body to light for approximately one second before the main exposure in an effort to reduce the size of a subject's pupils. Shutter speed synchronization is the same as for Auto flash sync.

⚡ + AUTO + SLOW - Auto flash with slow sync; in ◼ mode only, the flash fires as soon as the shutter has fully opened; the camera selects a shutter speed between 1 second and 1/200 second, automatically.

↯ + **◉** + **AUTO** + **SLOW** - Auto flash with slow sync and red-eye reduction; in **▣** only, the D60 uses the AF-assist lamp on the front right side of the camera body to light for approximately one second before the main exposure in an effort to reduce the size of a subject's pupils. Shutter speed synchronization is the same as for Auto flash with slow sync.

⊘ - Flash off; the flash will not operate even if the camera detects a low ambient light level, or the subject is backlit.

Note: If you attach an external Speedlight to the D60 when the camera is set to any of the Digital Vari-program mode options that support use of flash, except the **▣** mode, the only flash sync modes available are Auto flash sync, or Auto flash with red-eye reduction. If **▣** mode is selected the only flash sync modes available are slow sync, or slow sync with red-eye reduction.

Additional Flash Features and Functions

Flash Output Compensation
In P, S, A, and M exposure modes flash output compensation can be set on the D60 in increments of 1/3EV over a range of +1 to –3EV, via CS-08.

To set a flash output compensation on the D60 press the **◄⊞►** button to open the Shooting Information Display then press the **◄⊞►** button again to open the Quick Settings Display; use the multi selector button to highlight the flash compensation **↯⊠** option. Press the **◉** button to display the selected value. Press the multi selector up to select a positive compensation and down to select a negative compensation value, then press **◉** to set it.

An alternative and quicker route to select and set the flash output compensation is to press and hold the **↯⊠** and **⊠** buttons simultaneously, to show the flash compensation **↯⊠** highlighted in either the Shooting Information

Display, or Quick Settings; rotate the command dial to the left to select a positive value and to the right to select a negative value. To confirm the selection release the ⚡️ and ⊡ buttons. To restore normal flash output set the flash compensation to 0.0.

Note: Flash output compensation is not reset to 0.0 when the camera is switched off; always reset the value to 0.0 once you have finished flash shooting.

Hint: If you use the default i-TTL Balanced Fill-flash mode it will automatically set flash compensation based on scene brightness, contrast, focus distance, and a variety of other factors. The level of automatic adjustment applied by the D60 will often cancel out any compensation factor entered manually by the user. Since there is no way of telling what the camera is doing you will never have control of the flash exposure. To regain control set the flash mode to Standard i-TTL by selecting spot metering when using the built-in or an external Speedlight, or selecting Standard i-TTL mode directly on a compatible external Speedlight (currently the SB-800 and SB-600 only).

Flash Color Information Communication

The built-in Speedlight and external Speedlights (SB-800, SB-600, and SB-400) automatically transmit information about the color temperature of the light they emit to the camera. If the D60 is set to automatic white balance control, this information is used to determine the white balance setting in an attempt to match the color temperature of the flash output to the color temperature of any ambient light.

Limitations of Using the Built-In Speedlight

While the built-in Speedlight of the D60 is not as powerful as an external Speedlight, it can still provide a useful level of illumination at short ranges, especially for the purpose of fill-flash, since it supports flash output level compensation. However, if you want to use this built-in Speedlight as the main light source you should be aware of the following:

- The built-in Speedlight of the D60 has an ISO 100 Guide Number (GN) of 39 ft (12 m). Thus, at an aperture of f/5.6 this unit provides its full output at a range of little less than just 7.0 ft (2.1 m), as the maximum flash shooting distance is equal to the GN divided by the lens aperture.

- The flash head of the built-in Speedlight is much closer to the central lens axis than with an external flash; hence the likelihood of red-eye occurring is increased, significantly.

- Again, the proximity of the built-in Speedlight to the central lens axis often means that the lens obscures the output of the flash, especially if it has a lens hood fitted. If the camera is held in a horizontal orientation the obstruction of the light from the flash will cause a shadow to appear on the bottom edge of the picture.

- The angle of coverage achieved by the built-in Speedlight is limited, and only extends to cover the field of view of a focal length of 18mm. Using of a shorter focal length the flash will not be able to illuminate the corners of the frame and these areas will appear underexposed. Even at the widest limit of coverage it is not uncommon to see a slight fall off of illumination in the extreme corners of the full frame.

Aperture, Sensitivity (ISO), and Flash Range

The flash shooting range of the built-in Speedlight will vary depending on the values set for the lens aperture and sensitivity (ISO).

The flash shooting range will vary depending on the values set for the lens aperture and ISO sensitivity.

Lens aperture at ISO (sensitivity)					Range	
100	200	400	800	1600	Meters	Feet
1.4	2	2.8	4	5.6	1.0 - 8.5	3ft 3in - 27ft 11in
2	2.8	4	5.6	8	0.7 - 6.1	2ft 4in - 20ft
2.8	4	5.6	8	11	0.6 - 4.2	2ft – 13ft 9in
4	5.6	8	11	16	0.6 - 3.0	2ft – 9ft 10in
5.6	8	11	16	22	0.6 - 2.1	2ft – 6ft 11in
8	11	16	22	32	0.6 - 1.5	2ft – 4ft 11in
11	16	22	32	-	0.6 - 1.1	2ft – 3ft 7in
16	22	32	-	-	0.6 - 0.8	2ft – 2ft 7in

Maximum Aperture Limitation
According To ISO Sensitivity

It is important to understand that in addition to the general restrictions imposed on the control of exposure in the fully automated exposure modes the use of an external flash in these modes limits the maximum aperture value that can be selected. This will often negate the advantage of using a lens with a fast (low f# number) maximum aperture value. So those f/2.8 constant aperture zoom lenses become far less flexible in controlling depth of field to isolate a subject from its background. The maximum aperture (smallest f/number) is limited according to the ISO sensitivity set on the D60. In the 🅰, 🏃, 👤, 🏃, 🌷, 🌆 and Programmed-auto (P) exposure modes:

Maximum Aperture				
100	200	400	800	1600
4	4.8	5.6	6.7	8

In the 🅰 mode:

Maximum Aperture				
100	200	400	800	1600
5.6	46.7	8	9.5	11

> *Note:* Any flash unit places a high demand on the batteries used to power it; the built-in Speedlight draws its power from the camera's battery, so extended use will exhaust the battery quite quickly.

Lens Compatibility with Built-In Speedlight

Due to the proximity of the built-in Speedlight to the central lens axis when the lenses mentioned in the table below are used at the focal lengths and shooting ranges given, there is a possibility that they will obscure some light from the flash, and cause uneven exposure.

Lens Focal length / Minimum Shooting Range

Lens	Focal length	Minimum distance
AF-S DX 12–24mm	20 mm	9 ft. 10 in / 3.0 m
f/4G ED	24 mm	3 ft. 3 in / 1.0 m
AF-S DX VR 16-85mm f/3.5-5.6G	24mm of greater	No restrictions
AF-S 17–35mm f/2.8D ED	24 mm	6ft. 7 in / 2.0 m
	28mm	3 ft. 3 in / 1.0 m
	35mm	No restrictions
AF-S DX 17–55mm	28 mm	4 ft. 11 in / 1.5 m
f/2.8G ED	35 mm	3 ft. 3 in / 1.0 m
	45 mm	No restrictions
AF 18–35mm f/3.5–4.5D ED	24 mm	3 ft. 3 in / 1.0 m
	28 mm or greater	No restrictions
AF-S DX 18-70mm	18 mm	3 ft. 3 in / 1.0 m
f/3.5-4.5G ED	24 mm or greater	No restrictions
AF-S DX 18–135mm	18 mm	3 ft. 3 in / 1.0 m
f/3.5–5.6G ED	24 mm or greater	No restrictions
AF-S DX VR 18–200mm	24 mm	3 ft. 3 in / 1.0 m
f/3.5–5.6G ED	35 mm or greater	No restrictions

Lens	Focal length	Minimum distance
AF 20–35mm f/2.8D	24 mm	8 ft. 2 in / 2.5 m
	28 mm	3 ft. 3 in/ 1.0 m
	35 mm	No restrictions
AF-S 24–70mm f/2.8G ED	35 mm	4 ft. 11 in / 1.5 m
	50 mm	3 ft. 3 in / 1.0 m
AF-S VR 24-120mm f/3.5-5.6G ED	24 mm	3 ft. 3 in / 1.0 m
	28 mm or greater	No restrictions
AF-S 28–70mm f/2.8D ED	35 mm	4 ft. 11 in / 1.5 m
	50 mm or greater	No restrictions
AF-S VR 200-400mm f/4G ED	250 mm	8 ft. 2 in / 2.5 m
	300 mm	6 ft. 7 in / 2.0 m

Note: It is not possible to use the built-in Speedlight with the AF-S 14–24mm f/2.8G ED, as light is always obscured regardless of focal length.

Note: The built-in flash has a minimum range of 2-feet (60 cm); therefore it cannot be used at the close focus distances of macro zoom lenses.

Using a Single Speedlight Off-Camera with TTL Cord

When you work with a single external Speedlight it is often desirable to take the flash off the camera. Nikon produced a number of dedicated cords for this purpose: the SC-17 (now discontinued), SC-28, and SC-29. All three cords are 4.9 feet (1.5m) long: up to three, SC-17, or SC-28 cords can be connected together to extend the operating range away from the camera.

The benefits of taking a Speedlight off camera include:

• Increasing the angle between the central axis of the lens and the line between the flash head and a subject's eyes

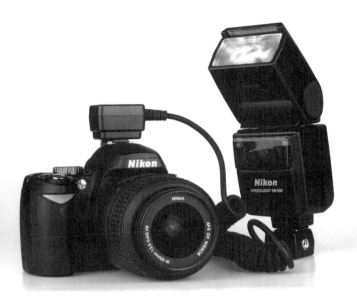

The D60 with SB-600 Speedlight connected via the Nikon SC-28 TTL flash cord; such a combination increases the flexibility of flash illumination by allowing the flash to be positioned away from the camera.

will reduce, significantly, the risk of the red-eye effect with humans, or eye-shine with other animals.

- In situations when it is not practical to use bounce flash, moving the flash off camera will usually improve the quality of the lighting. This is especially true for the degree of modeling the flash provides, compared with the rather typical flat, frontal lighting produced by a flash close to the central lens axis of the lens.

- By taking the flash off camera and directing the light from the Speedlight accordingly, it is often possible to control the position of shadows so that they become less distracting.

- When using fill-flash it is often desirable to direct light to a specific part of the scene to help reduce the level of contrast in that area.

Hint: Whenever you take a Speedlight off camera and use any flash mode that incorporates focus-distance information in the flash output computation, take care where you position the flash. If the Speedlight is located at a different distance from the subject than the camera, the accuracy of the flash exposure may be compromised. The TTL flash control system works on the assumption that the flash is located at the same distance from the subject as the camera.

Note: Compatible with either the SB-800, SB-600, or SB-400 Speedlights, the SC-29 has an AF-assist lamp in the terminal block that attaches to the camera accessory shoe; positioning an AF-assist lamp immediately above the central axis of the lens can help improve the accuracy of autofocus when using these Speedlights off the camera.

Note: An SB-800 Speedlight or SU-800 Commander unit connected to the D60 via one of Nikon's dedicated TTL cords can be used to control multiple, remote Speedlights, using the Advanced Wireless Lighting system.

Even though the Nikon D60 and SB-800 flash represent some of the ⇨ *most sophisticated photography equipment on the market today, the biggest secret to successful flash photography is still an experienced photographer. In order to make the most of your gear, you should practice and experiment with various flash techniques. Digital makes it even better since you can see the results and correct for image flaws while you are with the subject.*

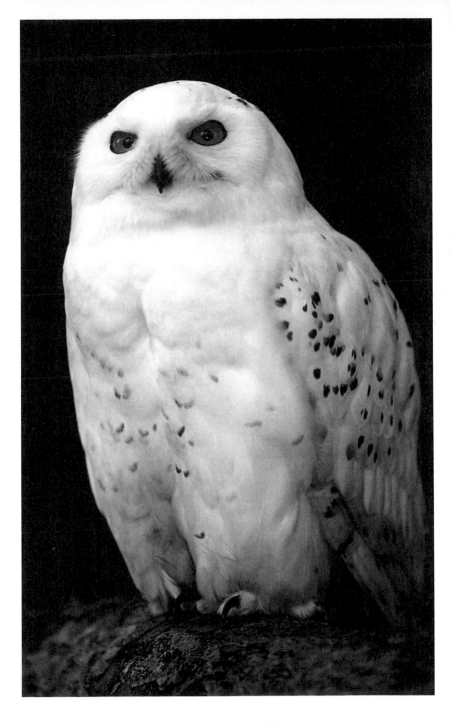

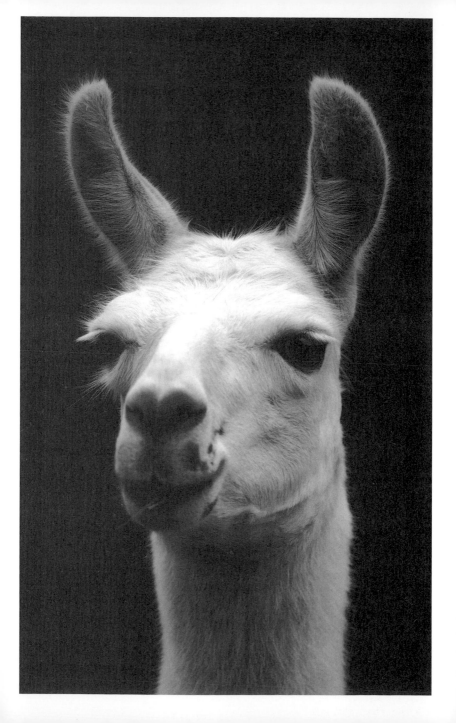

Nikon Lenses and Accessories

Nikon makes a huge range of lenses known by their proprietary name, Nikkor. Nikon's F mount for its Nikkor lenses is
legendary; it has been used on all Nikon 35mm film and
digital SLR cameras, virtually unchanged, since the introduction of the original Nikon F SLR in 1959. As such, a great
many of the lenses produced by Nikon in almost five
decades can be mounted on the D60; these include most
manual focus lenses produced since 1977 that conform to
the Ai lens mount standard and even earlier lenses, provided
they have been converted to the Ai standard. The fullest
level of compatibility is offered by modern autofocus Nikkor
lenses (D- and G-types); earlier autofocus Nikkor lenses can
still be used with the D60 but these must be focused manually. In common with the D40 and D40x models the D60
does not have a built-in motor for driving the lens focusing
mechanism. Excluding this motor reduces the weight of the
D60 by about an ounce (30 grams), and enables the lens
mount to be located closer to the base of the camera, help-
ing to reduce the overall height of the camera body. Consequently, the D60 only supports autofocus with AF-S and AF-I
types of Nikkor lenses (see page 61). Furthermore, the level
of compatibility between the camera and lens is restricted
severely if a non-CPU type lens (see page 275) is attached to
the D60.

*D- and G-type Nikkor lenses offer the fullest level of compatibility
with the Nikon D60.*

The DX-Format Sensor

The D60 has a sensor that Nikon refers to as the DX-format; you will often see this size of sensor also referred to as an APS-C sensor. At 15.6 x 23.7 mm it is smaller than a 35mm film frame, or FX format sensor of the Nikon D3 D-SLR camera (both are 24 x 36 mm), as a consequence the field of view covered by the DX-format sensor of the D60, regardless of the focal length of the lens mounted on the camera, is reduced (i.e. it is narrower) compared with the field of view produced by a lens of the same focal length on a 35mm film camera, or the D3.

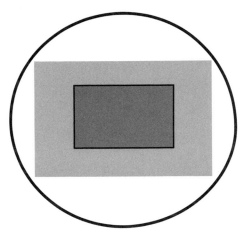

The circle represents the total area covered by the image circle projected from a lens designed for either the Nikon FX format digital sensor or 35mm film frame (24 x 36mm), while the pale gray rectangle is the approximate image frame for those two formats. The dark grey rectangle represents the area covered by the DX-format (15.6 x 23.7mm) sensor used in the D60.

While many photographers have become familiar with this concept, either though their experience of shooting with cameras of different formats, or being accustomed to shooting on the DX-format, there are still those who find the issue confusing. Furthermore, misconceptions persist as to what causes the altered field of view. Use of phrases such as, "it's like getting a free 1.4x teleconverter," or "the focal length is magnified by 1.5x," suggest, as if by magic, that the focal length of a lens when mounted on a camera with a DX-format sensor somehow increases by 1.5x. This is completely false. Using any lens, regardless of the size of the sensor, or piece of film it projects an image on to, its focal length remains constant; it is the field of view that alters.

For example, a lens with a focal length of 200mm will produce a specific field of view on the 24 x 36mm frame of 35mm film, or the FX-format sensor of the Nikon D3 camera but use the same focal length on the D60 and the field of view is reduced, so that it covers approximately the field of view produced by a lens with a focal length of 300mm used on a camera with a 24 x 36mm frame (film, or FX-format sensor). In other words, if you are accustomed to choosing a focal length based on the field of view it produces on a 24 x 36mm frame and want to estimate the coverage it will provide on the DX-format multiply that focal length by 1.5x (the actual factor is closer to 1.52x) and use the new value as a guide. Using the example of the 200mm focal length above, 200mm x 1.5 = 300mm. To put it another way if you where to shoot two pictures, one on a D60 and the other on a camera with a 24 x 36mm frame, mounted side-by-side pointing at exactly the same scene with the same focal length lens, and then cropped the image on the 24 x 36mm frame to the same area of the DX-format sensor of the D60 you would end up with identical pictures.

If you still find it easier to think in terms of the angle of view a particular focal length would give on a 24 x 36mm frame camera the following table provides an approximate operative focal length you can use to estimate the field of view on the DX-format sensor of the D60:

Focal length	12	14	17	18	20	24	28	35	50	60
Effective – Focal length DX-format	18	21	25.5	27	30	36	42	52.5	75	90

Focal length	70	85	105	135	180	200	300	400	500	600
Effective – Focal length DX-format	105	127.5	157.5	202.5	270	300	450	600	750	900

As a result of using the DX-format sensor in the D60 there is a beneficial side effect. Since only the central portion of the total image projected by lenses designed to cover is "seen" by the camera, the effects of optical aberrations and defects are kept to a minimum, as these are generally more prevalent toward the edge of the image circle. Some or all of the following can be reduced significantly, if not eliminated altogether:

- Light fall-off (vignetting) toward the edge and corners of the image area, which can be particularly troublesome at large lens apertures

- Appearance of chromatic aberration

- Linear distortion – both barrel and pin-cushion

- Effects of field curvature (i.e. centre and corners of frame are not in the same plane of focus)

- Light fall-off (vignetting) when using filters

Nikon also produces a range of Nikkor lenses designed specifically for use on their DX-format D-SLR cameras; known as DX lenses. Since they only need to project an image circle that covers the DX-format sensor these lenses can be made smaller and lighter compared with their counterparts designed for the 24 x 36mm frame cameras; however, it does mean that in most cases they cannot be used on the latter, so if you shoot on both formats bear this in mind.

Lens Types

Lenses are generally classified in to a number of different types dependent upon their focal length and/or design. Probably the most useful and popular are:

Wide-angle lenses – On the DX format these have focal lengths of less than 30mm. They offer a large field-of-view. While typically associated with landscape photography where they are used to capture sweeping vistas, but wide-angles are great for many other subjects. Their close focusing ability, and extended depth of field and angle-of-view can be combined to create some dynamic compositions if the subject is placed close to the lens, so it dominates the foreground and is set against an expansive backdrop.

Telephoto lenses – On the DX format these will have focal length of more than 30mm. They provide a narrower angle-of-view that magnifies a subject making them good for sport, action, and wildlife photography when it is usually difficult to be close the subject. The optical effects of a telephoto can be used in many other areas of photography such a portrait and landscape as they can help isolate a subject from its background due to their limited depth of field, particularly at large apertures.

Zoom lenses – These allow you to adjust the focal length range, which can be exclusively wide-angle, telephoto, or span both. Speaking strictly most modern lenses described as zooms are in fact vari-focal lenses; a true zoom lens maintains focus when the lens is zoomed in, which cannot be said of many lenses produced currently, so always check focus after you have adjusted the focal length on such a lens. Zoom lenses are extremely versatile, as you have several focal lengths available in one lens, which reduces the amount of lenses you need to carry and you spend less time changing lenses. However, convenience comes at a price; many zoom lenses have smaller (large f/ number) maximum apertures that often varies according to the focal length in use. These are usually around two-stops less than fixed focal length types. This can be an issue when shooting in low light. Zoom lenses with large, constant maximum apertures (small f/ numbers) tend to be expensive due to the complexity of their optical engineering.

I would suggest that for general photographic work a majority of D60 users will find that a lens, or lenses that offer focal lengths between say 18mm and 200mm will cover most shooting situations; for the greatest level of compatibility and functionality you should use either D-type, or G-type Nikkor lenses (see descriptions below).

Lens Compatibility

The D60 does not have an electric motor built-in to the camera to drive the focus action of those Nikkor AF lenses that do not have their own built-in AF motors; therefore, autofocus is only supported with either AF-S or AF-I type Nikkor lenses, which have a built-in autofocus motors. AF-S and AF-I type lenses can be identified by the presence of "AF-S" or "AF-I" at the beginning of the lens designation marked on the lens barrel. Other AF Nikkor lenses that do not have a built-in focus motor can be used with the D60 but focusing must be done manually.

Nikon classifies all AF-S, AF-I, and AF Nikkor lenses, plus manual focus Ai-P Nikkor lenses, as CPU-type lenses. These lenses can be identified by the electrical contact pins set around the edge of the lens mount bayonet flange. The following chart sets out the compatibility of Nikkor lenses with the D60:

Lens/accessory	Focus mode			Exposure mode		Metering system		
	S C	M (with electronic range finder)	M	P S	A M	3D	Color	
CPU lenses[1]								
Type G or D AF Nikkor[2] AF-S, AF-I Nikkor	•	•	•	•	•	•	—	•[3]
PC Micro 85mm f/2.8D[4]	—	•[5]	•	—	•[6]	•	—	•[3]
AF-S / AF-I Teleconverter[7]	•[8]	•[8]	•	•	•	•	—	•[3]
Other AF Nikkor (except lenses for F3AF)	•[9]	•[9]	•	•	•	—	•	•[3]
AI-P Nikkor	•	•[10]	•	•	•	—	•	•[3]
Non-CPU lenses[11]								
AI-, AI-S, AI-modified, or Series E Nikkor[12]	—	•[10]	•	—	•[13]	—	•[14]	•[15]
Medical Nikkor 120mm f/4 (IF)	—	•	•	—	•[16]	—	—	—
Reflex Nikkor	—	—	•	—	•[13]	—	—	•[15]
PC-Nikkor	—	•[5]	•	—	•[17]	—	—	•
AI-type Teleconverter[18]	—	•[8]	•	—	•[13]	—	•[14]	•[15]
PB-6 Bellows Focusing Attachment[19]	—	•[8]	•	—	•[20]	—	—	•
Auto extension rings (PK-series 11A, 12, or 13; PN-11)	—	•[8]	•	—	•[13]	—	—	•

1   *IX Nikkor lenses can not be used.*
2   *Vibration Reduction (VR) supported with VR lenses.*
3   *Spot metering meters selected focus point.*
4   *The camera's exposure metering and flash control systems do not work properly when shifting and/or tilting the lens, or when an aperture other than the maximum aperture is used.*
5   *Electronic range finder can not be used with shifting or tilting.*
6   *Manual exposure mode only.*
7   *Can be used with AF S and AF I lenses only (pg. 353).*
8   *With maximum effective aperture of f/5.6 or faster.*
9   *When focusing at minimum focus distance with AF 80 200mm f/2.85, AF 35¬70mm f/2.8S, new AF 28 85mm f/3.5 4.55, or AF 28 85mm f/3.5 4.5S lens at maximum zoom, in focus indicator may be displayed when image on matte screen in viewfinder is not in focus. Adjust focus manually until image in viewfinder is in focus.*
10 *With maximum aperture of f/5.6 or faster.*
11 *Some lenses can not be used.*

12 *Range of rotation for AI 80 200mm f/2.85 ED tripod mount is limited by camera body. Filters can not be exchanged while AI 200
400mm f/4S ED is mounted on camera.*

13 *If maximum aperture is specified using [Non CPU lens data] (pg.
198), aperture value will be displayed in viewfinder and control
panel.*

14 *Can be used only if lens focal length and maximum aperture are
specified using [Non CPU lens data] (pg. 198). Use spot or center
weighted metering if desired results are not achieved.*

15 *For improved precision, specify lens focal length and maximum
aperture using [Non CPU lens data] (pg. 198).*

16 *Can be used in manual exposure modes at shutter speeds slower
than 1/1255 If maximum aperture is specified using [Non CPU
lens data] (pg. 198), aperture value will be displayed in viewfinder
and control panel.*

17 *Exposure determined by presetting lens aperture. In aperture priority auto exposure mode, preset aperture using lens aperture
ring before performing AE lock or shifting lens. In manual exposure mode, preset aperture using lens
aperture ring and determine exposure before shifting lens.*

18 *Exposure compensation required when used with AI 28 85mm
f/3.5 4.5S, AI 35 105mm f/3.5 4.SS, AI 35 135mm f/3.5 4.SS, or AF
S 80 200mm f/2.8D. See teleconverter manual for details.*

19 *Requires PK 12 or PK 13 auto extension ring. PB 6D maybe
required depending on camera orientation.*

20 *Use preset aperture. In aperture priority auto exposure mode, set
aperture using focusing attachment before determining exposure
and taking photograph.*
PF 4 Reprocopy Outfit requires PA 4 Camera Holder.

Using Nikon AF-S / AF-I Teleconverters

The Nikon AF-S/AF-I teleconverters can be used with the
following AF-S and AF-I lenses:

AF-S VR Micro 105mm f/2.8G ED [1]
AF-S VR 200mm f/2G ED
AF-S VR 300mm f/2.8G ED
AF-S 300mm f/2.8D ED II
AF-S 300mm f/2.8D ED
AF-I 300mm f/2.8D ED
AF-S 300mm f/4D ED [2]
AF-S 400mm f/2.8D ED II
AF-S 400mm f/2.8D ED
AF-I 400mm f/2.8D ED

AF-S 500mm f/4D ED II [2]
AF-S 500mm f/4D ED [2]
AF-I 500mm f/4D ED [2]
AF-S 600mm f/4D ED II [2]
AF-S 600mm f/4D ED [2]
AF-I 600mm f/4D ED [2]
AF-S VR 70–200mm f/2.8G ED
AF-S 80–200mm f/2.8D ED
AF-S VR 200–400mm f/4G ED [2]
AF-S 400mm f/2.8G ED VR
AF-S 500mm f/4G ED VR [2]
AF-S 600mm f/4G ED VR [2]

1 *Autofocus is not recommended; at close focus distances the maximum effective aperture is likely to be less than f/5.6.*

2 *Autofocus not supported when used with TC-17E II/TC-20 E II teleconverter, the maximum effective aperture is less than f/5.6.*

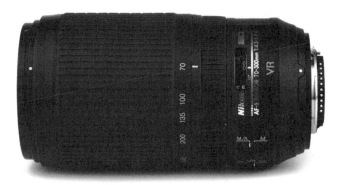

The Nikkor AF-S VR 70-300mm f/4.5-5.6G lens provides a wide range of focal lengths and the benefit of Nikon's Vibration Reduction (VR) system.

Using Non-CPU Lenses

Although the basic mechanical configuration of the Nikon F mount has remained unchanged, largely, for almost fifty years, the design of modern camera has moved on considerably! The introduction of electronic communication between the lens and camera for the purposes of exposure metering and autofocus has required a number of electrical contacts to be built-in to the modern version of the Nikon lens mount; consequently, older non-CPU type lenses (i.e., those lenses that do not have any electrical contact pins around the lens mount bayonet flange) offer a very restricted level of compatibility with the D60. In this case the camera can only be used in manual exposure mode (if you select another exposure mode the camera disables the shutter release automatically). The lens aperture must be set using the aperture ring on the lens, and the autofocus system, TTL metering system, electronic analogue exposure display, and TTL flash control do not function. However, the electronic range finder does operate, provided the maximum effective aperture is f/5.6, or larger (faster).

The following non-CPU type lenses can be used as described with the D60:

- Ai-modified, Ai, Ai-S, and E-series Nikkor lenses
- Medical Nikkor 120mm f/4 IF (only shutter speeds slower than 1/180 second can be used in order to synchronize with the flash unit of this lens)
- Reflex Nikkor lenses (electronic rangefinder does not operate)
- PC Nikkor lenses (electronic rangefinder does not operate if lens is shifted)
- Ai-type teleconverters (electronic rangefinder requires an effective aperture of f/5.6, or larger to operate).
- PB-6 Bellows focusing attachment
- Extension rings PK-11A, PK-12, PK-13, and PN-11

Incompatible Lenses and Accessories

The following accessories and lenses are incompatible with the D60. If you attempt to use them it may damage the camera.

- TC-16A AF teleconverter
- All non Ai-type Nikkor lenses (Ai-types introduced from 1977 onwards)
- Lenses that require the AU-1 focusing unit (400mm f4.5, 600mm f/5.6, 800mm f/8, 1200mm f/11)
- Fisheye-Nikkor (6mm f/5.6, 8mm f/8, OP 10mm f/5.6)
- 2.1cm f/4 (first type with protruding rear element)
- 180-600mm f/8ED (serial numbers 174041 – 1744180)
- 360-1200mm f/11 (serial numbers 174031 – 174127)
- 200-600mm f/9.5 (serial numbers 280001 – 300490)
- AF 80mm f/2.8, AF200mm f/3.5, TC-16 teleconverter (for F3AF camera)
- PC 28mm f/4 (serial numbers 180900 or earlier)
- PC 35mm f/2.8 (serial numbers 851001 – 906200)
- PC 35mm f/3.5 (early type)
- Reflex 1000mm f/6.3 (old type)
- Reflex 1000mm f/11 (serial numbers 142361 – 143000)
- Reflex 2000mm f/11 (serial numbers 200111 – 200310)

Features of Nikon Lenses

The designation of Nikkor lenses, particularly modern auto-focus types, is peppered with initials. Here is an explanation of what some of these stand for:

- **D-type** – these lenses have a conventional aperture ring and an electronic chip that communicates information about lens aperture and focus distance between the lens and the camera body. The 'D' designation appears on the lens barrel.
- **G-type** – these lenses have no aperture ring and are only compatible with Nikon cameras that allow the aperture value to be set from the camera body. They do contain an electronic chip that communicates information about

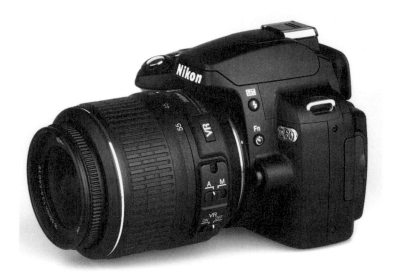

The Nikon D60 with AF-S DX VR 18-55mm f/3.5-5.6G.

lens aperture and focus distance between the lens and the camera body, similar to the D-type lenses. The "G" designation appears on the lens barrel.

- **AF-type** – these lenses are the predecessors to the later D, and G-type designs. The have a conventional aperture ring but do not communicate focus distance information to the camera.

- **DX** – lenses in the DX-Nikkor range have been especially designed for use on Nikon digital SLR cameras. They project a smaller image circle compared with lenses designed for the 35mm format cameras but the light exiting their rear element is more collimated to improve the efficiency of the photo sites (pixels) on the camera's sensor. The 'DX' designation appears on the lens barrel.

- **Non-CPU** – Nikon uses the term non-CPU lens type to describe any Nikkor lens that lacks the electrical connections and electronic components, which enable CPU-type lenses to communicate information about the lens to the camera (with the exception of the PC-Micro 85mm f/2.8D lens and Ai-P type Nikkor lenses all manual focus Nikkor lenses are non-CPU types).

- **AF-I** – predecessor to the AF-S type lenses that contain a silent-wave motor (SWM) for driving the focusing action. These lenses also have an internal focusing motor.

- **AF-S** – not to be confused with Single-servo autofocus, AF-S denotes the lens has a silent-wave motor (SWM) used for focusing; it uses alternating magnetic fields to drive the motor, which moves lenses elements to shift focus. This system offers the fastest autofocusing of all AF Nikkor lenses. Most AF-S lenses have an additional feature that allows the photographer to switch between autofocus and manual focus, without adjusting any camera controls, by just taking hold of the focus ring. The 'AF-S' designation appears on the lens barrel.

- **ED** – to reduce the effect of chromatic aberration Nikon developed a special type of glass known as Extra-low Dispersion to bring various wavelengths of light to a common point of focus.

- **IF** – to speed up focusing, particularly with long focal length lenses, Nikon developed their internal focusing (IF) system. This moves a group of elements within the lens so that it does not alter length during focusing, and prevents the front filter mount from rotating, which facilitates use of filters such as a polarizer.

- **N** (Nano Crystal Coat) – a specialized lens coating that is applied to the surface of some lens elements too help reduce the level of light reflection from them and thus improve overall image quality. The 'N' designation appears on the lens barrel.

- **Micro-Nikkor** – the name given to specialized lens designed specifically for close-up and macro photography; the optical formula of these lenses is optimized for close focusing

- **PC-E** – a special type of lens that offers the ability to shift and tilt the lens relative to the plane of the sensor in the camera to control perspective and depth of field. The 'PC-E' designation appears on the lens barrel.

- **VR** – Vibration Reduction is Nikon's name for a sophisticated technology that enables a lens to counter the effects of camera shake / vibration by using a set of built-in motion sensors that cause micro-motors to shift a dedicated set of lens elements to improve the sharpness of pictures. The 'VR' designation appears on the lens barrel.

Filters

I would always advocate trying to get as much right in the camera, apart from anything else it means you spend less time in front of a computer; time you can spend using your camera. As such optical filters, as opposed to the electronic filter effects of a digital camera, or those available in image editing software, are an integral part of any photographer's equipment, especially if they shoot on film. The white balance control of digital cameras such as the D60 obviates the need to carry a range of color correction, or color compensating filters that are be needed to control the color of light when shooting on film. Furthermore, the ability to blend two or more exposures together in digital imaging techniques, such as high-dynamic range photography, gets around the problem of how to contend with a scene that has a very high range of contrast between dark shadows and bright highlights. However, that is not to say that filters no longer have a place in a camera bag, as there are a few filter effects that you simply cannot achieve, or replicate post-exposure using a computer.

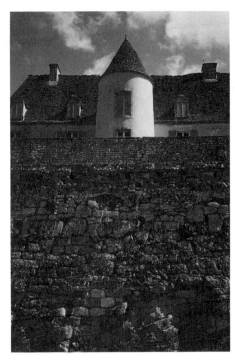

Polarizing filters are wonderful for travel photography. They create picture postcard skies with white billowy clouds, and improve color saturation throughout the scene.

One of the golden rules of filtration has always been to use a few as possible; this is even more applicable with digital cameras. The surface of the optical low-pass filter (OLPF) that is located in front of the camera's sensor is highly reflective, despite the anti-reflective coating that is applied to it, as a consequence some light that falls on the OPLF is bounced back into the lens and in turn can be reflected back down the lens; the risk of this occurring is particularly high if this reflected light encounters a flat optical surface, such as the rear surface of a filter, lens element (the coating applied to the rear element of newer Nikkor lens has been designed to help reduce this risk). The result of internal lens reflections is a lowering of image contrast and potential for flare effects. The good news for the digital photographer is you do not need that many filters; I would recommend that you consider just the three types, using them only when necessary:

Polarizing Filter

The most useful, and probably well-known filter is a polarizer. Often associated with their ability to deepen the color of a blue sky, a polarizer has many other uses. The unique effect of this filter type is one that makes it essential for digital photography; for example, it can remove reflections from non-metallic surfaces, including water, so the polarizer is a favorite with landscape photographers. Even on a dull, over cast day a polarizer can help reduce the glare from foliage, caused by the reflection of the sky, thereby intensifying its color.

Note: The automatic focusing and TTL metering systems of the D60 will not function properly if you use a linear-type polarizing filter; ensure you use a circular-type polarizer, such as the Nikon Circular Polarizer II (these also have the benefit of having a very slim filter mounting ring thus reducing the risk of vignetting).

Neutral Density Filters

At the base sensitivity of the D60 (ISO100) it is often not possible to set a lens aperture, or shutter speed to achieve the required results when shooting, especially in bright light conditions. Continuous tone neutral density (ND) filters help to reduce the overall exposure by lowering the amount of light that reaches the camera's sensor, so you can use longer shutter speeds and/or wider apertures under these conditions.

Note: Some manufacturers now manufacture ND filters that have a restricted transmission to eliminate IR and UV light that might otherwise adversely affect the images recorded by digital cameras.

Graduated Neutral Density Filters

Coping with the high contrast is one of the most difficult aspects of digital photography. For example the sky is often much brighter than the land, even at each end of the day, which can make shooting tricky. If you set the exposure in order to record the darker portion of the scene the lighter portion is often to bright to be recorded properly and ends up being overexposed.

No doubt someone will point out that another A popular way to solve this exposure problem is to make two, or more exposures of the same scene, shooting over a range of different exposure levels and then combining the series of pictures into a single image using a high-dynamic range software tool. For scenes that contain no moving elements this can be highly effective and produces a unique look to the shot. However, if an element in the scene moves between successive exposures the software is unlikely to be able to merge the all the separate images and the technique will fail!

The solution in such situations is to use a graduated neutral density filter; these are clear on one side and become progressively denser toward the other side, and are available in a variety of strengths and rates of change. If you use a slot-in type of filter system is easy to align these graduated filters, so their dense area darkens the bright area of the scene leaving the clear portion over the darker area, which is unaffected.

Hint: Nikon states that the 3D Color Matrix and Matrix metering of the D60 is not recommended when using for any filter with a filter factor over 1x. The filter factor is the amount of exposure compensation you need to apply to compensate for the reduction in light transmission caused by the filter. For example a filter factor of 2x is equivalent to one-stop, a factor of 8x is equivalent to three-stops. So this will apply to polarizing and neutral density filters - in these situations switch to center-weighted or spot metering.

Note: Nikon does not produce continuous (production has been discontinued), or graduated neutral density filters but many independent companies do – see the listings under Resources on page 288.

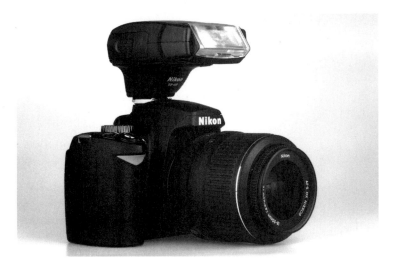

The Nikon D60 with AF-S DX VR 18-55mm f/3.5-5.6G and SB-400 Speedlight.

General Nikon Accessories

- **BF-1A** – body cap that will help prevent dust from entering the camera. Keep it in place at all times when a lens is not mounted on the camera.

Note: The earlier BF-1 type body cap cannot be used. It may damage the lens mount and electrical contacts around the lens mount of the D60; the designation of the body cap is stamped on its inside surface.

- **DG-2** – Viewfinder eyepiece magnifier provides an approximate 2x magnification of the central area of the viewfinder field. The DK-22 eyepiece adapter is required to enable the DG-2 to be fitted to the D60.

- **DK-3** – Circular rubber eyecup for the Nikon FM/FE-series cameras that can be attached via the square-to-circular DK-22 viewfinder eyepiece adapter, it also requires a viewfinder eyepiece filter for the FM3/FE-series camera to hold it in place. The circular eyecup provides a better light seal when held to the photographer's eye orbit than the DK-20 square eyecup fitted as standard to the D60.

- **DK-5** – Cover cap for the viewfinder eyepiece; it is essential to use when the D60 is operated remotely in automatic exposure modes, to prevent light entering the viewfinder and affecting exposure measurement.

- DK-20 – Standard square profile rubber eyecup supplied with the D60.

- DK-22 – A viewfinder eyepiece adapter that allows viewfinder accessories with a round attachment thread, such as the DG-2, to be mounted on the square frame of the viewfinder eyepiece on the D60

- DR-6 – Right angle viewer that can attach directly to the square frame of the D60 viewfinder eyepiece. It is useful when the camera is at a low shooting position, but is disproportionately expensive compared with the D60 camera!

- EH-5 / EH5a – Multi-voltage AC adapter for powering the D60; it is ideal for extended periods of shooting (requires the EP-5 DC power connector).

- EN-EL9 – 7.4V, 1000mAh, lithium-ion rechargeable battery for the D60, which at the time of writing is exclusive to this camera model (one battery is supplied with the camera).

- EP-5 – DC power connector that enables the D60 to be connected to an EH-5/EH-5a AC adapter to power the camera.

- MH-23 – Multi-voltage AC charger for a single EN-EL9 battery (supplied with the camera).

- ML-L3 Remote Control – Wireless infrared remote release for the D60. It requires one CR2025 (3V) battery.

- SB-400 – External Speedlight (flash unit) for D60; can be attached to camera's accessory shoe, or via SC-28/SC-29 TTL flash cord.

- SB-600 – External Speedlight (flash unit) for D60; can be attached to camera's accessory shoe, or via SC-28/SC-29 TTL flash cord.

- SB-800 – External Speedlight (flash unit) for D60; can be attached to camera's accessory shoe, or via SC-28/SC-29 TTL flash cord.

- SB-R200 – External Speedlight (flash unit) for D60 intended for close-up and macro photography; it cannot be attached to camera's accessory shoe, it requires use of the optional SU-800 Speedlight Commander unit to operate with the D60.

- SC-28 – TTL flash cord that maintains full functionality of compatible external Speedlight with the D60.

- SC-29 – TTL flash cord that maintains full functionality of compatible external Speedlight with the D60. The terminal unit that attaches to the camera has a built-in AF-assist lamp.

Resources

A number of other manufacturers and suppliers provide equipment to compliment and enhance the performance of the cameras and flash accessories produced by Nikon. The following is a list of some of a few you may find useful:

Gitzo – manufacturers of tripods, monopods, and general camera support accessories
http://www.gitzo.com/

HDRsoft – authors of the popular Photomatix high-dynamic range software
http://www.hdrsoft.com/

Kirk Enterprises – manufacturers of camera and flash accessories, including flash brackets
http://www.kirkphoto.com/

Lastolite – manufacturers of lighting accessories for portable flash units, and a wide range of reflectors, diffusers and other light modifying devices.
http://www.lastolite.com/

Lee Filters – manufacturers of both lens and lighting filters, including graduated filter types.
http://www.leefilters.com/

Lexar Media – manufacturers of Secure Digital (SD) flash memory cards compatible with the D60.
http://www.lexar.com/

Manfrotto – manufacturers of tripods, lighting stands and flash support accessories
http://www.manfrotto.com

Really Right Stuff – manufacturers of an extensive range of camera, flash, close-up, and panoramic photography accessories
http://www.reallyrightstuff.com/

SanDisk – manufacturers of Secure Digital (SD) flash memory cards compatible with the D60.
http://www.sandisk.com/

Singh-Ray – manufacturers of camera lens filters, including graduated filter types.
http://www.singh-ray.com/

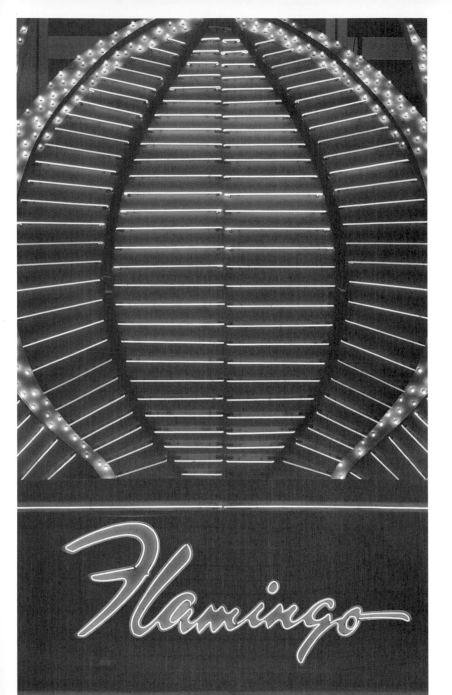

Working Digitally

Workflow

Shooting digitally instead of with film brings new aspects to your photography and provides a high level of user control, especially in processing and enhancing your image files. It is essential to develop a system to make sure you work in an efficient and effective way. The following 7-point workflow is a general guide to establishing a productive routine.

1. Preparation

- Familiarize your self with the camera. The more intuitive you become with your equipment, the more time you can spend concentrating on the scene/subject being photographed.
- Make sure the camera battery is charged and always carry a spare.
- Rather than save all your pictures to a single high capacity memory card, reduce the chance of a catastrophic loss due to card failure/loss by spreading the risk over several memory cards.
- Use the Clean Image Sensor function in the Set up menu of the D60 to clean the low-pass filter each time the camera is switched on. This will help reduce the amount of post-processing work necessary to remove the effects of dust on the filter's surface.
- Always format the memory card in the camera in which it will be used each time you insert a card.

Digital photography offers many clear advantages over film photography. One of the biggest is the ability to see the picture immediately so that you can make sure you got the shot.

2. Shooting

- Adjust camera settings to match the requirements of your shoot; choose an appropriate image quality, size, ISO, color space, and white balance.
- Set other camera controls such as metering and auto focus according to the shooting conditions.
- Use the Image Comment feature (see Setup menu) to assign a note about the authorship/copyright of the images you shoot.
- Review images and make any adjustments you deem necessary. The histogram display is extremely useful for checking on exposure values.
- Do not be in too much of a hurry to delete pictures unless they are obvious failures. It is often better to edit after shooting rather than "on the fly."

3. Transfer

- Before transferring images to your computer, designate a specific folder, or folders, in which the images will be stored so you know where to find them.
- Use a card reader rather than connecting the camera directly to the computer. It is much faster, more reliable, and reduces wear and tear on the camera.
- If your browser application permits you to assign general information to the image files during transfer (e.g. using appropriate fields in the XMP / IPTC) metadata) make sure you complete appropriate fields for image authorship and copyright.
- Consider renaming files, assigning further information, and adding key words to facilitate searching for images at a later date.

4. Edit and file

- Use a browsing application to sort through your pictures. Again, do not be in a hurry to edit out pictures. It is often best to take a second look at images a few days or even weeks after they were shot, as your opinions about images will often change.
- Print a contact sheet of small thumbnail images to help you decide which images to retain.

5. Processing

- Make copies of RAW files and save them to a working file format such as TIFF, or PSD (Adobe Photoshop).
- Do not use the JPEG format for post-processing.
- Make adjustments in an orderly and logical sequence, starting with overall brightness, contrast, and color. Then make more local adjustments to correct problems, or enhance the image.
- Save your adjusted file as a master copy to which you can then apply a crop, resizing, un-sharp mask, and any other finishing touches appropriate to your output requirements.

6. Archive

- Data can become lost or corrupted at any time for a variety of reasons so always make multiple back-up copies of your original files and the edited master copies.
- CD's have a limited capacity, so consider DVDs, or an external hard disk drive. No electronic storage medium is guaranteed 100% safe, nor does it have an infinite lifespan, so always check your back-up copies regularly and repeat the back-up process as required.

7. Display

- We shoot pictures for others to see and enjoy. Digital technology has expanded the possibilities of image display considerably; we can e-mail pictures to family, friends, colleagues, and clients; prepare digital "slideshows;" or post images to a web site for pleasure or profit.
- Home printing in full color is now reliable, cost effective, and above all, achievable. Spend some time to set up your system properly and work methodically; calibrate your monitor and printer, use an appropriate resolution for the print size you require, and choose paper type and finish accordingly.
- Once you have a high-quality print, be sure to present it in a manner befitting its status: Frame it or mount it securely. This will also help to protect it from the effects of light and atmospheric pollutants.

Using Memory Cards

Nikon has tested and approved only the memory cards listed in the table below for use with the D60. All cards from each manufacturer and of the designated capacity can be used regardless of the card speed; multi media cards (MMC) are not recommended and should not be used.

Nikon Approved Memory Cards For D60

Manufacturer	Capacity
Lexar	128MB, 256MB, 512MB and 1GB
	Platinum II series: 512MB, 1GB, 2GB [1], and 4GB [2]
	Professional (133x) series: 1GB and 2GB [1]
Panasonic	64 MB, 128MB, 256MB, 512 MB, 1GB, 2GB [1], 4Gb [2], and 8GB [2]
SanDisk	64 MB, 128MB, 256MB, 512MB, 1GB, 2GB [1], and 4GB [2]
Toshiba	64 MB, 128MB, 256MB, 512MB, 1GB, 2GB [1], and 4GB [2]

1   *If you use a memory card with a capacity of 2GB or more, ensure that your card reader or image storage device supports 2GB memory cards.*

2   *Make sure that the card reader or other storage device used with a memory card that has a capacity of 4GB or more supports the SDHC standard.*

While other brands and capacities of cards may work, Nikon will not guarantee their operation. If you intend to use a memory card not approved by Nikon, it is advisable to check with the manufacturer in respect of its compatibility. Should you experience any problems related to the memory card, use one of the approved cards for the purposes of trouble-shooting.

Memory Card Capacity

The table below provides information on the approximate number of images that can be stored on a 1GB memory card at the various image quality, and size settings available on the D60. All memory cards use a small proportion of their memory capacity to store data required for the card to operate, therefore the amount of memory available for storing image files will be slightly less than the quoted maximum capacity of the card.

Quality	Image Size	File Size [1]	No. Images [1]	Buffer Capacity [1,2]
NEF (RAW)	-	9.0	79	6
NEF (RAW) + JPEG Basic[3]	- / L	10.1 [4]	70	6
JPEG Fine	L	4.8	129	100
	M	2.7	225	100
	S	1.2	487	100
JPEG Normal	L	2.4	251	100
	M	1.3	431	100
	S	0.6	888	100
JPEG Basic	L	1.2	487	100
	M	0.7	839	100
	S	0.3	1500	100

1 *File size will vary according to the scene photographed, and the make of memory card used. Therefore, all figures are approximate.*
2 *This is the maximum number of image files that can be stored in the buffer memory. The number of images that can be stored before the buffer memory reaches capacity may vary with different makes of memory card. Capacity will be reduced if noise reduction is active.*
3 *Image size applies to JPEG file only; size of NEF file cannot be altered.*
4 *File size is the combined total for NEF and JEPG image files.*

Image Information

You may be surprised to learn that apart from image data the picture files generated by the D60 contain a wealth of other information that includes amongst other things, the shooting parameters and instructions about printing pictures. This information is tagged to the image file using a number of common standards depending on the sort of information to be saved with the image file.

Supported standards:

DCF (v 2.0): Design Rule for Camera File System (DCF) is a standard used widely in the digital imaging industry to ensure compatibility across different makes of camera.

DPOF: Digital Print Order Format (DPOF) is a standard used widely to enable pictures to be printed from print order created and saved on a memory card (see page 303).

EXIF (v 2.21): The D60 supports Exchangeable Image File Format for Digital Still cameras (EXIF); this standard allows information stored with image files to be read by software, and used for ensuring image quality when printed on an EXIF-compliant printer.

PictBridge: A standard that permits an image file stored on a memory card to be output directly to a printer without the need to connect the camera to a computer, or download the image file from a memory card to a computer first (see page 303).

Metadata

Metadata is any data that helps to describe the content or characteristics of a file. You may be familiar with viewing and perhaps adding some basic metadata through the File Info or Document Properties box found in many software applications and some operating systems. You may also use a digital image management application that can search some file properties and displays them for you.

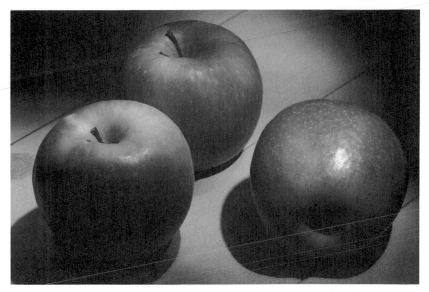

Nikon software supports the Digital Print Order Format (DPOF) standard used by many printers and photo finishers.

Exchangeable Image File Format (EXIF)

The D60 uses the EXIF (2.21) standard to tag additional information to each image file it records. Most popular digital imaging software is able to read and interpret the EXIF tags, so the information can be displayed but other software is not as capable, in which case some, or all of the EXIF data values may not be available. The information recorded includes:

- Nikon (the name of the camera manufacturer)

- D60 (the model number)

- Camera firmware version number

- Exposure information, including shutter speed, aperture, exposure mode, ISO, EV value, date/time, exposure compensation, flash mode, and focal length.

- Thumbnail of the main image

Examining EXIF data by either viewing the image information pages on the camera's monitor screen, or accessing the shooting data in appropriate software is a great teaching aid as you can see exactly what the camera settings were for each shot. By comparing pictures and the shooting data you can quickly learn about the technical aspects of exposure, focusing, metering and flash exposure control. Remember you can view some of this information using the Photo Information pages by pressing ⊚ up or down.

International Press Telecommunications Council (IPTC)

Other metadata (information) that can be tagged to an image file includes the use of a standard developed by the International Press Telecommunications Council (IPTC). Known as Digital Newsphoto Parameter Record (DNPR), it can append information including details of the origin, authorship, copyright, caption details, and key words for searching purposes, of images. Any application that is DNPR compliant will show this information and allow you to edit it. If you are considering submitting any pictures you shoot with the D60 for publication you should make use of DNPR (IPTC) metadata, as most publishing organizations require it to be present before accepting a submission.

Extensible Metadata Platform (XMP)

Adobe's Extensible Metadata Platform (XMP) is an open standard, digital labeling technology that allows metadata to be embedded into an image file. Any XMP-enabled software application, allows descriptions and titles, searchable keywords, plus author and copyright information to be stored in a format that is easily understood by other software applications, hardware devices, and even file formats. Since, XMP is extensible it can accommodate existing metadata schemes.

Note: Nikon Transfer, Nikon View NX and Nikon Capture NX all support the EXIF, IPTC, and XMP standards

Camera Connections

The Nikon D60 provides ports that facillitate connecting the camera directly to monitors, computers, and other devices. These are located on the left side of the camera.

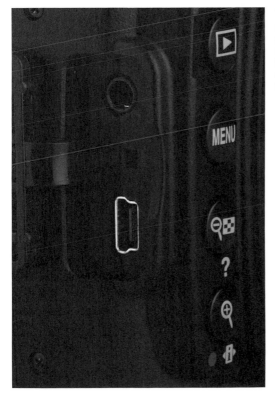

The D60 has connectors for video (top) and USB (bottom) beneath the rubber cover on the left side of the camera.

Connecting to a TV

The D60 can be connected to a television set or DVR/VCR for playback or recording of images. First, you need to obtain a Nikon EG-D100 video cable, as this accessory is not supplied with the D60.

To select the appropriate video standard open the Setup menu ☑ and navigate to the Video Mode item, then press the multi selector to the right and highlight the required option: NTSC (used in USA, Canada, and Japan) or PAL (most other countries), and press the multi selector to the right again, or press the ⏺ button, to confirm your selection.

Before connecting the camera to the video cord, make sure the camera power is switched off. Open the rubber cover on the left side of the camera body to reveal the ports for Video out (top), and USB (bottom). Connect the narrow jack-pin of the EG-D100 to the camera and the other end to the (yellow) video terminal of the TV/video player. Tune the TV to the video channel, and turn on the camera. Press the ⏺ button to start playback; the image that would normally be displayed on the LCD monitor will be shown on the television screen or can be recorded on a video recording device.

Note: The LCD monitor will remain blank but all other camera operations will function normally. So, you can take pictures with the camera connected to a TV set and carry out review/playback functions as you would on the LCD monitor. If you intend to use the camera for an extended period for image playback via a TV or DVR/VCR, it is probably best to use the EH-5 / EH-5a AC adapter with the EP-5 power connector to power the camera.

Connecting to a Computer

The D60 can be connected directly to a computer via the supplied UC-E4 USB cable. The camera supports the High-speed USB (2.0) interface that offers a maximum transfer rate of 480Mbps. You can download images from the camera using the supplied Nikon Transfer software, or alternatively, the D60 can be controlled from a computer and download pictures using the optional Nikon Camera Control Pro 2 software. Before connecting the D60 to a computer, for the purpose of downloading any pictures ensure that the supplied Nikon Transfer software has been installed on the computer.

Compatible Operating Systems:

• The Nikon D60 is compatible for direct connection to a computer provided it is running one of the following operating systems.

• Windows Vista (32-bit Home Basic, Home Premium, Business, Enterprise, or Ultimate editions).

• Windows XP Service Pack 2 (Home Edition, or Professional).

• Macintosh OS X (10.3.9, or 10.4.10).

Note: If the computer is running Windows 2000 Professional, it will be necessary to use a card reader or similar device to download pictures from a memory card used in the D60; the camera cannot be connected directly to a computer running this operating system.

Start the computer and ensure the camera is switched off. Open the rubber cover on the left side of the camera body to reveal the ports for Video out (top), and USB (bottom). With the camera turned off, connect the mini-USB plug of the UC-E4 USB cable to the USB port of the camera, and the other end of the cable to a USB port on a computer. Turn the camera on.

What happens next will depend on the operating system used by the computer:

- **Windows Vista:** When the AutoPlay dialog box is displayed, select "Copy pictures to a folder on my computer using Nikon Transfer". Nikon Transfer will start. To bypass this dialog in the future, put a check mark in the "Always do this for this device" selection box.

- **Windows XP:** When the AutoPlay dialog box is displayed, select "Nikon Transfer Copy pictures to a folder on my computer" and click OK. Nikon Transfer will start. To bypass this dialog in the future, put a check mark in the "Always use this program for this action" selection box.

- **Mac OS X:** Nikon Transfer will start automatically id Yes is selected in the Auto-launch setting dialog box when Nikon Transfer was first installed. You can always select this option by opening Nikon Transfer and clicking on the Preferences tab.

Using the preferences options in Nikon Transfer it possible to configure the application to close automatically once transfer is complete and automatically launch Nikon View NX (for more information on using Nikon Transfer click on Nikon Transfer help). Once transfer is complete turn the camera off and disconnect the USB cable, making sure you do not pull out the connectors at an angle.

Note: Nikon recommends that you do not use a USB hub to connect the D60 to a computer, as the camera may not be recognized.

Hint: If you use the D60 tethered via a USB cable to a computer for any function, be sure that the EN-EL9 battery is fully charged. Preferably, use the EH-5 / EH-5a AC adapter with the EP-5 power connector to prevent interruptions to data transfer by loss of power.

Card Readers

Although the D60 can be tethered directly to a computer via a USB cord for transferring image data, there are several reasons why you should consider using a memory card reader as an alternative:

• The connected camera drains battery power and lost or corrupted data may occur if the power fails.

• Data transfer from the memory card to the computer will usually be far faster using a card reader.

• A card reader allows you to run software to recover lost or corrupted image files while the card is mounted in the reader, as well as to diagnose problems with the memory card.

• You can leave a card reader permanently attached to your computer, which further reduces the risk of losing or corrupting files as a result of a poor connection due to the wear and tear caused by constantly connecting the camera.

Direct Printing

You can print individual pictures or a group of images directly from your D60 via a USB connection without the aid of a computer. However, this feature is only compatible with JPEG format image files, and a printer that supports the PictBridge standard.

Note: Direct printing from the D60 is only supported for JPEG files. Nikon recommends images destined for direct printing should be recorded in the sRGB color space. In P, A, S, and M exposure modes set the Color Mode in the Custom option of Optimize image in the Shooting menu to either Mode Ia (sRGB) or IIIa (sRGB). In and Digital Vari-progam modes pictures are always recorded in the sRGB color space.

Linking the D60 with a Printer

The D60 can be connected to a PictBridge compatible printer (PictBridge is an industry wide standard adopted by printer manufacturers) to print pictures directly from the memory card installed in the camera. First, turn the printer on and ensure the camera is switched off, and then connect the printer to the camera via the supplied UC-E4 USB lead. Nikon does not recommend connecting via a USB hub.

Note: It is essential that the camera battery is fully charged before starting direct printing from the camera to ensure no disruption to data transfer between the camera and printer should the battery become exhausted; preferably use the EH-5 / EH-5a AC adapter with the EP-5 power connector.

Turn the camera on and the PictBridge logo is shown briefly, followed by the PictBridge playback display on the camera's monitor screen. You can choose to print pictures one-at-time, or in multiples.

To scroll through the images saved on the memory card, press the multi selector to left or right. To view up to six images at a time press ⊞ . Use the multi selector to select a photograph (a yellow frame bounds the highlighted image) and press the 🔍 button to display the selected photograph full frame. Press the ⊞ button to return to the multiple image display. To show an enlarged section of the displayed image, press the 🔍 button. To return to the normal full frame or multiple image display press the ⊞ button.

Printing Pictures One At A Time

To print the image selected in the PictBridge playback display, press the 🆗 button. The PictBridge set up printing menu will be displayed. Use the multi selector to highlight the required option by pressing it up or down, and then press right to select it.

Option	Description
Page Size	Press the multi selector up or down to select the appropriate paper size from Printer Default item: 3.5 x 5in, 5 x 7in, (100 x 150 mm), 4 x 6 in, 8 x 10 in, (Letter, A3, or A4). Then press the ⊛ button to select and return to the print menu.
Number of Copies	Press the multi selector up or down to select the number of copies of the selected image that will be printed (maximum 99). Then press the ⊛ button to select and return to the print menu.
Border	Press the multi selector up or down to select Printer Default (uses default setting of current printer), Print with Border (prints picture with a white border but is only available if supported by printer in use), or No Border. Then press the ⊛ button to select and return to the print menu.
Time Stamp	Press the multi selector up or down to select Printer Default (uses default setting of current printer), Print Time Stamp (date and time image was recorded is printed in image area), or No Time Stamp. Then press the ⊛ button to select and return to the print menu.
Cropping	Press the multi selector up or down to select Crop (picture can be cropped in-camera), or No Crop (printed full frame). The press the ⊛ button to select and return to print menu. If Crop is selected the image is displayed with a frame border overlaid. Use the ⊛ , and ⊛ buttons to determine the size of the crop. To position the cropping frame use the multi select button. Then press the ⊛ button to select and return to print menu.

To print the image once you have selected the required options from the set up printing menu, highlight Start printing and press ⊛ ; the PictBridge playback display will be shown when printing is complete. Press the ⊙ button to cancel printing at anytime while it is in progress.

Note: If the date has been imprinted using the option available at CS-18 (Date imprint) select, No time stamp for Setup – Time stamp option in the Pictbridge set up printing menu to avoid the date being printed twice.

Note: If you select No border for the Border option in the Pictbridge set up printing menu, or depending on the setting selected for Cropping, the date imprinting may extend beyond the edge of the printing paper.

Printing Multiple Images

To print multiple images or an index print (contact sheet), press ⊙ button when the PictBridge playback display is shown on the monitor screen. A menu with three options will be presented:

- **Print Select** – The selected pictures are printed.

- **Print (DPOF)** – The current DPOF print order set is printed. See page 303 for more information.

- **Index Print** – Creates an index print of all pictures saved in the JPEG format.

Print Select

Press ⊙ button when the PictBridge playback display is shown on the monitor screen. Choose Print Select from the PictBridge menu; six thumbnail images will be displayed on the monitor screen. Use the multi selector to scroll through the images and press ⊙ to see the highlighted image full frame.

To select the highlighted image, press the multi selector up; the number of copies to be printed is set to one (each selected image will also be marked by a small icon of a printer). To specify the number of copies of each image for printing, press the multi selector up or down accordingly. To deselect a picture, press the multi selector down until "one" is displayed as the number of prints, and then press it left or right to highlight another picture. Repeat this process for each image to be printed. Display the print options and set page size, border type, and time stamp according to the instructions above for printing one picture at a time. To print selected images, highlight Start Printing and press the ⊛ button; the PictBridge playback display will appear when printing is complete. Press the ⊛ button to cancel printing at anytime.

Note: Images saved in the NEF RAW format will be displayed in the Print Selected menu, but cannot be printed.

Creating an Index Print
Press ⊛ button when the PictBridge playback display is shown on the monitor screen. Choose Index print from the PictBridge menu and press the multi selector to the right; six thumbnail images will be displayed on the monitor screen. Press ⊛ to display the PictBridge set up printing menu. Select and set the print options for set page size, border type, and time stamp according to the instructions above for printing one picture at a time; all pictures on the index print(s) will be printed at the same settings. Highlight Start printing and press the ⊛ button; the PictBridge playback display will appear when printing is complete. Press the ⊛ button to cancel printing at anytime.

Note: Index prints cannot be printed on some paper sizes; if the paper size is too small a warning message will be displayed.

Note: Up to a maximum of 256 pictures saved in the JPEG format can be printed; therefore if the memory card contains more than 256 JPEG format pictures some will not be printed.

Selecting Images For Direct Printing – DPOF

The D60 supports the Digital Print Order Format (DPOF) standard that embeds an instruction set in the appropriate EXIF data fields of an image file, which allows you to either print directly from the memory card installed in the camera, or to insert the memory card into any DPOF compatible home printer, or commercial mini-lab printer and automatically print a set of selected images. Obviously it is essential that the printer, or commercial mini-lab equipment support the DPOF standard.

To select images for printing, highlight the Print (DPOF) option from the playback menu ▶ and press the multi selector to the right. The Select/Set option will be highlighted; press the multi selector to the right to select it.

The camera will display a thumbnail of all the images stored on the inserted memory card, in groups of up to six pictures. Use the multi selector to scroll through the images; a yellow frame bounds the highlighted image. To view the highlighted image at a larger magnification, press and hold the 🔍 button.

To select the highlighted image for printing, press the multi selector up. A small icon of a printer and a number will appear in the upper right corner of the thumbnail image; the number of copies to be printed is set to one (the maximum is 99). To specify the number of copies of each image selected for printing, press the multi selector up to increase the number, and down to decrease the number. To deselect a picture from printing, press the multi selector down until one is displayed for the number of prints, and then press it left or right to highlight another picture. Repeat this process for of each image you require to be printed.
Once all images to be printed have been selected press the 🆗 button to save the selected group of images. A further two options are now displayed:

- **Data imprint** - to imprint shooting data (shutter speed and aperture setting) on all the pictures, highlight Data Imprint and press the multi selector to the right to place a check mark in the option box.

- **Imprint date** - to print the date/time of image recording on all the pictures in the print set, highlight Imprint Date and press the multi selector to the right to place a check mark in the option box.

Finally, to finish and save the print set order, highlight Done and press the ⊚ button.

To deselect an entire print set, select Print Set (DPOF) from the playback menu ▶ and highlight the Deselect All? option. Press the ⊚ button. A dialog box will appear with the following message "Marking removed from all images". The display will then return to the playback menu ▶ .

To print the DPOF print set using a PictBridge compatible printer connect the camera to the printer as described previously, and once the PictBridge playback display is shown on the monitor screen press the 🔘 button. Select Print (DPOF) and press the multi selector to the right. Then follow the steps for selecting and printing multiple pictures as described on page 306.

Note: The DPOF data and data imprint options are not supported when printing via a direct USB connection to a printer; to print the date of recording on a picture in the current DPOF print set use the PictBridge Time stamp option.

Note: If the date has been imprinted using the option available at CS-18 (Date imprint), select No time stamp for the Setup – Time stamp option in the Pictbridge set up printing menu to avoid the date being printed twice.

Note: The Print set option requires sufficient memory on the installed memory card to store the print order data as well as the image files, so the card must have spare capacity before creating a print order. These selections can only be made from JPEG format images stored on the memory card; if an image was shot using a NEF+JPEG option, only the JPEG image can be selected for printing.

Nikon Firmware

The initial firmware version for the D60 is version 1.0 (A and B), for Widows, including Vista 32-bit, and Mac OS X; however, Nikon may choose to release further updates whenever necessary. They are free for download from Nikon websites. I recommend you check the firmware version installed on your camera; open the Setup menu ⚒ and select the Firmware option then press the ⏺ button to display the firmware A & B versions. Compare these to the currently available versions, and update it if necessary. If you do not feel confident enough to do this for yourself, the update can be performed at any authorized Nikon service center.

Nikon Software

It is beyond the scope of this book to describe fully the features and functions of Nikon's dedicated software, fully; details can be obtained from the technical support sections of the Web sites maintained the Nikon Corporation. The following section is intended to provide a brief overview of the four Nikon applications in their current versions at the time of writing:

• Nikon Transfer: 1.1.0
• Nikon View NX: 1.1.0
• Nikon Capture NX: 2.0.0
• Nikon Camera Control Pro 2: 2.1.0

The D60 is supplied with copies of Nikon Transfer and Nikon View NX.

> **Note:** For information about Nikon software and to download updates to existing applications updates I recommend you visit the various technical support Web sites maintained by Nikon, which can be accessed via: http://www.nikon.com

Nikon Transfer

Nikon Transfer is Nikon's new utility for downloading images from camera or memory card to your computer. Nikon Transfer provides a simple intuitive workflow suitable for all users from beginners to professionals. Nikon Transfer is included with the latest Nikon cameras, such as the D60 and can also be downloaded fro free from Nikon web sites.

- Automatic recognition / auto start after camera connection or inserting CF/SD card.
- Transfer images from CD, external HD other removal media.
- Transfer images to computers hard drive.
- Easy selection and viewing of images on up to five external devices before transfer.
- Transfer image-data not only to a primary destination, but also to a backup location simultaneously.
- Add metadata during transfer, both XMP/IPTC standards are supported
- Select the application the images are displayed in after transfer.

Nikon View NX

View NX offers photographers a fast solution to the organization and classification of their digital images. This software uses the computer's file directory to display and browse images and incorporates the very latest features and design concepts of Capture NX. Nikon View NX is included with the latest Nikon D-SLR cameras, such as the D60 and can also be downloaded for free from Nikon web sites.

- High-speed thumbnail and preview display
- A simple way to choose images, operation similar to Explorer / Finder
- Fast sorting using image rating and labeling classification system
- Includes Picture Control Utility (including sharpening, contrast, saturation, hue, brightness, black and white conversion)
- Batch processing to convert file format, resize, rename, change settings, multiple destinations.
- Integration with Capture NX
- Integration with Nikon Transfer
- Printing and e-mail transmission
- IPTC/XMP data compatible (user settings retained when image opened in other supported applications)
- Quick Adjustment features for NEF (RAW) images including white balance, exposure, and creating custom curves

Nikon Capture NX

Capture NX represents a complete re-write by Nik Software, a wholly independent software company, of the original Nikon Capture application and incorporates their unique U-point technology that permits complex selections of an area(s) within an image to be made with an accuracy and speed that is far greater than can be achieved using current digital imaging software. The user has an extensive toolbox available to enhance and modify any image file regardless of whether it was saved in the NEF (RAW), TIFF, or JPEG format.

The intuitive Color Control Points allow you quickly select an entire image, or an area within it for enhancement to modify any aspect of a selected area including: Size, Hue, Brightness, Saturation, Contrast, Red, Green, Blue, and Warmth.

Black, White and Neutral Control Points can be used to set the dynamic range and correct color casts in your images. Neutral Control Points can also be used to set color balance in an image. Each Control Point appears on the image and can be easily dragged from point to point, for precise movement and positioning to achieve the desired effect. The Control Points' sliders let you adjust their effect for the respective Control Point areas. Neutral Control Points can be used to set a targeted color to any color available within the color picker. This is useful for removing colorcasts and toning, even without a neutral object in the scene. Use of multiple Neutral Control Points helps reduce multiple colorcasts and enhance selected colors in images. The drag, point and slider control is very easy to use, and very efficient.

Capture NX applies non-destructive image processing to NEF RAW files, which means that the original image data is never compromised. Each enhancement that is made is saved in an edit list with the original data and thumbnail. However, changes made to a JPEG or TIFF files will alter the data of the original image. To avoid this from occurring the image can be saved using a different file name, or converted into Nikon's NEF format.

Parameters set on any Nikon camera-produced NEF RAW file, such as white balance, sharpening, color mode, saturation are applied to the image when it is opened in Nikon Capture NX for editing, so the camera settings are preserved.

For a comprehensive set of hints and instructions on using Nikon Capture NX, together with some useful video tutorials go to: www.nikoncapturenx.com

Other key features of Nikon Capture NX:

- Advanced white balance control with the ability to select a specific color temperature, or sample from a gray point.

- Advanced NEF file control that permits attributes such as exposure compensation, sharpening, contrast, color mode, saturation, and hue to be modified after the exposure has been made, without affecting the original image data.

- The Image Dust Off feature, which compares an NEF file with a reference image taken with the same camera to help reduce the effects of any dust particles on the low-pass filter

- The D-Lighting tool, which emulates the dodge & burn techniques of traditional photographic printing to control highlight and shadow areas to produce a more balanced exposure

- A Color Noise Reduction tool, which minimizes the effect of random electronic noise that can occur, especially at high sensitivity settings

- An Edge Noise Reduction tool that accentuates the boundary between areas of the image to make them more distinct

- The Color Moiré Reduction feature helps to remove the effects of moiré, which can occur when an image contains areas with a very fine repeating pattern

- LCH Editor allows for control of Luminosity (overall lightness), Chroma (color saturation), and Hue in separate channels

- Fisheye Lens tool converts images taken with the AF Fisheye-Nikkor DX 10.5mm f/2.8G lens so they appear as though they were taken using a conventional rectilinear lens with a diagonal angle-of-view equivalent to approximately 120-degrees.

Camera Control Pro 2

Camera Control Pro 2 enables remote control of most functions of the D60 from a computer that is connected via USB cable. The Viewer feature in the application enables the preview and selection of images prior to transfer to a computer. It also integrates with Nikon View NX and Nikon Capture NX software.

- Key Features of Camera Control Pro 2:

- Most settings of the D60 camera, such as exposure mode, shutter speed and aperture can be controlled remotely

- Images in a camera buffer can be confirmed with thumbnail, or preview display on a computer prior to transferring, enabling deletion of unwanted images.

- Supports Picture Control System of the cameras. Picture Control parameters can be selected and adjusted on a computer, and custom curves (to modify contrast) can be created and saved.

- 3-point AF system can be controlled and displayed on a computer monitor

- Fine-tuning of white balance is available.

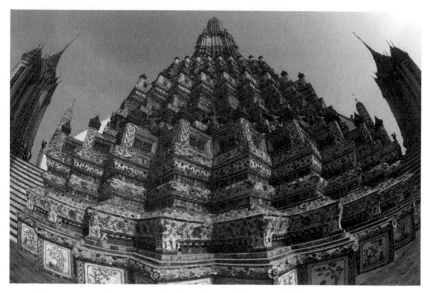

If you encounter an operation issue with your D60, refer to the fol-lowing pages to solve the problem.

Troubleshooting

On occasion your D60 may not operate as you expect. This could be due to an alternative setting(s) having been made (often inadvertently), or for some other reason. Many of the causes for these problems are common and the solutions are listed in the table on the next few pages:

Problem	Solution
All Shooting Modes	
Camera takes longer than expected to turn on	Delete files / folders
Shutter release will not operate	• CPU lens with aperture ring not set to minimum (highest f/number) value • Memory card not installed or full • Flash charging • Focus not acquired • Non-CPU lens attached: rotate mode dial to M
Final pictures shows more than viewfinder	Viewfinder coverage is limited to approx. 95% of full frame area
Image in viewfinder out of focus	• Camera unable to perform auto focus: use manual focus • Lens is not AF-S or AF-I: use manual focus • Manual focus selected: set auto-focus with AF-S and AF-I lenses; manual focus with all other types of Nikkor lens
Menu item not displayed	Select Full for CSM / Setup menu
Image size cannot be altered	RAW or RAW+B selected for image quality
Unable to select focus area	• Closest-subject selected for AF-area mode • Camera in stand-by: press shutter release halfway to activate camera
Camera is slow to record picture	• Turn off noise reduction • Turn off Active D-Lighting
Random bright pixels appear in image	• Use lower ISO setting • Use High ISO noise reduction • Shutter speed exceeds 1 second; use long exposure noise reduction
AF-assist lamp does not light	• Camera in M, or AF-C focus mode • Center focus point is not selected: select center focus point • Mode dial set to 🏞 , or 🏃 : select an alternative exposure mode • Select [On] at CS-9 (AF-assist) • Lamp has shut down automatically to cool down

Problem	Solution
No picture taken when release button of ML-L3 remote release is pressed	• Replace battery in ML-L3 • Select remote control mode • Flash is charging • Time selected for remote delay (CS-17) has elapsed; reset delay • Bright light is interfering with remote signal
Dark spots / blotches appear in pictures	• Dirt on lens • Dirt on low-pass filter
Menu item cannot be selected	Turn mode dial to another setting, or insert memory card, or ensure lens set to auto focus (AF-S / AF-I only)
Date cannot be imprinted	Date imprint disabled when image quality is set to RAW or RAW + B

In P, S, A, and M exposure modes

Shutter release will not operate	• Focus not acquired in AF-S (single-servo) AF • Non-CPU lens attached: rotate mode dial to M • Mode dial rotated to S after selecting **bu L b** in M exposure mode
Areas with a red tint appear in pictures	Long time exposure used; turn on long exposure noise reduction in Shooting menu when shooting at shutter speeds of (**bu L b** or "time".
Range of shutter speeds is limited	Flash in use – sync speed imposed
Focus does not lock when shutter release is depressed halfway	• Camera in AF-C focus mode: use AF-L/AE-L button • AF-A mode used to photograph a moving subject: use AF-L/AE-L button
Colors appear unnatural	• Adjust white balance to match light source. • Adjust [Optimize Image] settings
Unable to obtain WB measurement in Preset WB	Illumination of test target too dark or too bright
Source image cannot be selected for setting WB	Image not created with D60

Problem	Solution
Results with Optimize Image vary from image to image	Use [Custom] setting. Avoid Auto for Sharpening, Tone Compensation, and Saturation options
Metering cannot be changed	Auto-exposure lock active
Continuous shooting mode unavailable	Continuous shooting not available when built-in flash unit is in use
Playback	
NEF RAW image is not played back	Image quality set to NEF RAW + JEPG
Not all images displayed in Playback mode.	Select [All] for [Playback Folder]; note [Current] will be selected automatically when next picture is taken
Single image review selected: • Flashing area appears on image • Shooting data appears on image • Graph (histogram) appears on image	Press multi selector button up or down to scroll through photo information pages
Pictures shots in upright orientation (tall) displayed in horizontal (wide) orientation	• Select [ON] for [Rotate Tall] • [OFF] selected for [Auto Image Rotation] • Camera orientation was altered whilst shooting in continuous mode • Camera was pointed up / down when shooting
Unable to delete image	Image protection set; remove protection
Message displayed stating no images available in Playback mode.	Select [All] for [Playback Folder]; note [Current] will be selected automatically when next picture is taken
Image not displayed after picture is taken	Select On for Image Review in Custom Settings menu
Cannot retouch image	• Some retouch options cannot be applied to copies • Image created or modified with another device
Cannot change print order	Memory card is full: delete images

Problem	Solution
Unable to select image for direct printing	• Image saved as NEF (RAW) format file. Create a JPEG-format copy using Quick Retouch or NEF (RAW) processing in the ☑ menu • Transfer to a computer and print via Nikon View NX or Capture NX
Unable to display image on TV	Select correct video mode
Unable to transfer images to computer	D60 cannot be connected to a computer running Windows 2000 Professional
Unable to use Capture NX	Update software to latest version
Unable to use Camera Control Pro 2	Update software to latest version
Others	
Date of recording is incorrect	Set time and date
Cannot select menu item	Some menu items are not available depending on selected camera settings
Menu item is not displayed	Select Full for CSM/Setup menu
Displays turn off unexpectedly	Set longer delay for monitor off / meter off
Viewfinder appears out of focus	• Adjust viewfinder focus • Use diopter adjustment lens
Viewfinder display is unresponsive and dim	Response time and brightness of viewfinder display can be affected by high or low temperature

Error Messages and Displays

The D60 is capable of reporting a range of malfunctions and problems by way of indicators and error messages that appear in the viewfinder and LCD monitor. The following table will assist you in finding a solution should one of these indicators or messages be displayed.

Viewfinder	Message	Solution
FE E	Lock lens aperture ring at minimum aperture (largest f-number)	Lock ring at minimum aperture (largest f/number)
F- -/⊞ (blinks) F- -/⁴ (blinks)	Lens not attached Attach a lens	• Attach lens • Attached lens is not a CPU type lens: select M mode
⊏▭▬	Shutter release disabled Recharge battery	Turn camera off; recharge battery / replace with fully charged spare battery
⊏▬▬	This battery cannot be used. Choose battery designated for use in this camera	Insert Nikon EN-EL9 battery
⊏▬▬	Initialization error. Turn camera off and then on again	Turn camera off, remove and reinsert battery. Turn camera on again.
-	Battery level is low. Complete operation and turn camera off immediately	End the low-pass cleaning or inspection process and turn camera off immediately
⯗ (blinks)	Clock not set	Set camera clock from Setup menu
[- E -]	No SD card inserted	Insert appropriate SD memory card
⊏▬▬ (blinks)	-	Subject not in focus. Place focus brackets over subject and re-focus, or focus manually
[HR (blinks)	Memory card is locked. Slide lock to "write" position.	Slide memory card write protection switch to "write" position
[HR (blinks)	This memory card cannot be used. Card may be damaged. Insert another card	• Use Nikon approved card • Card may be damaged. Try reformatting. If error persists

Viewfinder	Message	Solution
		contact Nikon-authorized service center • If this message is displayed when creating a new folder, delete unwanted files. • Insert new memory card
[For] (blinks)	This card is not formatted. Format the card	Format memory card from the Setup menu
FuL (blinks)	Card is full	• Copy any images you want to keep from the card and/or delete unwanted images • Reduce image size and quality • Delete images and/or reset sequential file numbering then for format memory card • Insert new memory card
H i	Subject is too bright	• Choose lower ISO sensitivity • Increase shutter speed • Choose larger aperture (smaller f/ number) • Use neutral density (ND) filter
L o	Subject is too dark	• Choose higher ISO sensitivity • Use flash • Decrease shutter speed • Choose larger aperture (smaller f/ number)
ϟ (blinks)	-	Flash fired at full output. If picture is under

Viewfinder	Message	Solution
		exposed, try higher ISO, and/or larger aperture (lower f/ number), and/or move closer to subject
⚡/⏱ (blinks)	-	• Built-in flash lowered: raise flash • Try higher ISO, and/or larger aperture (lower f/ number), and/or move closer to subject • Flash head on SB-400 in bounce-flash position • SB-400 is unable to fully illuminate subject at current flash to subject distance (only displayed with SB-400)
⚡ (blinks)	Flash in TTL mode. Choose another setting or use a CPU lens	• Change flash control mode for optional Speedlight (CS-14) • Attach CPU lens
buL b (blinks) **- -** (blinks)	No bulb in S mode	Change shutter speed or select M mode.
no bd (blinks)	Unable to measure preset white balance. Please try again	Camera is unable to measure a value for preset white balance. Adjust exposure and try again
-	FOLDER CONTAINS NO IMAGES	• Insert another memory card • Set Playback folder to All
-	FILE DOES NOT CONTAIN IMAGE DATA	• Image files edited on a computer do not support DCF and cannot be played back

Viewfinder	Message	Solution
		• Image file is corrupted
-	CHECK PRINTER	Insert new ink or toner cartridge in printer. If error occurs with ink remaining in printer check printer settings
E r r (blinks)	Error. Press shutter release button again	Press shutter release button again if problem persists contact Nikon-- authorized service center.
E r r (blinks)	Initialization error. Contact Nikon-authorized service center.	Contact Nikon-author- ized service center

Electrostatic Interference

Operation of the D60 is totally dependent on electrical power. Occasionally, the camera may stop functioning properly, or display unusual characters or unexpected messages in the viewfinder and LCD display. Such behavior is generally due to the effects of a strong external electrostatic charge. If this occurs try switching the camera off, disconnecting it from its power supply (remove the EN-EL9 battery, or unplug the EH-5/ EH-5a AC adapter and EP-5 power connector), then reconnect the power, and switch the camera on again.

If this procedure fails to rectify the problem, turn the camera off, and open the rubber port cover on the left side of the camera. A small, square, recessed button is located between the video terminal and USB port; this is the reset switch. Press the reset switch but note that this resets the clock to its default time, so you will need to change the date/time settings appropriately. Should the symptoms persist the camera will require inspection by an authorized technician.

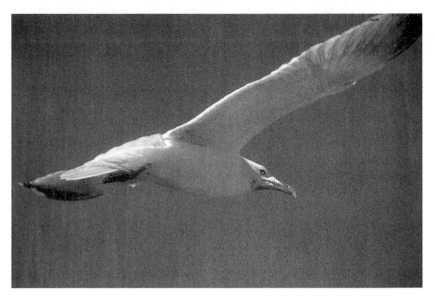

Nikon offers product support information on its corporate websites for various regions. For books on digital photo technique, go to www.larkbooks.com.

Web Support

Nikon offers product support information on-line at the following sites:

http://www.nikon.com–global gateway to Nikon Corporation
http://www.nikonusa.com–for continental North America
http://www.europe-nikon.com/support–for most European countries
http://www.nikon-asia.com–for Asia, Oceania, Middle East, and Africa

Glossary

AA
Auto aperture. Refers to a Nikon flash mode in which the flash level is automatically adjusted for aperture.

aberration
An optical flaw in a lens that causes the image to be distorted or unclear.

Active D-Lighting
A Nikon feature that detects high contrast before exposure and modifies the exposure levels to retain detail in highlights while preserving shadow and midtone values.

AF-D
AF Nikkor lenses that communicate the distance of the focused subject to a compatible camera body in order to improve the accuracy of exposure calculations for both ambient light and flash. (AF-G, AF-I, and AF-S lenses also perform this function.) AF-D lenses are focused by a motor mounted in the camera body.

AF-G
AF Nikkor lenses that lack a conventional aperture ring. They are only compatible with those cameras that permit the aperture to be set from the camera body.

AF-I
The first series of AF Nikkor lenses to have an internal focusing motor.

AF-S
AF Nikkor lenses that use a silent wave focusing motor mounted within the lens. The technology used in AF-S lenses permits faster and more responsive automatic focusing as compared to the AF-I and AF-D lenses.

AI
Automatic Indexing.

AI-S
Nikon F-mount lens bayonet for manual focus Nikkor lenses. They have a small notch milled out of the bayonet ring.

angle of view
The area seen by a lens, usually measured in degrees across the diagonal of the film frame.

anti-aliasing
A technique that reduces or eliminates the jagged appearance of lines or edges in an image.

aperture
The opening in the lens that allows light to enter the camera. Aperture is usually described as an f/number. The higher the f/number, the smaller the aperture; and the lower the f/number, the larger the aperture.

Aperture-priority mode
A type of automatic exposure in which you manually select the aperture and the camera automatically selects the shutter speed.

artifact
Information that is not part of the scene but appears in the image due to technology. Artifacts can occur in film or digital images and include increased grain, flare, static marks, color flaws, noise, etc.

artificial light
Usually refers to any light source that doesn't exist in nature, such as incandescent, fluorescent, and other manufactured lighting.

automatic exposure
When the camera measures light and makes the adjustments necessary to create proper image density on sensitized media.

automatic flash
An electronic flash unit that reads light reflected off a subject (from either a pre-flash or the actual flash exposure), then shuts itself off as soon as ample light has reached the sensitized medium.

automatic focus
When the camera automatically adjusts the lens elements to sharply render the subject.

available light
The amount of illumination at a given location that applies to natural and artificial light sources but not those supplied specifically for photography. It is also called existing light or ambient light.

backlight
Light that projects toward the camera from behind the subject.

bounce light
Light that reflects off of another surface before illuminating the subject.

bracketing
A sequence of pictures taken of the same subject but varying one or more exposure settings, manually or automatically, between each exposure.

brightness
A subjective measure of illumination. See also, luminance.

buffer
Temporarily stores data so that other programs, on the camera or the computer, can continue to run while data is in transition.

built-in flash
A flash that is permanently attached to the camera body. The built-in flash will pop up and fire in low-light situations

when using the camera's automated exposure settings.

built-in meter
A light measuring device that is incorporated into the camera body.

bulb
A camera setting that allows the shutter to stay open as long as the shutter release is depressed.

card reader
Device that connects to your computer and enables quick and easy download of images from memory card to computer.

CCD
Charge Coupled Device. This is a common digital camera sensor type that is sensitized by applying an electrical charge to the sensor prior to its exposure to light. It converts light energy into an electrical impulse.

chromatic aberration
Occurs when light rays of different colors are focused on different planes, causing colored halos around objects in the image.

close-up
A general term used to describe an image created by closely focusing on a subject. Often involves the use of special lenses or extension tubes. Also, an automated exposure setting that automatically selects a large aperture (not available with all cameras).

color cast
A colored hue over the image often caused by improper lighting or incorrect white balance settings. Can be produced intentionally for creative effect.

color space
A mapped relationship between colors and computer data about the colors.

contrast
The difference between two or more tones in terms of luminance, density, or darkness.

cropping
The process of extracting a portion of the image area. If this portion of the image is enlarged, resolution is subsequently lowered.

dedicated flash
An electronic flash unit that talks with the camera, communicating things such as flash illumination, lens focal length, subject distance, and sometimes flash status.

depth of field
The image space in front of and behind the plane of focus that appears acceptably sharp in the photograph.

diopter
A measurement of the refractive power of a lens. Also, it may be a supplementary lens that is defined by its focal length and power of magnification.

dpi
Dots per inch. Used to define the resolution of a printer, this term refers to the number of dots of ink that a printer can lay down in an inch.

DPOF
Digital Print Order Format. A feature that enables the camera to supply data about the printing order of image files and the supplementary data contained within them. This feature can only be used in conjunction with a DPOF compatible printer.

D-type Nikkor
A series of lenses that have a built-in CPU that is used to communicate the focus distance information to the camera body, improving the accuracy of exposure measurement.

DX
Nikkor lenses designed specifically for the Nikon DX format sensor.

electronic flash
A device with a glass or plastic tube filled with gas that, when electrified, creates an intense flash of light. Also called a strobe. Unlike a flash bulb, it is reusable.

electronic rangefinder
A system that utilizes the AF technology built into a camera to provide a visual confirmation that focus has been achieved. It can operate in either manual or AF focus modes.

EV
Exposure Value. A number that quantifies the amount of light within an scene, allowing you to determine the relative combinations of aperture and shutter speed to accurately reproduce the light levels of that exposure.

EXIF
Exchangeable Image File Format. This format is used for storing an image file's interchange information.

exposure
When light enters the camera and reacts with the sensitized medium. The term can also refer to the amount of light that strikes the light sensitive medium.

file format
The form in which digital images are stored and recorded, e.g., JPEG, RAW, TIFF, etc.

filter
Usually a piece of plastic or glass used to control how certain wavelengths of light are recorded. A filter absorbs selected wavelengths, preventing them from reaching the light sensitive medium. Also, software available in image-pro-

cessing computer programs can produce special filter effects.

FireWire

A high speed data transfer standard that allows outlying accessories to be plugged and unplugged from the computer while it is turned on. Some digital cameras and card readers use FireWire to connect to the computer. FireWire transfers data faster than USB. *See also, Mbps.*

firmware

Software that is permanently incorporated into a hardware chip. All computer-based equipment, including digital cameras, use firmware of some kind.

focal length

When the lens is focused on infinity, it is the distance from the optical center of the lens to the focal plane.

focal plane

The plane on which a lens forms a sharp image. Also, it may be the film plane or sensor plane.

focus

An optimum sharpness or image clarity that occurs when a lens creates a sharp image by converging light rays to specific points at the focal plane. The word also refers to the act of adjusting the lens to achieve optimal image sharpness.

f/stop

The size of the aperture or diaphragm opening of a lens, also referred to as f/number or stop. The term stands for the ratio of the focal length (f) of the lens to the width of its aperture opening. (f/1.4 = wide opening and f/22 = narrow opening.) Each stop up (lower f/number) doubles the amount of light reaching the sensitized medium. Each stop down (higher f/number) halves the amount of light reaching the sensitized medium.

full-frame

The maximum area covered by the sensitized medium.

full-sized sensor

A sensor in a digital camera that has the same dimensions as a 35mm film frame (24 x 36 mm).

gigabyte

Just over one billion bytes.

gray card

A card used to take accurate exposure readings. It typically has a white side that reflects 90% of the light and a gray side that reflects 18%.

gray scale

A successive series of tones ranging between black and white, which have no color.

guide number

A number used to quantify the output of a flash unit. It is derived by using this formula: GN = aperture x distance. Guide numbers are expressed for a given ISO film speed in either feet or meters.

histogram

A graphic representation of image tones.

IF

Internal Focusing. This Nikkor lens system shifts a group of elements within the lens to acquire focus more quickly without changing the overall length of the lens (as occurs with conventional, helical focusing mechanisms).

image-processing program

Software that allows for image alteration and enhancement.

infinity

In photographic terms, the theoretical most distant point of focus.

interpolation

Process used to increase image resolution by creating new pixels based on existing pixels. The software intelligently looks at existing pixels and creates new pixels to fill the gaps and achieve a higher resolution.

ISO

From ISOS (Greek for equal), a term for industry standards from the International Organization for Standardization. When an ISO number is applied to film, it indicates the relative light sensitivity of the recording medium. Digital sensors use film ISO equivalents, which are based on enhancing the data stream or boosting the signal.

i-TTL

A Nikon TTL flash control system that has a refined monitor pre-flash sequence and offers improved flash exposure control. See also, TTL.

JPEG

Joint Photographic Experts Group. This is a lossy compression file format that works with any computer and photo software. JPEG examines an image for redundant information and then removes it. It is a variable compression format because the amount of leftover data depends on the detail in the photo and the amount of compression. At low compression/high quality, the loss of data has a negligible effect on the photo. However, JPEG should not be used as a working format—the file should be reopened and saved in a format such as TIFF, which does not compress the image.

kilobyte

Just over one thousand bytes.

LCD

Liquid Crystal Display, which is a flat screen with two clear polarizing sheets on either side of a liquid crystal solution.

When activated by an electric current, the LCD causes the crystals to either pass through or block light in order to create a colored image display.

lens

A piece of optical glass on the front of a camera that has been precisely calibrated to allow focus.

lens hood

Also called a lens shade. This is a short tube that can be attached to the front of a lens to reduce flare. It keeps undesirable light from reaching the front of the lens and also protects the front of the lens.

light meter

Also called an exposure meter, it is a device that measures light levels and calculates the correct aperture and shutter speed.

lithium-ion

A popular battery technology (sometimes abbreviated to Li-ion) that is not prone to the charge memory effects of nickel-cadmium (Ni-Cd) batteries, or the low temperature performance problems of alkaline batteries.

low-pass filter

A filter designed to remove elements of an image that correspond to high-frequency data, such as sharp edges and fine detail, to reduce the effect of moiré. See also, moiré.

luminance

A term used to describe directional brightness. It can also be used as luminance noise, which is a form of noise that appears as a sprinkling of black "grain." See also, brightness, chrominance, and noise.

macro lens

A lens designed to be at top sharpness over a flat field when focused at close distances and reproduction ratios up to 1:1.

main light
The primary or dominant light source. It influences texture, volume, and shadows.

Manual exposure mode
A camera operating mode that requires the user to determine and set both the aperture and shutter speed. This is the opposite of automatic exposure.

Mbps
Megabits per second. This unit is used to describe the rate of data transfer. See also, megabit.

megabit
One million bits of data. See also, bit.

megabyte
Just over one million bytes.

megapixel
A million pixels.

memory
The storage capacity of a hard drive or other recording media.

memory card
A solid state removable storage medium used in digital devices. They can store still images, moving images, or sound, as well as related file data. There are several different types, including CompactFlash, SmartMedia, and xD, or Sony's proprietary Memory Stick, to name a few. Individual card capacity is limited by available storage as well as by the size of the recorded data (determined by factors such as image resolution and file format). See also, CompactFlash (CF) card, file format.

moiré
Occurs when the subject has more detail than the resolution of the digital camera can capture. Moiré appears as a wavy pattern over the image.

NEF
Nikon Electronic File. This is Nikon's proprietary RAW file format, used by Nikon digital cameras. In order to process and view NEF files in your computer, you will need Nikon View (version 6.1 or newer) and Nikon Capture (version 4.1 or newer).

Nikkor
The brand name for lenses manufactured by Nikon Corporation.

noise
The digital equivalent of grain. It is often caused by a number of different factors, such as a high ISO setting, heat, sensor design, etc. Though usually undesirable, it may be added for creative effect using an image-processing program. See also, chrominance noise and luminance.

overexposed
When too much light is recorded with the image, causing the photo to be too light in tone.

pan
Moving the camera to follow a moving subject. When a slow shutter speed is used, this creates an image in which the subject appears sharp and the background is blurred.

perspective
The effect of the distance between the camera and image elements upon the perceived size of objects in an image. It is also an expression of this three-dimensional relationship in two dimensions.

pixel
Derived from picture element. A pixel is the base component of a digital image. Every individual pixel can have a distinct color and tone.

pre-flashes
A series of short duration, low intensity flash pulses emitted by a flash unit immediately prior to the shutter opening. These flashes help the TTL light meter assess the reflectivity of the subject. See also, TTL.

Program mode
In Program exposure mode, the camera selects a combination of shutter speed and aperture automatically.

RAW
An image file format that has little or no internal processing applied by the camera. It contains 12-bit color information, a wider range of data than 8-bit formats such as JPEG.

RAW+JPEG
An image file format that records two files per capture; one RAW file and one JPEG file.

rear curtain sync
A feature that causes the flash unit to fire just prior to the shutter closing. It is used for creative effect when mixing flash and ambient light.

red-eye reduction
A feature that causes the flash to emit a brief pulse of light just before the main flash fires. This helps to reduce the effect of retinal reflection.

resolution
The amount of data available for an image as applied to image size. It is expressed in pixels or megapixels, or sometimes as lines per inch on a monitor or dots per inch on a printed image.

RGB mode
Red, Green, and Blue. This is the color model most commonly used to display color images on video systems, film recorders, and computer monitors. It displays all visible colors as combinations of red, green, and blue. RGB mode is the most common color mode for viewing and working with digital files onscreen.

saturation
The intensity or richness of a hue or color.

short lens
A lens with a short focal length—a wide-angle lens. It produces a greater angle of view than you would see with your eyes.

shutter
The apparatus that controls the amount of time during which light is allowed to reach the sensitized medium.

Shutter-priority mode
An automatic exposure mode in which you manually select the shutter speed and the camera automatically selects the aperture.

slow sync
A flash mode in which a slow shutter speed is used with the flash in order to allow low-level ambient light to be recorded by the sensitized medium.

SLR
Single-lens reflex. A camera with a mirror that reflects the image entering the lens through a pentaprism or pentamirror onto the viewfinder screen. When you take the picture, the mirror reflexes out of the way, the focal plane shutter opens, and the image is recorded.

small-format sensor
In a digital camera, this sensor is physically smaller than a 35mm frame of film. The result is that standard 35mm focal lengths act like longer lenses because the sensor sees an angle of view smaller than that of the lens.

Speedlight
The brand name of flash units produced by Nikon Corporation.

standard lens
Also known as a normal lens, this is a

fixed-focal-length lens usually in the range of 45 to 55mm for 35mm format (or the equivalent range for small-format sensors). In contrast to wide-angle or telephoto lenses, a standard lens views a realistically proportionate perspective of a scene.

stop down
To reduce the size of the diaphragm opening by using a higher f/number.

stop up
To increase the size of the diaphragm opening by using a lower f/number.

strobe
Abbreviation for stroboscopic. An electronic light source that produces a series of evenly spaced bursts of light.

synchronize
Causing a flash unit to fire simultaneously with the complete opening of the camera's shutter.

telephoto effect
When objects in an image appear closer than they really are through the use of a telephoto lens.

thumbnail
A miniaturized representation of an image file.

TIFF
Tagged Image File Format. This popular digital format uses lossless compression.

tripod
A three-legged stand that stabilizes the camera and eliminates camera shake caused by body movement or vibration. Tripods are usually adjustable for height and angle.

TTL
Through-the-Lens, i.e. TTL metering.

USB
Universal Serial Bus. This interface standard allows outlying accessories to be plugged and unplugged from the computer while it is turned on. USB 2.0 enables high-speed data transfer.

vignetting
A reduction in light at the edge of an image due to use of a filter or an inappropriate lens hood for the particular lens.
The ground glass surface on which you view your image.

VR
Vibration Reduction. This technology is used in such photographic accessories as a VR lens.

wide-angle lens
A lens that produces a greater angle of view than you would see with your eyes, often causing the image to appear stretched. See also, short lens.

zoom lens
A lens that can be adjusted to cover a wide range of focal lengths.

Index